Hello App Inventor!

Android programming
for kids and the rest of us

PAULA BEER
CARL SIMMONS

MANNING
SHELTER ISLAND

For online information and ordering of this and other Manning books, please visit
www.manning.com. The publisher offers discounts on this book when ordered in quantity.
For more information, please contact:

    Special Sales Department
    Manning Publications Co.
    20 Baldwin Road
    PO Box 261
    Shelter Island, NY 11964
    Email: orders@manning.com

Manning Publications Co.   Development editor: Susanna Kline
20 Baldwin Road   Copyeditor: Tiffany Taylor
PO Box 261   Proofreader: Alyson Brener
Shelter Island, NY 11964   Technical proofreader: Jerome Baton
                                              Typesetter: Marija Tudor
                                          Cover designer: Leslie Haimes

ISBN 9781617291432

Printed in the United States of America

1 2 3 4 5 6 7 8 9 10 – EBM – 19 18 17 16 15 14

To anyone who really, really tries.
Come on, keep going, you're nearly there.

—P.B.

To Frank, who treated us like geniuses and loved us fiercely.

—C.S.

Brief contents

Contents

15 Publishing and beyond   312

Preface

We think writing computer programs is fun and that those who can do it can make a difference to the world around them—sometimes in an almost magical way. But when you start out, it's often hard to see how the programs you write can make any difference to anyone—for example, you might just be drawing simple shapes or adding up a bunch of numbers.

Back in 2012, we started using App Inventor with teachers and children and discovered it was a brilliant way to make computer programs that worked in the real world. Beginners could perform useful, imaginative, and fun tasks like a GPS treasure hunt or a homework excuse generator. The App Inventor books that helped us learn were great, but we wanted to focus on helping school-age kids and beginners become app creators. Paula proposed that we write a book, and within a day we had the original contents page and app list. This initial speed lulled Paula into a false sense of security, and colleagues now remind her that she waved her arms around and said "It'll only take us 12 weeks!" She was only off by a factor of 8 …

But what a couple of years it has been! Throughout the book, we've woven in key facts and resources useful to beginning programmers and always tried to develop original (or inspired!) working examples. We feel that the power of visual programming languages is brought out through the concepts and the huge variety of apps that can be produced by users of the book. Our companion website provides great graphics and sounds for each of the apps and a really useful table layout so users can set up their designs quickly and get down to learning to program with App Inventor right away.

We've used the resources from this book to teach App Inventor to primary-age kids, secondary-age kids, trainee teachers, experienced programmers, and experienced teachers—and what we always see is fun, satisfaction, and engagement.

We hope you get a lot out of the book and make fun apps for you and your friends. Who knows? You might even make the next award-winning killer app!

Acknowledgments

Many people helped bring this book to fruition—mentors, colleagues, reviewers, editors, friends, and family. We thank you all.

Thanks to the reviewers who read the manuscript in various stages of its development and provided invaluable and encouraging feedback: Aditya Sharma, Alain Couniot, Andrei Bautu, Brent Stains, Chris Davis, Ezra Simeloff, Ian Stirk, John D. Lewis, Mark Elston, Michael Knoll, Phanindra V. Mankale, Richard Lebel, Rick Goff, and Ron Sher.

Thanks to the student reviewers from Avon Grove Charter School, West Grove, PA, whose comments helped make this a much better book for our target audience: Alex Wilson, Ian Khan, Jacob Snarr, Jake Kerstetter, James Cottle Vinson, Lewis Arscott, Rhys Cottle Vinson, and their teacher Jacqueline Wilson.

Thanks to Diane Blakeley and the brilliant pupils of Wellfield College for trying out the early chapters of this book and coming up with brilliant ideas for apps, especially the Homework Excuse Generator.

Thanks to the readers of Manning's Early Access Program (MEAP) for their comments and their corrections to our chapters as they were being written. You helped us to improve our manuscript.

Thanks to Shay Pokress at MIT for keeping us in the App Inventor loop. Thanks for your encouragement and also to the team at MIT who continue to support App Inventor as a great educational tool.

Our Manning editor, Susanna Kline, always made great suggestions and knew when to push and when to wait with patience and understanding while we grappled with difficult chapters; thanks for being a constant and encouraging presence.

Finally, thanks to the super-professional and efficient team at Manning who worked with us and supported us throughout: Marjan Bace, Scott Meyers (for taking a chance on us), Cynthia Kane, Candace Gillhoolley, Jerome Baton, Kevin Sullivan, Tiffany Taylor, Mary Piergies, and many others who helped along the way.

Paula Beer

I would like to give huge thanks to my friends and family. In roughly "how long I have known them" order: my mum, Carol, who taught me the white-hot fear of not having a good book on the go; my dad, Bernie, who taught me how to teach using confidence-building examples; my brother, Andy "Analogy Man," who taught me how to explain myself clearly; my sister, Netty, who taught me about priorities and how to juggle (career and family, not batons; she is rubbish at that); and my twin cousin Stephen and best chum Janet, who have always convincingly feigned interest in my progress and inspired me with their own achievements. Thanks to my in-laws, Gillian and John, and my friend Jeff whose own love of writing inspired me toward this possibility. To my Edge Hill colleagues Claire, Dawn, and Colette: your encouragement means so much.

To my coauthor and sparring partner Carl: it's been fun, especially as I won the last round (don't you dare edit this out!). To my three delicious children, Sam, Ella, and Sophia: thanks for testing my apps, telling me when they were up to the mark, and making everything wonderful. Thank you for not spilling juice on my keyboard when occasionally I sat among you writing apps on treat night while watching Harry Hill. Finally, to my incredible husband Rufus: it is impossible to fail at anything with a man like you in my life.

Carl Simmons

Thank you to our Edge Hill colleagues who supported us throughout and patiently endured our bizarre conversations about hungry spiders, cheeky hamsters, and amazing penguins. Thanks also to the many teachers and students who tried out chapters and gave us great feedback.

To Mum and Dad: thanks for indulging my early geekhood. Not only for all the computers, disk drives, monitors, and books, but also for the self-esteem that comes from constant encouragement and support. Huge thanks to my family for putting up with the long hours I sat staring at screens of various sizes, my wandering around holding a phone trying to get a

GPS signal, and my occasional shouts of frustration or triumph. Also for offering lots of helpful advice about ideas, characters, games, and graphics. Special thanks to the children for testing the apps, especially A-Mazeing Penguin, which needed lots of play-testing to get right. To Daniel: thanks for the brilliant Zombie picture and for testing the early chapters to see whether a 10-year-old could follow them. To Ellie: thanks for ensuring that I didn't become a total hermit, dragging me away from the computer to have fun with the family and providing a constant soundtrack of music and dance while I worked. To Lynne: without your support, this simply wouldn't have happened; thanks for being the chauffeur, chef, and chief of our home to give me the space to write.

Finally, thanks to my coauthor, Paula: you've made this a huge amount of fun, and that's kept me going throughout. But just remember, it's not the last round that counts, it's the total score!

About this book

This book will help you become an App Inventor—someone who doesn't just use a phone or tablet, but takes control of it! You'll learn to create some fun apps, and along the way you'll also learn programming skills that you can use in lots of other programming languages. We wrote this book for kids, but anyone who's curious about programming and mobile devices will find it useful.

We aren't expecting you to have any programming knowledge at all—we'll start from the very beginning (you'll be surprised how quickly you learn). You need to know your way around a keyboard and mouse, how to save files, and how to use a web browser like Chrome, Firefox, or Safari. You'll also find it useful to know how to use an Android smartphone and access its menu settings. If you can do that, you can jump right in and get started making apps.

What is an App Inventor?

Before we answer that question, we need to answer this one: *"What is an app?"*

An *app* is a computer program—a list of instructions that tells a computer what to do. Normally, the word *app* is used to talk about programs written for smartphones and other mobile devices like tablets. It's going to get a bit longwinded to keep talking about "smartphones and other mobile devices like tablets," so throughout this book we'll use the term *phone* or *smartphone* to mean any mobile Android device such as a smartphone or tablet.

An *App Inventor* is two things:

- App Inventor is a programming language you can use via an internet browser to design and make apps for Android phones. It's a graphical environment—that means you don't have to type complicated code. Instead, you drag and drop objects on screen and plug blocks of code together like a jigsaw puzzle. If you've used the Scratch programming language, this will be familiar.
- *You* are an App Inventor. Once you've done the first exercise in chapter 1, you can proudly claim, "I am an App Inventor!" That's someone who can create code that runs on a phone.

What is Android?

We've mentioned Android a couple of times already. Android is an operating system (OS) that runs on lots of mobile devices. An OS manages a computer's *hardware*—that's all the bits you can touch, including computer chips and circuit boards and cameras and touch screens.

Windows, Mac OS, and Linux are OSs that are mainly used in desktop and laptop machines. Android, iOS, and Windows Phone are the main OSs you find in mobile devices. So App Inventor lets you program pretty much any Android device, but it won't work on iPhones or Windows phones.

Why should you be an App Inventor?

Learning to program computers is fun! It can sometimes be frustrating when things aren't working, but the joy you get from solving these problems is huge.

Programming is a great skill to learn because it helps you think in a certain way—this is sometimes called *computational thinking*. What this really means is that once you can program, you can solve lots of problems in the real world, too. Even if you become an architect, an artist, an engineer, or a scientist, the skills you learn from programming are useful. These skills are things like

- Thinking creatively
- Problem solving
- Sequencing steps
- Logic and math skills
- Understanding people's needs

- Patience and tenacity (sticking with it)
- At the moment, the world needs computational thinkers and good programmers, and becoming an App Inventor is a great place to start a career as a coder, game designer, or entrepreneur.

Why choose the App Inventor language?

There are loads of choices of programming languages—LOGO, Python, Small Basic, JavaScript, Logo, Scratch, and Kodu. We think you should try them all! What's different about App Inventor is that it gives you access to some powerful hardware that you can carry in your pocket—a smartphone. That means you can create apps that

- Can do very cool things like use your GPS location, make phone calls, send texts, read barcodes, and take pictures or videos.
- Are useful in the real world. You might make an app that
  - Reminds you to do important things, like take medication
  - Sends an alert text with your phone's location
  - Uses pictures to tell small children what time of day it is
- Being able to create apps that your friends and family can use on their phones is an amazing motivator to learn to program and to make your apps the best they can possibly be. If you get really good, you can even sell your apps—for example, on the Google Play store.
- The other reason we're excited about App Inventor is that because it's a drag-and-drop graphical language, beginners tend to make fewer mistakes, and it's easier to spot them when you do (this is true of languages like Scratch and Kodu, too). It can be frustrating to hunt down missing periods or capital letters in typed programming languages—and that's one thing you don't need to worry about when you're starting out in App Inventor.

What you need

We've included setup instructions in chapter 1, and there's more on the App Inventor website. To get started, you'll need

- A computer running Windows, Mac OS X, or Linux (we used Windows).
- A web browser. Firefox, Chrome, or Safari is fine (Internet Explorer doesn't work at the moment, but there are plans for an update soon).
- An Android phone isn't essential, but it makes things a lot more fun! A wireless internet connection or USB lead from your phone to your computer is required too.

- A Google account (more about this in chapter 1).
- Website resources. All the files we use (like graphics and sound clips) can be found at www.manning.com/HelloAppInventor.
- Good ideas and a little patience!

Ways of using this book

We've written this book in sequence so you get the essential ideas of computing and programming in an order that we think makes sense. The early examples in the book include step-by-step instructions (walkthroughs). Later, we assume you already know lots of things; and as you progress, the activities become more challenging as your skill level increases. The apps tend to get more complicated as you go through the book, too, and those in chapter 14 bring all the ideas you've learned together in two quite big and complicated apps.

If you're a beginner, we suggest that you work through the book in order; it probably makes the most sense that way. If you know a little about programming, you might find it useful to skip around and try different sections that interest you.

We've included "Try It Out" and "Taking It Further" sections that give you additional challenges. This is how you find out just how much you know! It's easy to follow a set of instructions, but can you apply those skills to something else? We strongly suggest that you try these exercises and suggestions. You'll also find some quiz questions at the end of each chapter to check that you understand the computing concepts covered.

Symbols you'll see

We've used these symbols to highlight important information throughout the book:

Learning points give you general computer science concepts that you can research further. They explain the "Why is this important?" questions and give you keywords that you'll see in this book and others. They're also useful for teachers in planning lessons.

The *Let's invent!* symbol indicates the beginning of a practical activity. You'll see this whenever we start a new app.

 Some apps only work properly on a real phone—you can make a phone vibrate, but that won't work if you use the onscreen *emulator* (more about this in chapter 1). The *Phones only!* symbol means this part of an activity can only be tested on a phone rather than in the emulator.

Code conventions and downloads

All source code in listings or in text is presented in a `fixed-width font like this` to separate it from ordinary text. Code annotations accompany many lines of code, highlighting important concepts.

The code used in this book, along with graphics and sound clips, is available from the publisher's website at www.manning.com/HelloAppInventor.

Author Online

Purchase of *Hello App Inventor!* includes free access to a private web forum run by Manning Publications where you can make comments about the book, ask technical questions, and receive help from the authors and from other users. To access the forum and subscribe to it, point your web browser to www.manning.com/HelloAppInventor.

This page provides information on how to get on the forum once you're registered, what kind of help is available, and the rules of conduct on the forum. Manning's commitment to our readers is to provide a place where a conversation between individual readers and between readers and the authors can take place. We invite you to visit the forum and to share your questions and comments with the authors and other readers of this book.

OK, that's enough introduction—now let's go be App Inventors!

CHAPTER 1

Getting to know App Inventor

Any sufficiently advanced technology is indistinguishable from magic.

—Arthur C. Clarke's Third Law of Prediction[1]

First a little history …

The first handheld cell phones were large, heavy, and very expensive. Here's Martin Cooper, a technical wizard (note the white beard). He is one of the inventors of the first cell phones—and is holding his original prototype phone. In his other hand is a modern smartphone, but more than the size and weight have improved. Mobile devices today do an incredible range of jobs, from simple things like waking you up in the morning to complicated stuff like telling you where you are on the planet and providing anyplace access to the World Wide Web. Human beings have never before carried around so much power in their pockets. Even a basic smartphone operates hundreds of times more quickly and stores tens of thousands more bytes of data than the Apollo Guidance Computer that landed men on the Moon! Most of us just accept and use this power—these

© Fundación Príncipe de Asturias

---

[1] In the essay "Hazards of Prophecy: The Failure of Imagination," in *Profiles of the Future* (Gollancz, 1962).

things happen as if by magic. App Inventor lets you become the magician, writing the spells that transform your world.

The language of spells (or programming, as we call it) can be hard to learn in some cases. Fortunately App Inventor was designed to help you bridge the gap between the complicated tasks that mobile phones do and learning to write simple but powerful computer programs.

What can an Android smartphone do?

In this illustration, you can see some of the smartphone features that you can take control of through App Inventor. The exciting thing is that it was previously impossible for beginning programmers to program a single device that has all these features.

Imagine building a Wish You Were Here app that uses the device's camera and Global Positioning Satellites (GPS) to send photo-texts to people on your contact list. Or, using a combination of touch-screen technology and orientation sensing, you could create fun games that respond to you touching, shaking, and tipping the phone—and why not put the leader board of high scores on the internet for all to see? The possibilities are endless … almost!

App Inventor setup

App Inventor was developed by Google and is now owned and developed by the Massachusetts Institute of Technology (MIT) and can be accessed through this website: http://appinventor.mit.edu/explore/. We suggest you head over there for the most up-to-date setup instructions, because things do change from time to time, but we'll give you a brief rundown of the setup options at the time we're writing this. If you're already set up, you can skip this section.

You need three things to use App Inventor:

- *A computer*—Windows, Macintosh, or GNU/Linux.
- *An internet connection and browser*—Chrome, Firefox, or Safari. (Internet Explorer support is planned for the future.)
- *A Google account*—Free, and available at https://accounts.google.com/signup. Note that to set up your own account, you have to be age 13 or older in most countries. If

you're under 13, a parent can sign up for an account and work alongside you. (We know—the kids will teach the grownups!) Schools can manage groups of Google email accounts (which can include those under 13) by setting up Google Apps for Education: www.google.com/enterprise/apps/education/.

The fourth item we recommend that you have is an Android phone or tablet—but you can use an onscreen emulator if you don't have one.

Next, we'll tell you about the options you have for connecting to App Inventor.

Option 1: Using Wi-Fi with the App Inventor companion phone software

If you have access to Wi-Fi, then the good news is that you can run App Inventor without having to download any software to your computer. *This is by far the easiest option.*

You do need to install an app on your phone called AICompanion, which is available from the App Inventor website and the Google Play Store. And both your phone and your computer need to be able to access the same network router Wi-Fi network.

Before you begin, it's always a good idea to completely uninstall any previous versions of App Inventor that you have on your system. Then follow these steps to configure your phone for working with App Inventor:

1. On your phone or tablet, go to System Settings > Applications and select Unknown Sources. This option lets you use a phone or tablet to "live test" apps that weren't downloaded from the Google Play Store.
2. Choose Development on the Applications page, and select both the USB Debugging and Stay Awake options. It's helpful for the screen to stay awake when you have it plugged in to your computer so you can program without having to constantly tap the screen.
3. Install the AICompanion app on your phone. This link will give you a QR code you can scan to download the free app: http://mng.bz/3eV2.

Option 2: using the onscreen emulator

If you don't want to test on a phone or tablet, you can run a virtual phone called an *emulator* on your computer screen. To do this, you need to install the App Inventor setup software.

Once this software is installed, any time you want to test an app, you must run the aiStarter program (which will be installed automatically as part of the setup). We explain more about the emulator later in the chapter.

Before you begin, it's always a good idea to completely uninstall any previous versions of App Inventor that you have on your system. Then follow these steps:

1   Install the App Inventor setup software. Follow this link, and go to the Install the App Inventor Setup Software section of the page: http://mng.bz/tk58. Then follow the steps for your operating system.

2   Launch aiStarter. You need this piece of software to communicate between the computer and the emulator. When you installed the App Inventor setup software in step 1, aiStarter was automatically installed.

Windows and Linux users need to manually launch it from either the Start menu or the Programs menu every time you want to use App Inventor. Mac users will find that it launches automatically.

Option 3: connecting via USB cable

You can plug your phone directly into your computer via a USB cable. This has the advantage that your phone is charging while you're working. You need the same setup as for option 2, plus you may need to install the right USB driver for your phone on the computer you're using.

Before you begin, it's always a good idea to completely uninstall any previous versions of App Inventor that you have on your system. Then follow these steps:

1   Install the App Inventor setup software. Follow this link, and go to the Install the App Inventor Setup Software section of the page: http://mng.bz/3eV2. Then follow the steps for your operating system.

2   If you are using a Windows PC, you'll probably need to install the device driver for your Android phone or tablet. A *device driver* is a little program that lets computers "talk" to

compatible devices like mice, keyboards, and smartphones. The App Inventor setup software includes drivers for some common Android phones, but if yours doesn't appear on the list at http://mng.bz/YXxg, you'll need to install a driver manually.

3   Configure your phone for working with App Inventor, as follows:

   a   On your phone or tablet, go to System Settings > Applications and select Unknown Sources. This option lets you use a phone or tablet to "live test" apps that weren't downloaded from the Google Play Store.

   b   Choose Development on the Applications page, and select both the USB Debugging and Stay Awake options. It's helpful for the screen to stay awake when you have it plugged in to your computer so you can program without having to constantly tap the screen.

   c   Install the AICompanion app on your phone. This link will give you a QR code you can scan to download the free app: http://mng.bz/3eV2.

4   Launch aiStarter. You need this piece of software to communicate between the computer and the phone via USB. When you installed the App Inventor setup software in step 1, aiStarter was automatically installed.

Windows and Linux users need to manually launch it from either the Start menu or the Programs menu every time you want to use App Inventor. Mac users will find that it launches automatically.

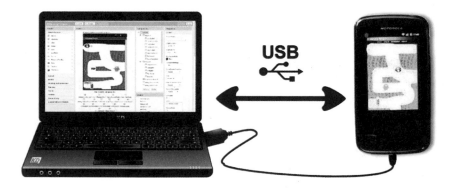

Using all three options

If you want to be able to use all three options to test or teach, you need to ensure that you've downloaded the free App Inventor software from the website and installed the AICompanion app on your phone. You can either go straight to the website (http://appinventor.mit.edu/explore/ai2/setup.html) and follow the instructions or use the steps we just listed in option 3.

Troubleshooting

If you run into any problems along the way, the Web is a powerful tool for troubleshooting. The MIT App Inventor site has its own troubleshooting page as well as an App Inventor Forum where users and experts help each other overcome difficulties: http://mng.bz/FwKK.

The App Inventor juggling act

In this section, we'll walk you through the main parts of App Inventor, and then you'll build your first app. In all the App Inventor apps you build, you'll use the same three steps with three different screens:

1 Design the app screen by using the app *Designer*.
2 Tell the app what to do by programming the *Blocks Editor*.
3 Test the program using your *phone* or *emulator*.

Here's what those steps look like.

1. Designing the app screen

In the App Inventor Designer, you'll start a new project. Then you'll design the app screen (even if it's only a rough draft).

The App Inventor Designer lets you

- Create a new project
- Add components
- Design the look of the app

You access the Designer through your web browser (such as Chrome, Firefox, or Safari) by clicking the Designer button.

2. Telling the app what to do

Next, you'll program the Blocks Editor to tell the app what to do. The Blocks Editor lets you control how the app works by using programming blocks.

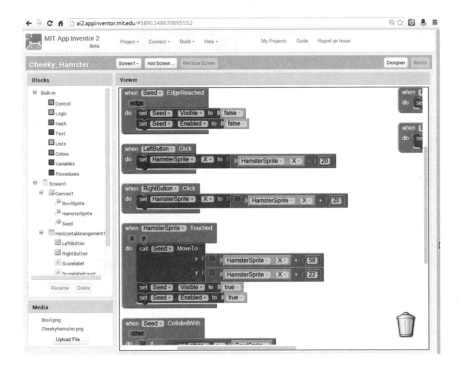

You write apps through your web browser by clicking the Blocks button. You can toggle between Designer and Blocks as you program.

3. Testing the program

Finally, you'll test the program on your phone (shown on the left) or in the emulator (right):

You can see if the app looks OK and works by watching your phone or the emulator (a virtual phone that you see on your computer screen). Either way, you can test the program in real time.

TIP

If you lose the emulator window onscreen, look for the Android in your toolbar.

In the next three sections, we'll look at each of these three steps in turn, and then you'll put them together and build your first app: Hello World! It might help to have an example in mind, so imagine that you want to create an app that plays tic-tac-toe (or noughts and crosses).

How will it look? App Inventor Designer

The first step in creating an app is to set up a new project and then design it. Designing means both laying out what the app looks like and also deciding which small components you need to make the app work—things like buttons and labels and sounds (more on this in chapter 2). The place to do both of these jobs is the App Inventor Designer.

Think about tic-tac-toe. What do you need the game to look like? Probably a grid with nine spaces (3 x 3). You also need some way of letting the player touch a space in the grid; and then you'll put an X or an O in that space (as long as it's still free). You might also want to play some sounds and keep score.

To do these things in App Inventor, you would start a new project called TicTacToe. You'd put a grid on the screen, along with buttons to detect which box was touched, a score label, and some sounds. All these components would be dragged into the app from a section called the Palette, where there are more than 50 components to choose from. In chapter 2, you'll see them all listed.

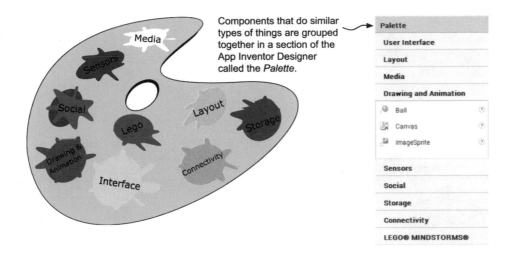

Components that do similar types of things are grouped together in a section of the App Inventor Designer called the *Palette*.

Component properties

In chapter 2, you'll learn that components have *properties* like how big they are, their color, or what flavor they are when you lick the screen (we made the last one up—but one day, who knows?). Each component has its own unique set of properties. As you work through the book, you'll use components from most of the component groups, so very soon you'll be a component expert.

How will it work? The Blocks Editor

OK, imagine you've designed a beautiful interface full of buttons, backgrounds, and images. What can it do? As it stands, your app doesn't do anything—you'll become a programmer once you tell the app what to do using the Blocks Editor.

In tic-tac-toe, you would write a program to detect which box the player touched, display an X or an O, work out a countermove, and display an O or an X. You'd also detect when someone wins or there's a draw, and play some sounds. These rules need to be programmed into App Inventor, and you can't do that in the Designer part—you need the Blocks Editor.

TIP

The App Inventor screen has two buttons on the right side that let you toggle between the Designer and the Blocks Editor (shortened to Blocks onscreen).

The Blocks Editor is a drag-and-drop interface, which means you can begin programming right away without needing to learn lots of unfamiliar words. So in the tic-tac-toe example, you could drag programming blocks to detect when a button was pressed without having to write a bunch of code. Programming using blocks that are close to your natural language (in this case, English) is a form of *abstraction* (see the upcoming Learning Point).

The Blocks Editor screen is split in two, with all the blocks to choose from on the left and a large empty workspace on the right.

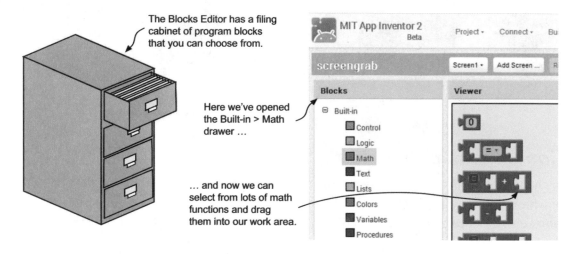

The Blocks Editor has a filing cabinet of program blocks that you can choose from.

Here we've opened the Built-in > Math drawer ...

... and now we can select from lots of math functions and drag them into our work area.

Some of the block drawers (like Math) are very deep, so you'll need to scroll down once you're in the drawer to see all the blocks. Also, there are two categories of blocks—*built-in* and *component-specific*—and they have an important difference:

- Built-in blocks are *static*. They're always available, no matter what kind of app you're creating. They include things like functions to add or subtract.
- Component-specific blocks are *dynamic*. They become available as you add components and definitions to your app (in the Designer screen). For example, if you add a button, you'll see a new set of blocks appear, named after your button.

Built-in blocks

Here's a brief overview of each of the tools in the Built-in blocks drawer.

Block drawer	Blocks you'll find in there	Explanation and example
Control	**Decision** blocks that tell the program what to do next based on some kind of test **Loops**, which are a powerful way of repeating tasks	**Decision**: If you clicked the Happy button, the phone sends a ☺ tweet. If you clicked Sad, it sends a ☹ tweet. **Loop**: When you text a group of contacts, the phone executes a loop from the first contact to the last, sending a single text each time. Doing this manually would be tedious!

Block drawer	Blocks you'll find in there	Explanation and example
Logic	The logic values **True** and **False** Logical tests: **AND, OR, NOT, =**	**True** and **False** can set properties. For example, setting a button's **Visible** property to **False** makes the button disappear. Logical tests are used for more complicated **Decision** blocks. For example, you might want to make sure the user's age is more than 8 **AND** less than 12.
Math	Blocks that create and compare numbers, plus all the functions you would find on a calculator	For example, in a game you could use **Math** blocks to add up the number of coins collected and convert this to a score. You could also use **Math** blocks to work out whether this score was greater than the current high score.
Text	Blocks that create, change, add, join, split, replace, and compare text	Any piece of text you want to display is created in a **Text** block. For example, you could join the name a user typed and a text message—something like, "Hello Amy, how are you today?"
Lists	Blocks that store, display, and work with lists of things	For example you might want to give the user a menu of choices that they can click.
Colors	A choice of standard colors to use[a]	You can set or change the color of anything you see on screen, like text, a button, or the background.
Variables	Blocks to create variables	A *variable* is a named storage space for a small piece of data like your name or age or a game score.
Procedures	Blocks to create and run procedures	A *procedure* is a kind of mini program that other blocks can start. For example, you might have a procedure that resets the screen whenever a game is over.

a. You can also mix your own colors using the color chart at http://mng.bz/qhY3.

Don't worry about understanding all of these right away. We'll say a lot more about the blocks as you work through the book.

Component-specific blocks

The contents of the Blocks Editor change in response to the components you add to the Designer. Say you've created a simple interface with two components: a button called **PressButton** and a sound called **BeepSound**. When you look in the **Screen1** drawer (which contains component-specific blocks) in the Blocks Editor, inside will be **BeepSound** and **PressButton** drawers.

TIP
You'll always see **Screen1** in the Blocks Editor. This component is there for all apps—it's the blank screen that opens when you open the app.

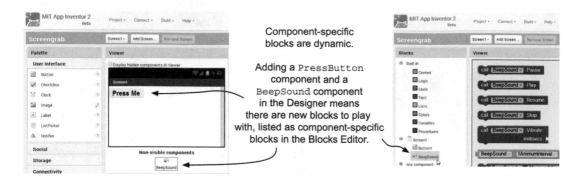

Component-specific blocks are dynamic.

Adding a `PressButton` component and a `BeepSound` component in the Designer means there are new blocks to play with, listed as component-specific blocks in the Blocks Editor.

Learning Point: What is abstraction?

Abstraction is a way of simplifying programming. It lets a programmer use or *call* high-level functions using a descriptive name such as "play sound". Another way of saying this is that it lets programmers program using language which is closer to their "natural language."

Behind each of the blocks is hidden Java code (Java is a programming language) that you can re-use lots of times. If it weren't for the blocks abstraction, every time you wanted to play a sound you'd have to write some Java code like this:

```
import java.net.URL;
import javax.swing.*;
import javax.sound.sampled.*;
public class LoopSound {
    public static void main(String[] args) throws Exception {
        URL url = new URL(
            "http://pscode.org/media/leftright.wav");
        Clip clip = AudioSystem.getClip();
        // getAudioInputStream() also accepts a File or InputStream
        AudioInputStream ais = AudioSystem.
            getAudioInputStream( url );
        clip.open(ais);
        clip.loop(Clip.LOOP_CONTINUOUSLY);
        SwingUtilities.invokeLater(new Runnable() {
            public void run() {
                // A GUI element to prevent the Clip's daemon Thread
                // from terminating at the end of the main()
                JOptionPane.showMessageDialog(null, "Close to exit!");
            }
        });
    }
}
```

Even this Java code is an abstraction of the binary 1s and 0s that turn things on and off inside your smartphone. Later you'll learn how you can use abstraction to make your own programs efficient and quicker to write.

Running and testing programs

In App Inventor you test a bit of design and coding at a time—don't wait until the end to make sure it all works (this is a useful tip, no matter what programming language you use). As you drag objects onto the screen in the Designer or make changes in the Blocks Editor, you'll see the app on your phone or emulator change in real time. For example, in the tic-tac-toe game, as you developed the app you could check that buttons appeared in the right place or that the program detected a win and played a sound.

Running and testing: emulator vs. smartphone

Chances are, if you've bought this book, you already have a smartphone or tablet you can use with App Inventor. But there may be times when it's not available or you want to show an app to someone who doesn't have an Android device.

The emulator is a program that runs on your PC, Mac, or Linux machine and that acts like your phone. But some smartphone-specific features don't work on the emulator. These include the following:

- Touch-screen technology (although you can use your mouse for some actions)
- GPS
- Texting and calling
- Camera
- Barcode scanner
- Internet connection
- Sensing and responding to what is physically happening to the phone

Throughout the book, when you come to a tutorial, we'll tell you whether its functionality works fully on the emulator or the phone only (using the Phones Only Android symbol from "How to Use this Book"). For example, one of the games you're going to program lets you move characters by physically tilting the phone from side to side—which isn't going to work on a computer. Believe us, picking up your computer screen and tilting doesn't work.

Your first app: Hello World!

Let's jump right in and create your first app. You'll start with something simple: a Hello World! app that displays a pop-up message saying "Hello World!" This isn't going to make your fortune as an app designer, but after you've done it, you can rightly claim that you've written your own computer program (and not just any old program—an app!). You can also build on this basic app to learn more useful stuff later.

It's kind of a tradition that programmers write a Hello World! program whenever they use a new language. This is because it's very simple, and you can check that you've understood the basics before doing the hard stuff. (Carl used to sneak into computer shops in the 1980s to try to run the Hello World! program on as many computers as possible before the store manager threw him out!) The following sections walk you through the steps to create the app.

TIP

In this book we'll often refer to *the user*. That means anyone who might use the app (you, your friends, or other people who download it).

---

1. Opening App Inventor

Once you've set up App Inventor on your computer, select the Create section of the App Inventor website (http://appinventor.mit.edu) to get started. This opens the App Inventor Designer.

If you've never used App Inventor before, you'll see a blank list of projects and a welcome message like this:

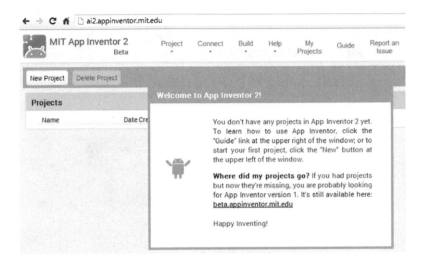

2. Starting with a new project

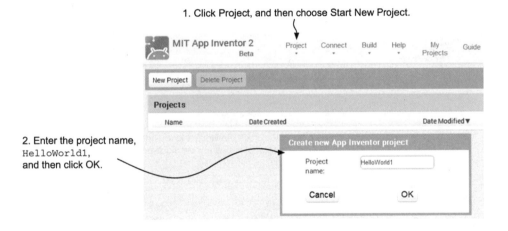

1. Click Project, and then choose Start New Project.

2. Enter the project name, `HelloWorld1`, and then click OK.

TIP

No spaces are allowed in project names, and you'll see the same is true of component names, too. One way to separate words is to use capital letters to indicate the start of each word. That's what coders call *camel case*. See the humps in *CamelCase*?

Once you've created or opened an app, the design page opens. This is where you add components to your app and design the appearance of the app screen on the phone. You can return to the list of your apps in My Projects at any time by clicking the link at the top of the page.

3. Adding a Notifier component to the project

You can use the useful `Notifier` component for all kinds of pop-up messages and warnings.

3. You're finished in the Designer, so open the Blocks Editor by clicking the Blocks button.

1. From the Palette, drag the `Notifier` component onto `Screen1` here.

Tip: If you can't spot Notifier in the Palette, make sure you're looking in the User Interface section.

2. You should see the Notifier icon appear in the Components list above and also down here.

You see **Notifier**s in lots of computer programs and apps—they're the little windows that pop up to give you information or warnings on your phone, consoles, computers, and TVs. Sometimes they just have an OK button, sometimes they give you a choice like OK or Cancel, and sometimes they ask for more information and provide a list to choose from or a box to type into.

4. Writing the program using blocks

Normally, apps do nothing until the user does something—such as clicking a button. This is called an *event*. The special blocks that detect an event and then do something are called *event handlers*. You can recognize an event handler because it has the words **when** and **do** at the left side of the block. After the **when**, you always see two words separated by a period (or full stop): the first word is the name of the component the event handler is working with, and the second word is the action the event handler is waiting for (also called a *trigger*). That might sound complicated, but we bet you can figure out what this event handler is looking for:

```
when StartButton.Click
```

Did you work it out? The event handler looks for when the user clicks **StartButton**—when they do, it will carry out whatever is in the **do** part of the block.

In this simple app, you want a message to appear as soon as the app starts. You'll use a special event handler called **Screen.Initialize** to do this. This means the app will do something right away—even if the user hasn't clicked a button.

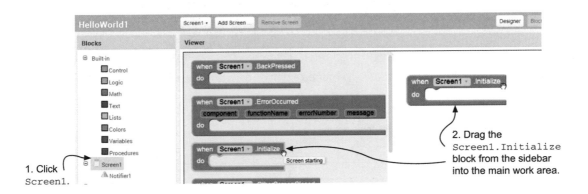

What do you want the app to do? Pop up a notifier that says "Hello World!" You'll see that there are lots of different kinds of **Notifier** actions (purple blocks). In this case, you'll use one that shows a message until the user clicks an OK button to make it go away. It's called **ShowMessageDialog**, and it displays an alert message with a single button. (You could

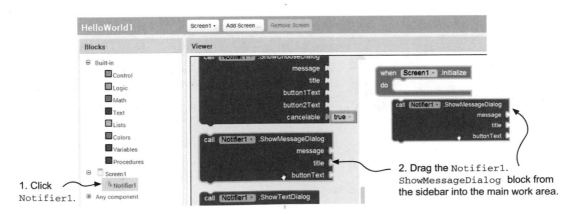

probably figure that out from the name `ShowMessageDialog`—App Inventor blocks have logical, descriptive names.)

Now you join the blocks.

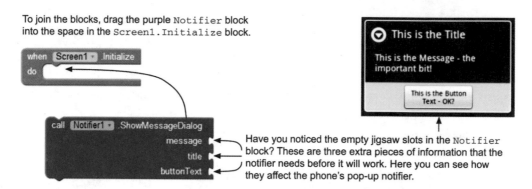

To join the blocks, drag the purple `Notifier` block into the space in the `Screen1.Initialize` block.

Have you noticed the empty jigsaw slots in the `Notifier` block? These are three extra pieces of information that the notifier needs before it will work. Here you can see how they affect the phone's pop-up notifier.

The message, title, and button text that the notifier needs are all pieces of text—in programming, we call them *text strings*. To make text strings, you use a Built-in Text block.

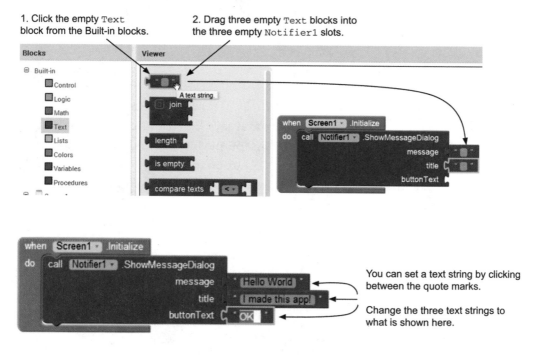

1. Click the empty `Text` block from the Built-in blocks.

2. Drag three empty `Text` blocks into the three empty `Notifier1` slots.

You can set a text string by clicking between the quote marks.

Change the three text strings to what is shown here.

That's it—you're an App Inventor, computer programmer, and wizard! Now let's see if your app works.

5. Testing the app

It's incredibly easy to make a mistake when you're programming—you can grab the wrong block, forget a step, or even miss plugging blocks together by a few millimeters. So it's important to test the app yourself before you hand it over to users. You can test the app using a smartphone or the onscreen Android emulator. App Inventor will *translate* your Designer components and program blocks into a bunch of binary code that the emulator or phone can understand. You'll test the app by using a direct connection between the Blocks Editor and your phone or emulator. This is the way you'll test most of your apps while you build them—later we'll look at how you can package an app so that it works even if the phone isn't plugged in to your computer.

You connect a smartphone or run the emulator from the Connect menu at the top of your screen.

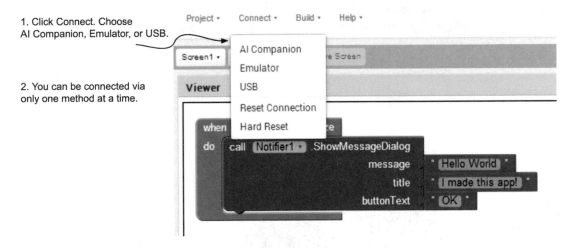

If you have a phone, you can connect wirelessly (Wi-Fi), which is the easiest option. Alternatively, you can plug it in via a USB cable (you probably got this when you bought the phone). If you don't have a phone, then use the emulator. Do one of the following:

- *For a wireless connection* to your phone, choose AI Companion. A code will appear on your computer screen. You can enter or scan this code into your phone by running the AI Companion phone app.
- *For a USB cable connection*, the process depends on what kind of computer you're using. Start by connecting your phone to your computer with a USB cable, and then follow the instructions for your operating system (Windows, Mac OS X, or GNU/Linux) at http://mng.bz/3eV2.

1. Choose AI Companion from the Connect menu.

2. A unique app code appears in both QR and text form.

3. On your phone, start the MIT AI2 Companion app.

4. Either type the app code and click Connect with Code or click Scan the QR Code and point your phone at the QR code on your computer screen.

- *If you don't have a phone to test with*, the process depends on what kind of computer you're using. Follow the instructions for your operating system (Windows, Mac OS X, or GNU/Linux) at http://mng.bz/tk58. It takes a little while for the emulator to load, so let it complete this uninterrupted. You'll see the Android icon appear at the bottom of your screen. Once the emulator is open, you can use your mouse to slide across the virtual screen lock.

You should see the Hello World! notifier appear on your phone or emulator. Here's how it looked on our emulator:

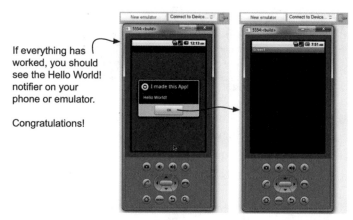

If everything has worked, you should see the Hello World! notifier on your phone or emulator.

Congratulations!

But clicking OK leaves you staring at a blank screen.

That's because the notifier knows it should disappear when OK is clicked, and you haven't told the app to do anything else.

To quit the app, click the Menu button on the phone or emulator, click Stop This Application, and then choose Stop and Exit.

If you wanted to run Hello World! a second time, you would need to quit the app on the phone or emulator, reset the phone or emulator connection by clicking Connect > Reset Connection, and then restart the whole process manually by going back to the start of step 5. This is clumsy and takes time; surely there's a better way. How about creating a button the user can click to see the "Hello World!" message? To do that, you need to understand a little more about how the phone can detect when something happens—an event. In the next section, we'll look at why understanding events is so important and how you can rerun the app at the touch of a button.

Computers never sleep: why you use events

App Inventor is an event-driven programming language. This means the app sits there constantly watching for an event to happen. An app is a bit like an alert watchdog: if you tell it to listen for an intruder and bark when it hears one, then it will spend all its time and resources doing just that. Unlike a watchdog, it never gets tired and will listen for an intruder thousands of times each second! Apps can watch for lots of different event triggers, so you could write an app that watches all the time to see when a user clicks a button or tips the phone or receives a text, and the app could respond differently to each event.

The problem in the Hello World! app is that the `Screen1.Initialize` event handler you use to trigger the app only happens once: when the app first runs. It would be better to have an event like a button press that the user can touch to trigger the event handler whenever they want to see the message.

Adding a button to the Hello World! program is simple, but before you get to that, it would be a good idea to save a new version of the Hello World! app. That way, you can always go back to the original version if you need to. Learning about saving projects now will save you from getting in a tangle later on.

Saving in the cloud and using checkpoints

Before we get to *how* to save, it's important to understand *what* you're saving. App Inventor projects contain your screen designs, blocks designs, and assets (graphics, sounds, videos, and so on that your app needs). App Inventor projects only work when opened in App Inventor running on your computer. To get an app to work on your phone without being connected to App Inventor, you need to turn it into an Android Application Package (APK) file—and we'll look at these files at the end of the chapter.

App Inventor projects are automatically saved every few seconds as you work on them; you might have noticed that this happens in other programs you use, too, like word processors or graphics programs. One difference with App Inventor is that the projects are saved online out in the cloud—this means they're on a server connected to the internet somewhere, and you don't need to worry about the details. This is handy because you don't lose much work if something goes wrong (like a power outage, for example). There are two potential problems, though:

- If you're experimenting and making lots of changes, and you forget what you did and then want to go back to an earlier version, you're often stuck with the last version that saved ☹.
- If the server breaks (unlikely), you have no local copies of your projects on your own computer.

To solve the first problem, App Inventor lets you save projects and use *checkpoints*.

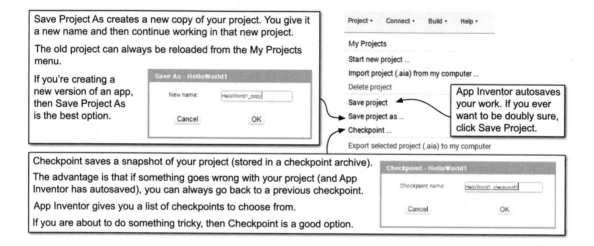

Using Save As and Checkpoint saves project copies in the cloud—but what if you want a copy on your own computer as a backup? You can save the project files of all your projects in one zip file; or you can select the one you want to back up, which is saved as an App Inventor App (.aia) file. To do that, click My Projects and then do the following:

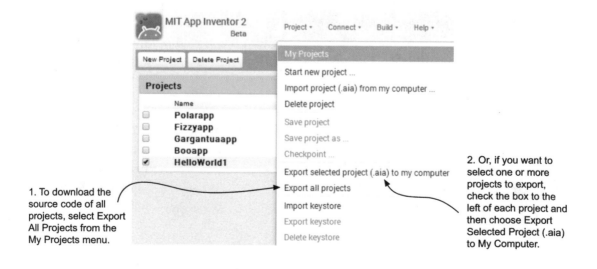

The resulting .aia file will be saved in your computer's Downloads folder. From there you can keep a local copy and share the project file with other App Inventors for them to work on, which they can do by importing your .aia file.

Button click: Hello World! app, version 2

Adding a button to the Hello World! program is a simple four-step process:

1 Save a new copy of the app.
2 Add a button to the screen in the App Inventor Designer.
3 Change the event trigger for the notifier so it watches the button (instead of the **Screen1.Initialize** event).
4 Test the app.

1.   Saving a new copy of Hello World!

You call the new project **HelloWorld1_Button** so that when you look at the list of projects, you know what makes this version different from any others. Giving items sensible names will help you later when things get more complicated and you've created lots of different projects.

2.   Adding a Button component

In the Designer screen, click and drag a button from the Palette onto your phone screen.

You need to tell the user what to do with the button. Change the button text to say **Click Me!**

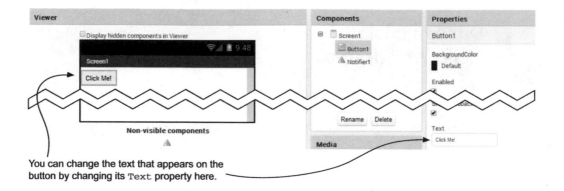

You can change the text that appears on the button by changing its Text property here.

3. Programming the blocks

You've already written the blocks to pop up the notifier. The only thing you need to change is the event trigger—instead of **Screen1.Initialize**, you're going to use a **Click** event triggered by the button. You'll add the event as a new block and then drag and drop the notifier's code blocks from **Screen1.Initialize** into **Button1.Click**.

Switch to the Blocks Editor. Drag out a **Button1.Click** event:

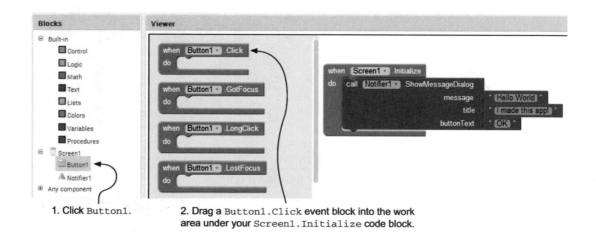

1. Click Button1.

2. Drag a Button1.Click event block into the work area under your Screen1.Initialize code block.

Now drag the **Notifier** block's code from **Screen1.Initialize** into **Button1.Click**:

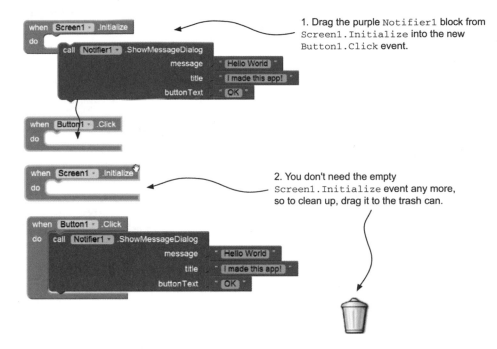

1. Drag the purple Notifier1 block from Screen1.Initialize into the new Button1.Click event.

2. You don't need the empty Screen1.Initialize event any more, so to clean up, drag it to the trash can.

4. Testing your app

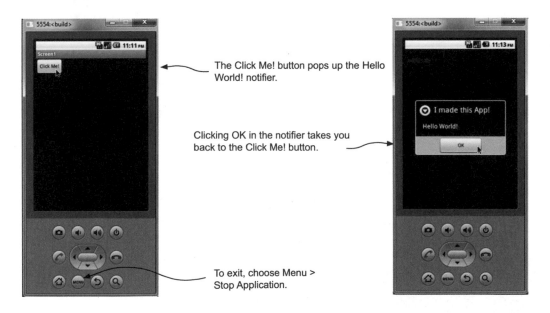

The Click Me! button pops up the Hello World! notifier.

Clicking OK in the notifier takes you back to the Click Me! button.

To exit, choose Menu > Stop Application.

Taking it further

1 Add a new button and notifier to your app. Make the notifier say "Goodbye World" if the user clicks the second button.

2 Try changing the color properties of **Screen1** and **Button1**. Also change the **Font** and **Size** properties of **Button1**.

Packaging an app for your phone

Your first app or two are finished, and they run fine as long as you're connected to App Inventor via Wi-Fi or USB. To get them to run independently on your phone, you need to package them as Android Application Package (APK) files. An APK is the same kind of file you download from the Google Play Store (the online shop where you can download apps to your phone).

You can either download your APK directly to your phone or download it to your computer and then transfer it to your phone over USB or via SD card. The first option (direct download) is an easy way to download a single copy onto a single phone. The second option (download to computer) is a good way to share your app with friends—you can email the APK to them to install on their own phones—or even upload it to a website.

IMPORTANT

APK files can't be loaded back into App Inventor. To change apps, you need to use the project .aia files in My Projects. Think of it this way: project files are like recipes and ingredients, and APKs are like the final cakes. If a baker wants to change the flavor of their cakes, they need to go back to the recipe and bake a new batch. Tinkering with the cakes once they're baked and iced never ends well!

Downloading APKs directly to your phone or computer

To create an APK, do the following:

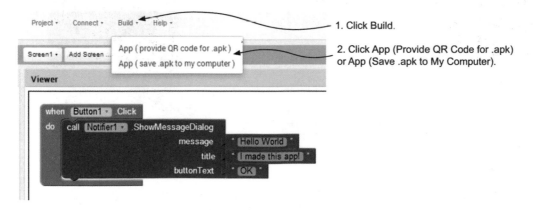

If you select App (Provide QR Code for .apk), you'll see a progress bar. After a bit, you'll see the QR code on your computer screen. You can scan it with the AI Companion app on your phone. When you scan the QR code, the APK will be automatically downloaded to your phone, ready for you to install:

1. Open the MIT AI2 Companion app on your phone.
2. Click Scan the QR Code, and scan the code on your computer screen.
3. The file will download and run.

4. Select Package Installer.

5. Click Install and then Done.

6. The new Hello World! app is in your phone's app list.

Note that your steps may look slightly different depending on which version of the Android operating system is on your phone.

Once the download has finished and the app is installed on your phone, you don't need to use App Inventor to run it. Click the new icon, which looks like this:

Downloading APKs as files to your computer

If you chose to download the APK file to your computer, do this:

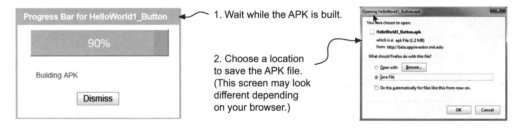

1. Wait while the APK is built.

2. Choose a location to save the APK file. (This screen may look different depending on your browser.)

You can now share the file with others via email and transfer the file to your phone. Opening it using a file browser on your phone will run the app installer.

Changing the app's icon

The App Inventor icon is cute, but you probably don't want all your apps to look the same. You can choose your own image as an icon before you package your APK. It's best if you use an icon that's about 48 x 48 pixels in PNG or JPEG format. Add it to your app like so:

1. In the Designer, click the `Screen1` component.

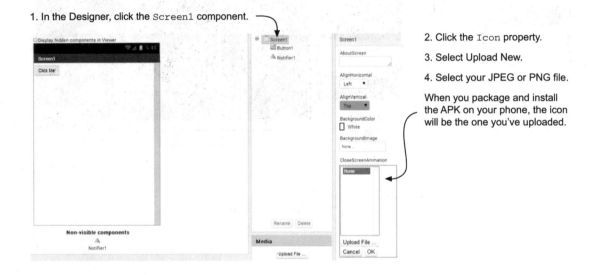

2. Click the `Icon` property.

3. Select Upload New.

4. Select your JPEG or PNG file.

When you package and install the APK on your phone, the icon will be the one you've uploaded.

What did you learn?

In this chapter, you learned about the following:

- The capabilities of Android smartphones
- The three parts of App Inventor: the App Inventor Designer, the Blocks Editor, and the phone or emulator
- The difference between the emulator and a phone
- Using the **Notifier** pop-up and **Button** components
- Event-driven programming
- Saving projects and packaging them for your phone and friends

Test your knowledge

1 What is the difference between Save As and Checkpoint?

2 Which of these actions can't be tested using the emulator?

   a Getting GPS coordinates

   b Playing a sound

   c Clicking a button

   d Capturing a barcode

3 Which of these actions do you do in the App Inventor Designer, and which do you do in the Blocks Editor?

   a Starting a new project

   b Connecting to your phone

   c Using an event handler

   d Adding a button component

   e Changing the app's icon

   f Saving a backup of your app

   g Packaging your app

Try it out

1 Try connecting your phone by USB and Wi-Fi. Which is fastest to connect?

2 Draw a world icon for your app in a simple drawing program, and then package your app using this icon.

CHAPTER 2

Designing the user interface

The chapter 1 apps were simple, but they taught you a lot about how the different parts of App Inventor fit together. In this chapter, you'll build on this to make apps that look fun and do interesting things using graphics and sound. The basic app you'll make is called Getting to Know Ewe. Prod the sheep, and it makes a cute "baa!" sound. You'll then improve the app to make the sheep disappear in fright if you shake the phone—an app called Ewe Scared Her!

People choose to download apps because the apps do something useful, look attractive, and are as easy to use as possible. The "doing something useful" bit is what this book is all about. This chapter focuses on the second two aspects—making an app that looks attractive with a really simple user interface.

What is a user interface?

One of the most popular Android game series is Angry Birds by Rovio. Angry Birds does something useful: it provides challenging puzzles (plus you get to blow stuff up). This isn't the only reason it's popular though—a lot of work has gone into the user interface.

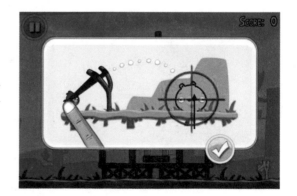

First, it looks great: the characters, artwork, sounds, and text all work together flawlessly. Second, it's incredibly simple to play: the user only needs to tell the game at what angle and speed their next bird should be fired. The game *could* ask the user to type these values on a number pad and press Enter. Instead, the game designers came up with the brilliant idea of having the player drag the bird away from a catapult at an angle and then let go— just like you would if you used a catapult in real life. This is one of the reasons people play the game for hours—it's so easy to play again, and again, and again.

The final thing that Angry Birds does incredibly well is give feedback to the user about the results of flinging the bird. So you see the bird fly and crash and pop, you hear the sound effects, and you feel your phone vibrate.

We call this combination of things the *user interface*, or *UI* for short:

- How the app looks—graphic design, typography (fonts), and color
- How people tell the app what they want to do
- How the app gives information back to the user through the screen, speakers, or *haptic* feedback (buzzing the phone's little motor)

Learning Point:
Input > process > output

Input
The user tells the phone to do something: for example, by touching an object and dragging.

Output
The phone does something like showing a bird flying and crashing, changing the score, or playing a sound.

Process
In Angry Birds, when the user lets go of the bird, the computer inside the phone (called the *processor*) works out where the bird will fly and land and how the landscape will be affected.

Using the Designer to make a UI

The way App Inventor works means you need to do the following:

1. Design the UI first in the Designer window (even if it's only a rough draft).
2. Program the Blocks Editor to tell the app what to do.
3. Test the program on your phone or emulator.

You'll spend most of your time as an app inventor flipping backward and forward between these three activities, like this:

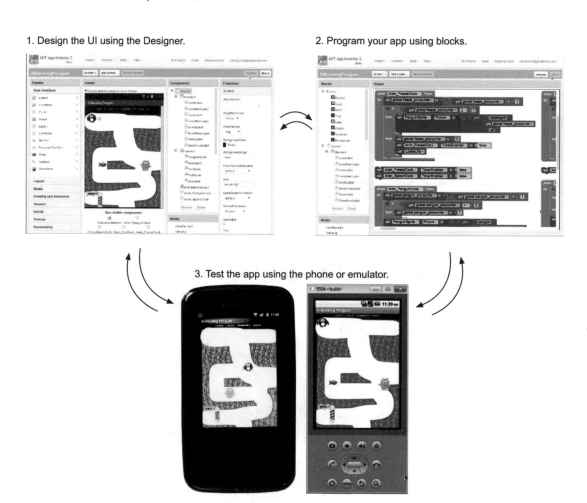

1. Design the UI using the Designer.

2. Program your app using blocks.

3. Test the app using the phone or emulator.

Learning Point: Working from the top down

In App Inventor, you design the UI first and then write a computer program. This is an example of a *top-down* approach.

An alternative way of doing things in other programs is to start with the nuts and bolts of the program and worry about the UI later—*bottom-up*.

Both approaches have advantages and disadvantages, and in practice you'll probably find yourself doing a little of each as you build apps.

Speeding along: built-in components

As a computer and smartphone user, you'll recognize lots of the components in App Inventor's Palette. Elements like buttons, screen labels, and text boxes are common in web pages, desktop programs, and smartphone applications. Because App Inventor has these ready-made elements, you can speed up the process of creating apps.

These are all the App Inventor components. Don't let the number of components overwhelm you. There are a lot to choose from, but we'll help you quickly decide what's best for each app.

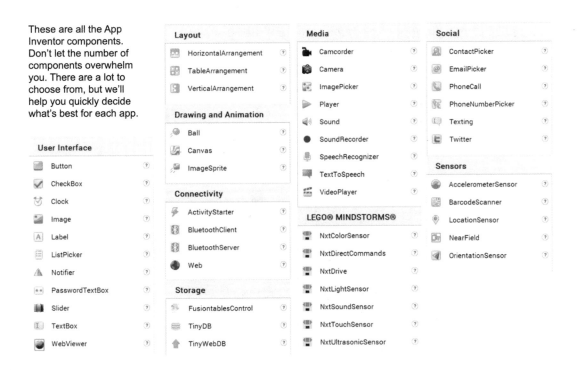

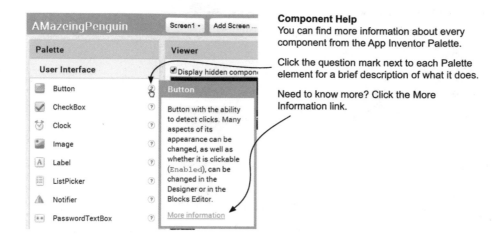

Component Help
You can find more information about every component from the App Inventor Palette.

Click the question mark next to each Palette element for a brief description of what it does.

Need to know more? Click the More Information link.

In this chapter, you'll use only a few of the components. You'll say hello to more and more of them as you go through the book, but feel free to dip in now and take a look at some of the more exotic components and what they do by using the built-in component help.

Now, let's use some components to build your fun little app.

Getting to Know Ewe app

PURPOSE OF THIS APP
This app displays a picture of a sheep in a field. When the user prods the sheep, it baas.

APP RATING

ASSETS YOU'LL NEED
Images: green pasture background and sheep. Sounds: "baa!"

1. Setting up the project

Start a new App Inventor project by choosing Project > Start New Project. Give it the name `GettingToKnowEwe`, and click OK. You should see the familiar four columns: Palette, Viewer, Components, and Properties.

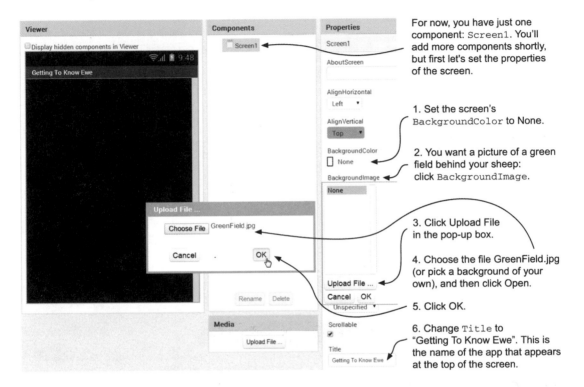

For now, you have just one component: `Screen1`. You'll add more components shortly, but first let's set the properties of the screen.

1. Set the screen's `BackgroundColor` to None.

2. You want a picture of a green field behind your sheep: click `BackgroundImage`.

3. Click Upload File in the pop-up box.

4. Choose the file GreenField.jpg (or pick a background of your own), and then click Open.

5. Click OK.

6. Change `Title` to "Getting To Know Ewe". This is the name of the app that appears at the top of the screen.

You can see that the App Inventor screen has changed. This is only a rough draft of how the app will look on your emulator or phone. You can check out the differences by connecting your phone or starting an emulator; as you make changes in the Designer, those changes will appear immediately on the phone.

Learning Point: Setting properties

All components have *properties*—things you can change about that component. Some components have many properties (such as **Screen**), others have only a few (such as **Sound**), and some have none (such as **Camera**). The Properties column on the right side of your screen lets you set the properties of components when your app first starts.

Later, the programs you write will be able to both read and change properties. This is called GETting and SETting properties—you'll notice that many blocks start with the word **get** or **set**.

---

2. Adding a sheep image

You need two components to complete your app's UI: a sheep picture and a "baa!" sound. Looking at the component options shown next, which one do you think will let you insert your sheep?

CHOOSING THE COMPONENT

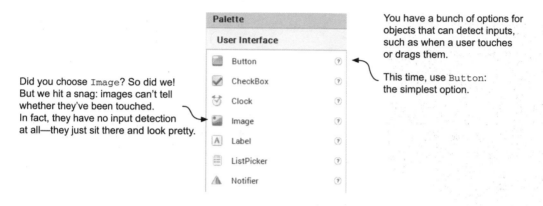

You have a bunch of options for objects that can detect inputs, such as when a user touches or drags them.

This time, use Button: the simplest option.

Did you choose Image? So did we! But we hit a snag: images can't tell whether they've been touched. In fact, they have no input detection at all—they just sit there and look pretty.

ADDING AND RENAMING THE BUTTON

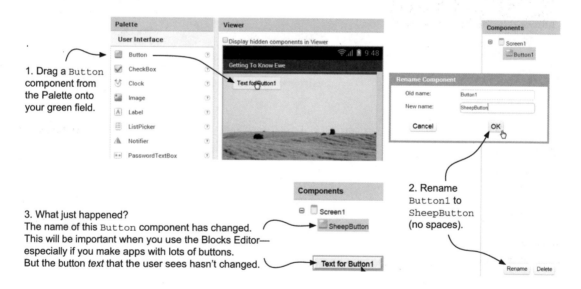

1. Drag a Button component from the Palette onto your green field.

2. Rename Button1 to SheepButton (no spaces).

3. What just happened? The name of this Button component has changed. This will be important when you use the Blocks Editor—especially if you make apps with lots of buttons. But the button *text* that the user sees hasn't changed.

MAKING THE BUTTON LOOK LIKE A SHEEP

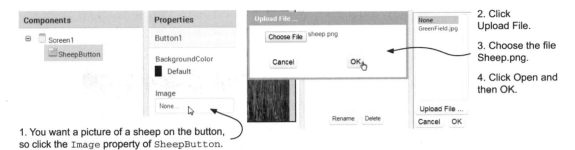

2. Click Upload File.

3. Choose the file Sheep.png.

4. Click Open and then OK.

1. You want a picture of a sheep on the button, so click the Image property of SheepButton.

Learning Point:
Portable Network Graphics (PNG) format

We're using a PNG formatted image of a sheep with a transparent background. This means the sheep won't have a white box around it.

The sheep has button text written across its eyes and is rather large. So, change the **Text**, **Width**, and **Height** properties to fix these problems. We've zoomed in on the relevant properties to help you find them:

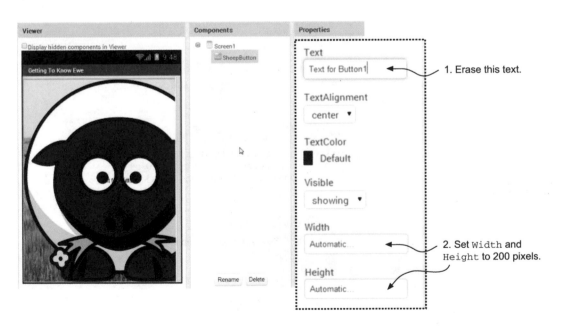

1. Erase this text.

2. Set Width and Height to 200 pixels.

3. Adding a "baa!" sound

The last component you need is the "baa!" sound:

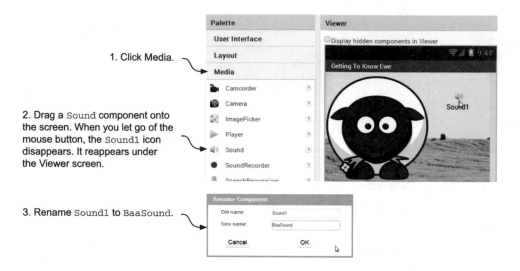

1. Click Media.

2. Drag a Sound component onto the screen. When you let go of the mouse button, the Sound1 icon disappears. It reappears under the Viewer screen.

3. Rename Sound1 to BaaSound.

Finally, you need to attach a sound source file to your **BaaSound** component. App Inventor can use sound files in a variety of formats; we suggest you use PCM/WAV files or MP3s because they should work on all phones.

WARNING

It's easy to forget this step with sounds. If a button or background doesn't have a media file attached, it's obvious in the screen preview. But if you forget a sound, you may only realize it when you run the program later.

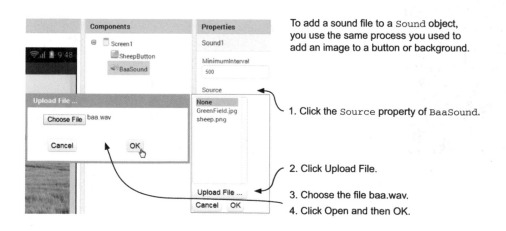

To add a sound file to a Sound object, you use the same process you used to add an image to a button or background.

1. Click the Source property of BaaSound.

2. Click Upload File.

3. Choose the file baa.wav.

4. Click Open and then OK.

Learning Point: Nonvisible components

A sound is a *nonvisible component*—you don't see it on the screen. Other nonvisible components include input devices like the camera, the barcode scanner, and the accelerometer and orientation sensors that detect movement and direction (shaking or tipping the phone). When you design your UI, drag over the desired components and drop them onto the screen. You'll see them appear in the Non-Visible Components section beneath the Viewer screen.

That's it! Your UI has all the elements you need to make the basic version of the Getting to Know Ewe app. You've chosen and added all the objects, attached media to them (images and sound), and set some of their other properties like `Size` and `Text`. The finished UI should look like this:

4. Programming the blocks, part 1: playing the sound

Remember how in chapter 1 you used a `Button.Click` event to tell the program you wanted it to do something? This app works exactly the same way—when a user prods the sheep, they're really clicking a button.

Switch to the Blocks Editor, and, if you haven't already, connect a phone or emulator as you did in chapter 1. Create the blocks like this:

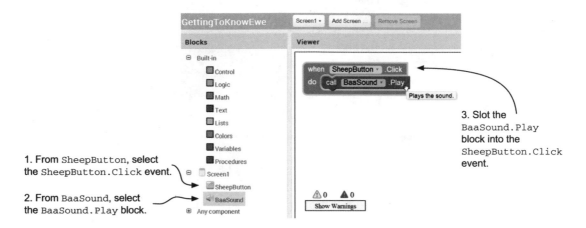

1. From `SheepButton`, **select** the `SheepButton.Click` **event.**

2. From `BaaSound`, **select** the `BaaSound.Play` **block.**

3. Slot the `BaaSound.Play` block into the `SheepButton.Click` event.

Now try it—click the sheep on your phone, and you should be rewarded with a bleating sheep!

Learning Point: Calling procedures

In this app, you play the "baa!" sound using a built-in procedure, `Play`. This is known as *calling* a procedure. You can spot procedures because their blocks are purple and include the word `call`. In chapter 5, you'll learn how to create and call your own procedures.

5. Programming the blocks, part 2: vibrating the phone

Click the `BaaSound` section in `MyBlocks`, and you'll see lots of purple procedures such as pausing, resuming, and stopping the sound. There is also a procedure to vibrate the phone. You'll use this so that in addition to playing the "baa!" sound, the phone will vibrate.

Phones only!

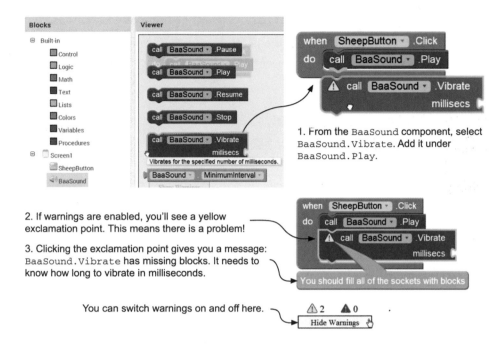

1. From the BaaSound component, select BaaSound.Vibrate. Add it under BaaSound.Play.

2. If warnings are enabled, you'll see a yellow exclamation point. This means there is a problem!

3. Clicking the exclamation point gives you a message: BaaSound.Vibrate has missing blocks. It needs to know how long to vibrate in milliseconds.

You can switch warnings on and off here.

ENTERING A VALUE

There are 1,000 milliseconds in 1 second, so enter **1000** into the **BaaSound.Vibrate** block. You have two options for entering values: choose the one that you find easiest.

Option 1: Use a Built-in > Math block.

To create a Number block with the value 1000, do this:
1. Click Built-in > Math.
2. Select the Number block, which contains a zero.
3. Click 0, and change it to 1000.

Option 2: Use a keyboard shortcut.

1. Click anywhere in the blank work area of the Blocks Editor.
2. Type 1000.
3. Press Enter on your keyboard.

Now plug your **Number** block (with the value 1000) into the empty socket of **BaaSound.Vibrate**. You'll see the yellow exclamation point disappear, and the app will now work on your phone—try it.

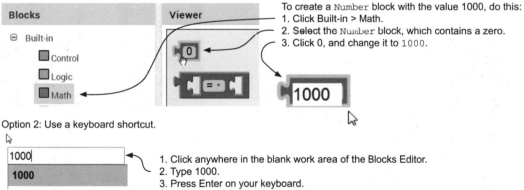

Experiment with different values for `BaaSound.Vibrate`. Try these challenges:

- What's the shortest time you can enter and still feel the phone vibrate?
- How many milliseconds do you need to enter to make the vibration last exactly as long as the "baa!" sound?

Extra challenge: Ewe Scared Her! app

PURPOSE OF THIS APP
Click the sheep, and she baas. Shake the phone, and the sheep disappears, and the message "Ewe scared her!" appears on a reset button. The user clicks this button to start again.

APP RATING

ASSETS YOU'LL NEED
A completed version of the Getting to Know Ewe app.

Click the sheep, and she baaas!

Shake the sheep, and she disappears. A button appears.

Click the button, and …

… she reappears!

1. Saving a new project

To get started, save a copy of **GettingToKnowEwe**.

1. Choose Project > Save Project As.
2. Change the name to `EweScaredHer`.
3. Click OK.

2. Adding components: accelerometer, reset button, and screen arrangement

To make this app, you need to go back to the Designer screen and think about inputs and outputs. The *input* is easy—you need to know if the phone is shaking. Most phones have an accelerometer that can detect movement. The **AccelerometerSensor** component in the Sensors section of the Palette can detect a **Shaking** event. You also need a **ResetButton** input; this detects when a user clicks the reset button, just like in Getting to Know Ewe.

Next is the *output*. When the phone is shaken, you'll hide **SheepButton** and show **Reset-Button**. When the reset button is clicked, you'll hide it and show the sheep.

For the overall layout, it would be helpful to be able to arrange things in a grid. To do this, you can center the button at the top of the screen and the sheep at the bottom using a **VerticalArrangement** component.[1]

You can see how all this looks in the Designer.

---

[1] You'll find more on screen arrangement and a mini project to practice in the next chapter.

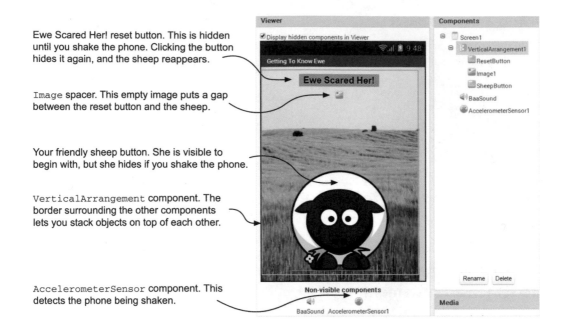

Ewe Scared Her! reset button. This is hidden until you shake the phone. Clicking the button hides it again, and the sheep reappears.

`Image` spacer. This empty image puts a gap between the reset button and the sheep.

Your friendly sheep button. She is visible to begin with, but she hides if you shake the phone.

`VerticalArrangement` component. The border surrounding the other components lets you stack objects on top of each other.

`AccelerometerSensor` component. This detects the phone being shaken.

Add the components by dragging them from the Palette onto your Designer screen, like so:

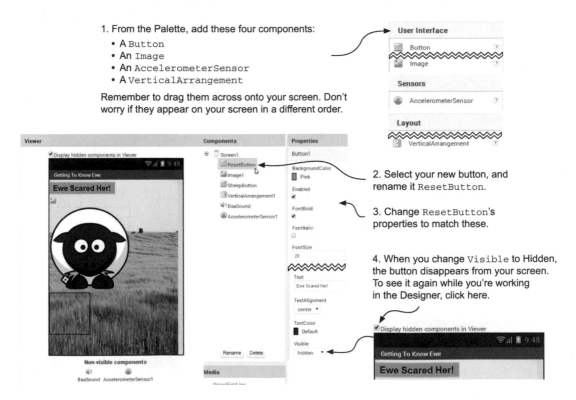

1. From the Palette, add these four components:
   - A `Button`
   - An `Image`
   - An `AccelerometerSensor`
   - A `VerticalArrangement`

Remember to drag them across onto your screen. Don't worry if they appear on your screen in a different order.

2. Select your new button, and rename it `ResetButton`.

3. Change `ResetButton`'s properties to match these.

4. When you change `Visible` to Hidden, the button disappears from your screen. To see it again while you're working in the Designer, click here.

3. Arranging the screen

Select the **VerticalArrangement** component, and set its **Height** and **Width** properties to **Fill Parent**. Set its **AlignHorizontal** property to **Center**. Select the image component (**Image1**), and set its **Height** to 150 pixels; this will be a spacer, so the sheep appears to stand on the grass.

Drag your components into the
VerticalArrangement1 box
in this order:

1. ResetButton
2. Image1
3. SheepButton

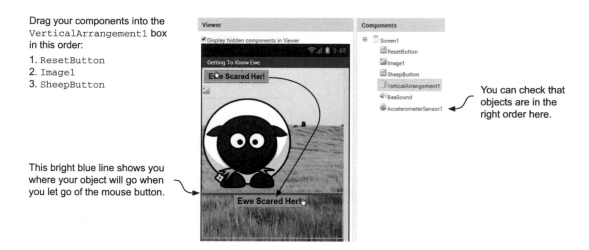

This bright blue line shows you
where your object will go when
you let go of the mouse button.

You can check that
objects are in the
right order here.

4. Programming the blocks

Switching to the Blocks Editor, you need two new blocks for your two new input events. From the **AccelerometerSensor1** and **ResetButton** blocks, add these events to the workspace:

- **AccelerometerSensor1.Shaking**
- **ResetButton.Click**

You want to set the **Visible** property of **SheepButton** and **ResetButton** depending on which event happens. A table will help here:

Event	SheepButton	ResetButton
AccelerometerSensor1.Shaking	Hidden	Visible
ResetButton.Click	Visible	Hidden

To change an onscreen component so it's visible or hidden, you set its **Visible** property to True (for visible) or False (for hidden).

HINT
Blocks that set properties are green.

Get the **set** blocks shown from the **SheepButton** and **ResetButton** sections of the blocks. To add the **true** and **false** blocks, you can either type **true** or **false** into a blank area of the Blocks Editor and press Enter, or go to the Built-in > Logic section.

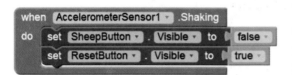

This is the block for hiding the sheep and showing the reset button. Now—can you figure out how to do **ResetButton.Click**?

Are you done? Wow, congratulations! You're truly on your way to being an amazing app designer.

As you go through the book, you'll see how you could make improvements to this app, like animating the sheep to move off the screen instead of just disappearing—or how about a walking sound effect? In chapter 3, we'll look at how you can use your phone to draw graffiti and how to create a customizable sound FX machine you can carry around in your pocket.

Taking it further

Adapt Ewe Scared Her! so that instead of hiding the sheep, you change the image to an angry sheep and change the reset button to say Ewe Made Her ANGRY!?

What did you learn?

In this chapter, you learned about the following:

- What makes a good user interface
- Input, process, and output
- Switching between the Designer screen, the Blocks Editor, and your phone (or emulator) to make an app
- Top-down versus bottom-up program design
- App Inventor's built-in components and how to find out about what they do

- Renaming components
- Setting properties
- Adding an image to a screen or a button
- Hiding and showing objects
- Playing sounds by calling a **Play** procedure
- Detecting when the phone is shaken, using an accelerometer
- Creating a simple screen arrangement using a **VerticalArrangement** component

Test your knowledge

1 Pick a device in your house. What are its inputs, and what are its outputs?

2 Why do apps sometimes look different in the Designer than they do in the emulator?

3 What event is triggered when a button is clicked?

  a **Button.Press**

  b **Button.Touch**

  c **Button.Click**

4 What color are these blocks?

  a Events

  b Procedure calls

  c Values (numbers)

  d Set property

Try it out

1 Create a Whipcrack app that plays the sound of a whip cracking whenever you make a whipping movement with the phone (use the **Accelerometer.Shaking** event).

2 Create a Canned Laughter, Drum Roll, or Rim Hit app with a button to activate the corresponding sound effect.

3 Create a simple sound-clip player app with Play, Pause, and Resume buttons. At this stage it will work only with the sound clip you specify in the sound properties.

CHAPTER 3

Using the screen: layouts and the canvas

Getting objects to appear in the right place onscreen can be tricky—especially because Android devices come in all shapes and sizes. Also, you never know when a user will tip the screen and the display will change from portrait to landscape. In the Ewe Scared Her! app in chapter 2, you used a basic vertical layout to make sure items appeared in the right order top to bottom; you also used an invisible spacer to separate the sheep from the button. In this chapter, we'll take these ideas further by looking at more screen properties and also layout components in the Palette. You'll practice these skills by making a Spooky Sound FX app.

In the second half of the chapter, we'll begin to look at the canvas, a powerful tool for organizing graphical elements anywhere onscreen. You'll also see that the canvas lets you interact with the screen in ways other than just the single touch you've used so far with buttons. In the Graffiti Artist app, you'll be dragging paint all over the screen (coveralls optional).

Layout

In this section, you'll take control of the screen, organizing eight elements in a grid to make a Sound FX app that plays spooky noises. It looks simple, but you need to make sure that

- The app copes with the user tilting or rotating the phone. If the layout also rotates, then some buttons will disappear off the bottom of the app.
- The buttons appear in a centered grid and are sized correctly.

Dealing with phone rotation is easy—there's an option to allow or stop rotation in the screen's properties. For this app, you won't allow the display to rotate (see the section "1. Set the screen properties" for the Spooky Sound FX app for how to do this).

Arranging elements in a grid is trickier. Unless you tell it what to do, App Inventor defaults to piling components on top of each other. Drag three objects onto the screen in the App Inventor Designer, and they pile up like a stack of pancakes. You can change the order, but if you want the objects next to each other, what do you do?

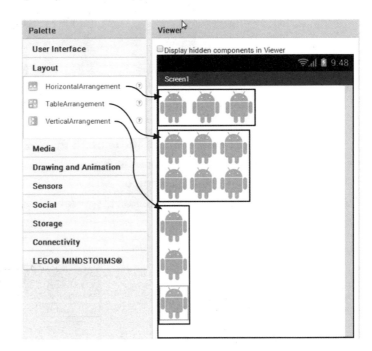

You can choose from three components to help you, in the Layout section of your Palette:

- **HorizontalArrangement** should be used when you want components placed left to right across the screen.
- **TableArrangement** lets you arrange components in a grid. You can put only one component in each cell—if you squash a couple or more in, only the last component will be displayed.
- **VerticalArrangement** lets you stack components on top of each other.

Learning Point: Testing layouts

Always test layouts on the emulator or a phone. In all the apps in this chapter, you'll see differences such as lines around the layout components that are invisible on the phone.

Layout: mini-project

Try to reproduce the sentence layout above using the **HorizontalArrangement**, **VerticalArrangement**, and **TableArrangement** components. Each word should be created on a separate label—so you'll end up with 15 labels in your project. For **Horizontal-Arrangement** and **VerticalArrangement**, you can drag and drop labels into the correct place using the blue indicator to help see where the label will appear.

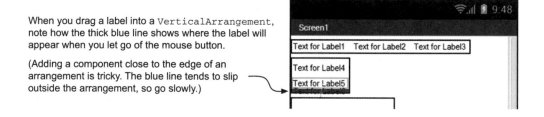

When you drag a label into a VerticalArrangement, note how the thick blue line shows where the label will appear when you let go of the mouse button.

(Adding a component close to the edge of an arrangement is tricky. The blue line tends to slip outside the arrangement, so go slowly.)

When you create the **TableArrangement**, you specify the number of columns and rows in Properties. In this case, you want three columns and three rows. Then drag in components just like with **HorizontalArrangement** and **VerticalArrangement**.

When you're finished, your screen should look like this:

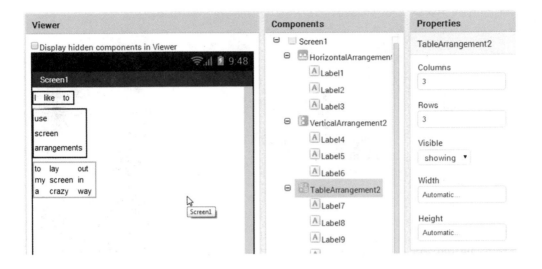

WARNING: QUIRKY GRAPHICAL EFFECTS

TABLES

At the time of writing, the **Layout** component in App Inventor can be a little quirky because empty cells are ignored. For example, if you create a 3 x 3 table and put something in the top-middle cell and something else in the bottom-middle cell, they will be spaced apart in the Designer—but on your phone, the space in the center will be ignored.

In addition, image elements in a table try to match the width of the widest element. So if an image at the top is wide and another at the bottom is narrow, the bottom image will appear stretched—or disappear. You can fix these image issues by manually setting the **Height** and **Width** properties of each image.

TRANSPARENCY

While we're on the subject of quirky graphical effects, transparency can sometimes misbehave. For example, if you set your screen's **BackgroundColor** property to a color (rather than None) and then insert a background image and a component with some transparency (like the sheep in chapter 1), then on the phone the transparent areas will be a solid block of color (whatever the original screen background was). Change the screen's **BackgroundColor** property back to None to restore image transparency.

Now that you understand the three layout components, you'll put the table component to practical use in a Spooky Sound FX app. Then, in the Graffiti Artist app, you'll use a horizontal arrangement to give the user a neat bar of buttons for picking colors.

Spooky Sound FX app

PURPOSE OF THIS APP
This is a sound-board app that lets you play eight spooky sound effects by touching an icon. You could use the app to scare your friends (or your computer teacher). It could also provide sound effects for a ghost story, play, or movie that you record.

APP RATING
3

ASSETS YOU'LL NEED
Eight spooky button images and sounds. Rumors that Paula provided the witch's cackle are entirely unfounded.

In previous chapters, we showed you every single app-building step. We figure you're getting the hang of things by now. To help you build apps quickly from this point on, we'll give you a summary of the components you need to drag onscreen and then concentrate on the tricky parts in the explanations. If you're feeling adventurous, you can try setting up the app from just the following table and see how far you get before reading further. It's important that each new app start as a new project with a sensible name (for example, **SoundFx**). If you don't name your projects something meaningful, then later on you'll be left with a list of projects that you'll have to open one by one to find out what they do. This quickly becomes tedious—so get into the habit of naming things properly now.

Spooky Sound FX app			
Screen1 properties	**AlignHorizontal**: Center **ScreenOrientation**: Portrait **Scrollable**: Yes (selected) **Title**: Sound FX: Spooky **Icon**: ghost_button.png (downloaded from our website) **BackgroundColor**: Black (A black background makes gridlines hard to see, so only set this after you've arranged all the other components onscreen.)		
Components	**What do I rename it?**	**What does it do?**	**What properties do I set?**
TableArrangement Palette group: Layout	**TableArrangement1**	Creates a 2-column x 4-row grid that organizes your buttons on the screen.	**Columns**: 2 **Rows**: 4 **Width**: Automatic **Height**: Fill Parent

Components	What do I rename it?	What does it do?	What properties do I set?

8 **Button**s
Palette group:
User Interface
	`GhostButton`
	`BatButton`
	`OwlButton`
	`FootstepButton`
	`CatButton`
	`WolfButton`
	`CackleButton`
	`ThunderButton`
		These are the buttons the user clicks to hear a sound.	**Image**: Upload the matching media file for each button: ghost_button.png for `GhostButton`, bat_button.png for `BatButton`, and so on.
			Text: Nothing—delete the text.
			Width: 90 pixels
			Height: 90 pixels

8 **Sound** objects
Palette group: Media
	`GhostSound`
	`BatSound`
	`OwlSound`
	`FootstepSound`
	`CatSound`
	`WolfSound`
	`CackleSound`
	`ThunderSound`
		Creates eight sound objects you can play using the Blocks Editor, just like you played the "baa" sound in Getting to Know Ewe.	**Source**: Upload the matching media file for each sound: ghost.wav for `GhostSound`, bats.wav for `BatSound`, and so on.

Media files			
8 sound files downloaded from our website: ghost.wav bats.wav owl.wav cackling.wav thunderclap.wav cat.wav wolf.wav footstep.wav		Each sound object's **Source** property will be set to one of these matching files so that when you play the sound, you hear the correct file.	
8 image files downloaded from our website: bat_button.png lightning_button.png cat_button.png owl_button.png footsteps_button.png witch_button.png ghost_button.png wolf_button.png		Each button's **Image** property will be set to display one of these images.	

1. Setting the screen properties: alignment, orientation, and scrolling

Sometimes you want an app to change its orientation when the phone is rotated (you'll see examples in later chapters). But for this app, you want to make sure the app stays in portrait alignment (even if the user tips the phone). You also want the user to be able to scroll around and see all the icons if they have a very small Android screen. Finally, you want the table and buttons to be centrally aligned. All this is controlled in the `Screen` component's properties. Use the table at the start of this section to set all the properties for `Screen1` except `BackgroundColor`. The properties you haven't come across before are as follows:

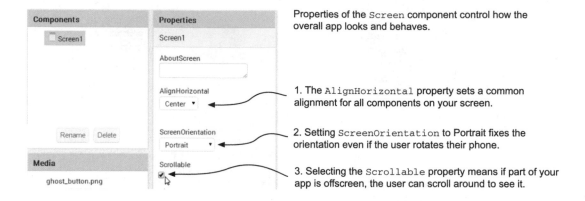

Properties of the `Screen` component control how the overall app looks and behaves.

1. The `AlignHorizontal` property sets a common alignment for all components on your screen.

2. Setting `ScreenOrientation` to Portrait fixes the orientation even if the user rotates their phone.

3. Selecting the `Scrollable` property means if part of your app is offscreen, the user can scroll around to see it.

2. Setting up the table arrangement and eight buttons

Once you've added the **TableArrangement** component to the screen, make sure its properties are set exactly as described in the app table at the start of this section. You should see an empty box with a green outline appear. Add the eight buttons, placing one in each section of the table. Don't forget to delete the buttons' text and set their width and height to 90 pixels as you did in chapter 2.

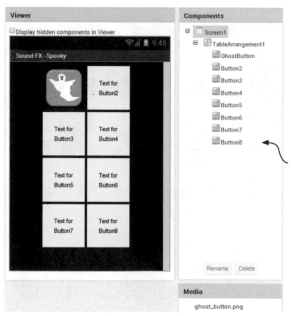

Once you've set up the buttons in the table arrangement, do this:

1. Resize them: `Height` and `Width` = 90 pixels.
2. Delete the text from the `Text` property of each button.
3. Rename them.
4. Set each button's `Image` property to one of the spooky icons we've provided.

You can see that all the buttons are in the `TableArrangement1` component by looking at the Components list.

When the layout is complete, set **Screen1**'s **BackgroundColor** property to Black. Now you should see a black screen with eight green icons, as shown in the screenshot in the next section.

3. Adding the eight Sound components and their source files

The final part of this setup is to add eight **Sound** components (remember that these are found in the Media section of the Palette and that you drag-and-drop them anywhere on the screen). Rename them, and set their **Source** properties to match their names—for example, the **WolfSound** component's source file is called wolf.wav. Your Spooky Sound FX app design is complete and should look like this.

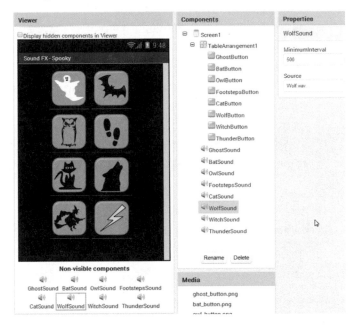

4. Coding the blocks

You already know the code you need here—it's exactly the same as for the baaing sheep in Getting to Know Ewe. The difference is that instead of choosing **SheepButton.Click**, you'll need eight **Button.Click** events—one for each spooky sound. When you've added the eight **Button.Click** events and the eight **Sound.Play** functions, the final result should look something like this:

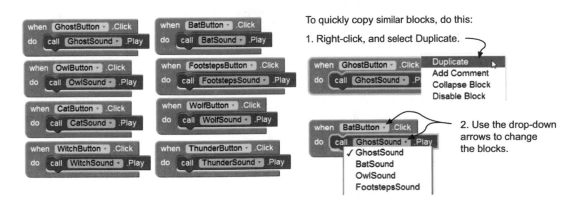

Taking it further

Here are some creative ways you could change or rebuild this app:

- Add more rows and columns of buttons—and find your own favorite button images and sounds.
- Create a sound board using sound effects from your favorite movie or videogame genre, such as sci-fi, action, or comedy.
- Create a sound board of your favorite movie quotes and snippets.
- Make a friends and family sound board with recorded messages and photos.
- Make a beatbox app with your favorite drum loops and instrument hits. What happens if you click the same button multiple times? What happens if you click one button right after another?
- Make a sound board of your favorite jokes—don't forget to include an Applause button and a Canned Laughter button just in case nobody gets them!

TIP

In addition to finding sound clips on the web, you could record yourself using a microphone.

There are lots of internet sites where you can download sound effects and clip art for your buttons. For the Spooky Sound FX app, we used mainly www.clker.com for the graphics and www.freesound.org for the sound clips. We edited the sound clips using the brilliant and free Audacity software: http://audacity.sourceforge.net.

Learning Point: Copyright, Creative Commons, and public domain

Copying and using images and sounds from the internet is easy to do, but you need to be careful that you aren't stealing someone else's work. This becomes especially important if you plan to make your apps widely available—that is, sharing them through your own website or the Play Store rather than creating apps for your personal use or to share with a few friends. Broadly speaking, images and sounds usually fall into one of three categories:

- *Copyrighted material* ©—When you see the copyright symbol, it means you need to seek permission from the copyright owner before you can copy or use the item. You may find that the original creator is happy for you to use their work—particularly when it's an individual rather than a large corporation. They may ask that you don't change it and that you make it clear that they created the original (this is called *attribution*).
- *Public domain*—Items in the public domain are copyright free and can be freely copied and reused without attribution or payment.   ➤

- *Creative Commons* ©—Content marked with the double CC logo has a Creative Commons license. Creative Commons is a way content creators can easily license their work so that other people can use it. Content creators can choose

  - Whether their work may be changed or just copied (called *derivative*)
  - Whether their work can be sold as part of something else (called *commercial*)
  - Whether you have to state who made the original (called *attribution*)

Creative Commons uses symbols to say which of these things are allowed. You can find out more here: http://creativecommons.org.

When you've created your own apps, Creative Commons is a good way to make it clear to others what they're allowed to do with them.

WARNING: SOUND AND GRAPHICS FILE FORMATS

App Inventor's **Sound** component generally likes sounds in WAV or MP3 format. It sometimes has a problem with audio files that are large or that have embedded tags. So if you have problems with an audio file, try these things:

- Check that it's short—say, less than 30 seconds.
- Convert it to a different format. For example, if it's an MP3, convert it to a WAV. You can use Audacity or a free online service to do this, like http://media.io.
- Use Audacity to make the file smaller by reducing its bit rate (quality). You'll find this setting at bottom right on the screen. 11,025 Hz or lower is fine.
- Close your App Inventor windows, disconnect your phone, and then restart everything. (You'll be surprised how often this works!)

For graphics files, we usually stick to JPEGs or PNGs. Resizing them in a graphics editor before uploading is usually better than uploading a large image and then reducing it in App Inventor.

Now that you know how to make grid layouts, we'll look at the **Canvas** component. It deals with screen layout and interaction in a much more flexible fashion.

Introducing the Canvas component

Canvas is a component that provides more advanced graphical components, animations, and user interactions. What are the differences between the canvas and the screen?

Each app has a screen that is generated as soon as you select New Project. You can't change the name of **Screen1**. This screen is a container for all the components the user interacts with—it's essentially a box for putting things into.

The canvas is both a container for things *and* a two-dimensional touch-sensitive rectangular panel. It can detect events like touching, dragging, and flinging (more on this in chapter 4).

You can draw on a canvas, and *sprites* (animated figures) can move around on it. In fact, if you want any animation in your app, you have to include a `Canvas` component. In addition to the usual color, width, height, and background image properties, `Canvas` also allows you to set a default paint color and line width.

Graffiti Artist app

PURPOSE OF THIS APP
When the user drags their finger (or the mouse, in the emulator) across the wall, they draw lines. The user can also touch the screen to make dots. They can choose the paint color by tapping a color button. Clicking Clean It Off! clears all the graffiti.

APP RATING

3

ASSETS YOU'LL NEED
Image: Wall.png.

Create a new app called Graffiti Artist.

Graffiti Artist app			
Screen1 properties	**AlignHorizontal**: Center **AlignVertical**: Center **ScreenOrientation**: Portrait **Scrollable**: No (unselected) **Title**: Graffiti Artist **BackgroundColor**: None		
Components	**What do I rename it?**	**What does it do?**	**What properties do I set?**
HorizontalArrangement Palette group: Layout	ColorBar	Contains the five color-change buttons at the top of the screen	**Width**: Fill Parent **Height**: Automatic **AlignHorizontal**: Center
5 **Buttons** Palette group: User Interface	**RedButton** **GreenButton** **WhiteButton** **PinkButton** **BlueButton**	Change the paint color	**BackgroundColor**: Match this to the button name. **FontSize**: 14 **Text**: Same as **BackgroundColor** **TextAlignment**: Center **Width**: Automatic **Height**: Automatic

Components	What do I rename it?	What does it do?	What properties do I set?
Canvas Palette group: Drawing and Animation	`WallCanvas`	Enables the user to draw and dot on the wall with their finger	**BackgroundColor**: Black **BackgroundImage**: Wall.png **PaintColor**: Red **Width**: Fill Parent **Height**: Fill Parent
Button Palette group: User Interface	`WipeButton`	Clears the graffiti	**FontSize**: 16 **Text**: "Clean it off!" **TextAlignment**: Center **Width**: Automatic **Height**: Automatic

1. Setting up the user interface

In this app, it's important that the graffiti wall fill as much of the screen as possible. A current working standard size for a small phone is 320 pixels x 480 pixels (width x height). But the screen size of the devices (phones, tablets, and so on) that you might want to use your app on will vary. Generally, experimenting with the Fill Parent and Automatic options for width and height is a good idea. This means the **Layout** component will attempt to fill the screen space available. You can see from the table that you use these settings for most of the components. The other tricky part of this arrangement is making sure the five buttons at the top go into the **HorizontalArrangement** and everything else sits below it.

Follow the table to design your screen. It should end up looking like this.

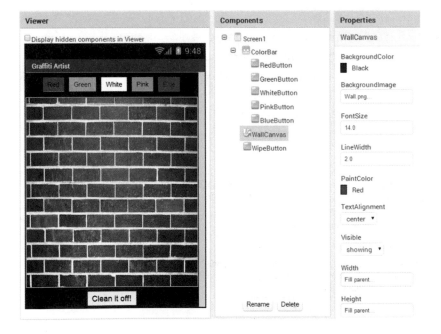

2. Coding the blocks

Now that you have your user interface set up with your canvas, arrangement, and buttons, it's time to think about how the user will interact with the app. A user can trigger four types of events in your app:

- They touch the wall in a single spot and then let go, drawing a dot.
- They drag their finger across the wall, drawing a line.
- They change the paint color by clicking one of the color buttons.
- They click the Clean It Off! button to clear the wall of graffiti.

DRAWING: MAKING DOTS

When the application is complete, you want users to be able to draw dots on the screen. In order to make this work in the app, you use the **Touched** event trigger. It works just like the **Click** event for buttons, but it also tells the program where the user touched the screen. That's useful here because you can tell where the user touched and then draw a dot at that location. When an event gives you extra information like this, it's called an *event argument*. Event arguments are *local variables*—only that event can see them. We'll discuss these ideas more in chapter 6.

Switch to the Blocks Editor. From **WallCanvas**, select the **WallCanvas.Touched** event-handler block. Did you notice that the block has three additional orange rectangles just under its name? These are the event arguments—useful pieces of information about the location on the canvas that the user touched. In Graffiti Artist, the event arguments you're interested in are x and y coordinates—knowing these means you can draw a dot at a specific position. To use these orange block values in other parts of your program, you need to *hover* your mouse pointer over them (don't click yet) and then click the **get** option. You're probably wondering about the third orange block, **touchedSprite**. This would tell you the name of any sprite the user touched, but you don't have any sprites in this app—so it isn't something you need to worry about until chapter 4.

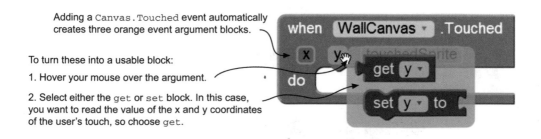

Adding a `Canvas.Touched` event automatically creates three orange event argument blocks.

To turn these into a usable block:

1. Hover your mouse over the argument.

2. Select either the `get` or `set` block. In this case, you want to read the value of the x and y coordinates of the user's touch, so choose `get`.

To draw a dot (called a circle in App Inventor) at the position where the user touched, follow these steps:

1 From **WallCanvas**, select the **WallCanvas.DrawCircle** block, and plug it into the **WallCanvas.Touched** event handler.

2 Select the **get x** and **get y** blocks from the **WallCanvas.Touched** orange event arguments, and drop them into the **x** and **y** slots in the purple **WallCanvas.DrawCircle** block.

3 There is still one gap to fill: the **r** (radius) of the dot or circle you're drawing.

   Add a number block with the value 5. You can either click **WallCanvas.Touched**, type 5, and press Enter; or, from the Built-in blocks, choose Math (the blue zero block) and then change the value to 5.

The finished dotting block should look like this.

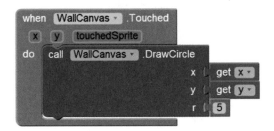

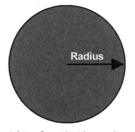

Learning Point: Math terms—coordinates and radius

X,Y COORDINATES

The canvas is a table of pixels. A *pixel* is the smallest dot that can appear on the phone. Each of these pixels has a location on the canvas, which is set using an x,y co-ordinate system. The x tells you where the dot is in the left-right plane (horizontal), and the y tells you where it is on the up-down plane (vertical).

RADIUS

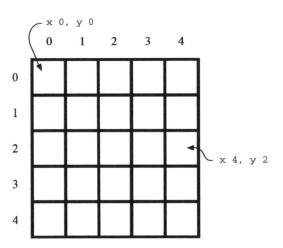

A bit of math! The *radius* of a circle is the distance from the center of the circle to the edge of the circle. In this case, it's measured in pixels.

DRAWING: DRAGGING LINES

When you use your finger to draw lines or curves on a screen, you're actually drawing lots of small straight lines. To do this, you use the **Dragged** event trigger. The event is triggered when a user moves their finger across the screen. From the **WallCanvas** blocks, select the **WallCanvas.Dragged** event handler:

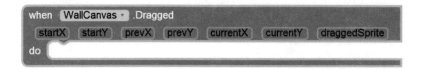

Just like the **Touched** event, you'll see it has created lots of new event arguments. It's a bit tricky to understand these, because doing a drag on your phone is easy, but describing it in a programming language (or even in English) isn't!

A **Dragged** event is triggered whenever the user moves their finger over the screen. Unlike a button, which registers once per click, a **Dragged** event keeps triggering as the user moves their finger around—right up until the moment they lift their finger off the screen.

In the orange event arguments, you'll see **startX** and **startY**—these are special because they only change when a user starts a new drag. The current position of your finger is always stored in **currentX,currentY**. When your finger pauses or changes direction (even for a moment), its position is stored in **prevX,prevY**.

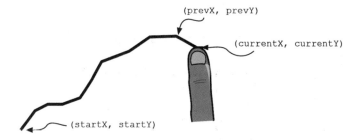

A dragged line is made up of lots of tiny straight lines, with the values of **prevX,prevY** and **currentX,currentY** constantly changing.

To draw a line at the place where the user is dragging, follow these steps:

1 From the **WallCanvas** block, choose the call **WallCanvas.DrawLine** block and plug it into the **WallCanvas.Dragged** block.

2 From the **WallCanvas.Dragged** event arguments, insert **prevX**, **prevY**, **currentX**, and **currentY** into the matching gaps on the **WallCanvas.DrawLine** block.

3   Your blocks should now look like this:

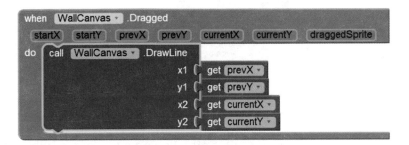

Learning Point: Arguments

Arguments (in computer science) are special values that a function must know before it can work. In this app, the arguments for dotting and dragging are the screen coordinates of the user's finger when they touch or drag the screen.

CHANGING THE PAINT COLOR

The current color that is painted on the canvas is a property of the canvas that can be set to any color:

1   From the **BlueButton** block, select the **BlueButton.Click** event.

2   From the **WallCanvas** block, select the **WallCanvas.PaintColor** block and insert it into the **BlueButton.Click** event handler.

3   From the built-in colors, select the blue block and insert it into the **set Wall-Canvas.PaintColor** block.

4   Repeat this for all the colors to enable the user to change the paint color. A quick way of doing this is to duplicate the block you've just created (right-click and choose Duplicate) and then change the button name and color.

We chose red, green, white, pink, and blue, but of course you can change these—or add more.

CLEARING THE WALL

After the user has written graffiti all over the wall, they're going to want a way to clear it and start again. Clearing a canvas is easy—you just need to call a

Clears anything drawn on this Canvas but not any background color or image.

`Canvas.Clear` function. In this case, call `WallCanvas.Clear` when the user clicks `WipeButton`. Put them together as shown here.

Notice how hovering over a block gives you useful information about what that block does.

What did you learn?

In this chapter, you learned the following:

- `VerticalArrangement`, `HorizontalArrangement`, and `TableArrangement` help you organize elements onscreen.
- You can prevent the phone display from rotating when the device is rotated.
- A canvas is a touch-sensitive drawing area that can detect different user actions like touching and dragging.
- The `Touched` and `Dragged` events store the location the user last touched in a set of automatically created event arguments.

That's a fantastic amount to learn in a short time—well done! Can you feel your App Inventor powers growing?

Test your knowledge

1. What will happen if you put two buttons in the same `TableArrangement` cell?
2. What is the difference between a `Dragged` and a `Touched` event?
3. Why does the `Dragged` event need start, previous, and current coordinates?

Try it out

Experiment with different dot radiuses and line thicknesses in the Graffiti Artist app (hint: add a `set WallCanvas.LineWidth` block).

CHAPTER 4

Fling, touch, and drag: user interaction with the touch screen

One of the great things about phone apps that is different from PC-based games is the use of touch-screen technology, which enables the user to interact in a direct way with your apps. In this chapter, we'll show you how to put together a catchy app called Fling It! that uses touch screen-based **Touched**, **Dragged**, and **Flung** events. You'll also build a mini app to demonstrate the use of the **Dragged** and **Flung** events.

As you get more experienced with App Inventor, you'll see that different components (labels, buttons, image sprites, and so on) can do different things. This chapter is about some of the ways in which your user physically interacts with the components on your phone screen.

For example, labels are just that: labels. A label can't sing or dance; you can't drag it or click it. A label can only display text to tell the user what something else is. The user can't physically interact with it at all. The same goes for an image component.

But other components are more fun to play with, such as buttons, the canvas, balls, and sprites. The following table lists the three main events you'll use in this chapter and which components they can be used with.

Event/Component	Button	Canvas	Ball	Sprite	Accelerometer
Dragged—Collects coordinates related to the position of the user's finger when they have dragged it across the screen		✓	✓	✓	
Flung—Provides arguments such as the initial position and velocity of the swipe when a fling gesture (or a quick swipe) is made on the screen		✓	✓	✓	
Touched—Provides position coordinates when touch-down and touch-up have occurred		✓	✓	✓	

In previous chapters you've used images, labels, buttons, the canvas, and the accelerometer but not the animation components, which are called *balls* and *sprites*. (In the computing community in the 1970s, the word *sprite* was adopted to describe an image that is capable of movement on the screen.) If you're creating an app that uses a sprite or a ball, you must use a canvas to hold these components on the app. The difference between a ball and a sprite is that the only appearance changes you can make to a ball are its size and color, whereas you can assign an image to your sprite.

A sprite is usually an animated character in a game, such as Sonic The Hedgehog, Super Mario, or Pacman. But sprites can also be objects that are capable of movement, such as the coins in Super Mario, the space ship in Defender, and the asteroids in … ummm … Asteroids.

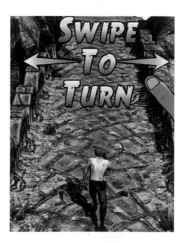

You used the **Touched** and **Dragged** events in the Graffiti Artist app, but **Flung** is new. Have you heard of the game Temple Run? The graphics are incredible, but what makes the game different from many others are its fast pace and the flexible use of **Flung** (or, as the game calls it, *swipe*) to make the sprite turn, jump, or duck.

It's good to know up front what a component does, before you put it in your Designer, so you don't discover in the Blocks Editor that something can't be flung! Some of these events work in the emulator, and some don't. The good news for this chapter is that you can use **Touched**, **Dragged**, and **Flung** successfully in the emulator.

The helpful and clever people at the Massachusetts Institute of Technology (MIT) who constantly update and improve App Inventor have provided a great resource for checking out what each component can do. You can find it at http://ai2.appinventor.mit.edu/reference/components. We can't recommend these pages highly enough for you app inventors out there.

Events up close

When you built the Graffiti Artist project in chapter 3, we looked in detail at the **Dragged** event you used for drawing. Now let's look at the **Flung** and **Dragged** events you can use for action!

Flung event

Because the **Flung** event is one of the more complicated physical events, we have provided a table that explains each of the arguments reported by the event.

Argument	What does it mean?
x	The x coordinate (horizontal axis) of where the user begins the **Flung** event. The bigger the value, the further to the right the position of the sprite.
y	The y coordinate (vertical axis) of where the user begins the **Flung** event. The bigger the value, the further down the screen the position of the sprite.
speed	How many pixels per second the ball or sprite is travelling.
heading	The direction in which the ball is travelling (measured in degrees). Right is 0 degrees.
xvel	The sprite's rate of change in the x direction.
yvel	The sprite's rate of change in the y direction.

You may remember we pointed out that in order to effectively use an event handler, your methods don't have to use all the arguments it provides. You can produce an effective fling by using just the speed and heading. The mini app in the next section will demonstrate this.

Drag event

In order to allow the user to reposition a sprite, you only need to use the current x and current y arguments that indicate where the user's finger leaves the screen after dragging the sprite.

Flingflung app

PURPOSE OF THIS APP
This mini app demonstrates the use of the **Flung** and **Dragged** events. The user flings the ball toward the block, which, when hit, changes to a *bang!* graphic. The ideas used in this mini app can be used in a fully formed game.

APP RATING

 2

ASSETS YOU'LL NEED
Image sprite: **Blocksprite**. Two image files: Bigblueblocksprite.png and Bang.png.

The following table sets out the components needed for setting up the Flingflung app. We have kept the interface simple to allow you to set it up and start coding the blocks quickly.

Learning Point: Intervals

The *interval* of the sprite you're going to fling—in this case, the ball—is important. The interval means how often (in milliseconds) the sprite's position is updated. For example, if the interval is 50 and the speed is 10, then the sprite will move 10 pixels every 50 milliseconds. One thousand milliseconds is one second. The speed is measured in how many pixels per interval the sprite (or ball) moves. To get a smooth fling movement, an interval of 10 works well. We'll sort out the speed side of things in the Blocks Editor.

Flingflung			
Screen1 properties	**AlignHorizontal**: Center **Scrollable**: No **Icon**: Bang.png (downloaded from our website) **AlignVertical**: Center **Title**: Flingflung **ScreenOrientation**: Portrait		
Components	**What do I rename it?**	**What does it do?**	**What properties do I set?**
Canvas	**Canvas**	Allows you to position sprites	**BackgroundColor**: Yellow
Ball Palette group: Animation	**Ball1**	Can be flung toward the block target	**Radius**: 10 **Interval**: 10
Imagesprite Palette group: Animation	**Blocksprite**	Stays still unless repositioned by the user, who can drag it anywhere on the screen to provide a target toward which to fling the ball	**Picture**: Upload the matching image file for the **imagesprite**, Bigblueblocksprite.png. This **imagesprite** has another image called Bang.png that you need to upload to Media. You access it from the Blocks palette.
Media files			

Image files downloaded from our website:
   Bigblueblocksprite.png
   Bang.png

1. Dragging out the Ball1.Flung event handler from the Ball1 drawer

This diagram shows an empty event handler for the **Flung** event.

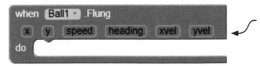

Open the Ball1 drawer, and pull out the Ball1.Flung block. You'll see that it's populated with x, y, speed, heading, xvel, and yvel arguments.

2. Giving the ball velocity

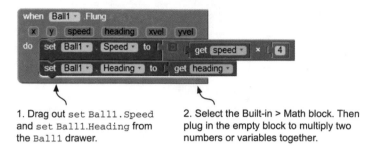

1. Drag out set Ball1.Speed and set Ball1.Heading from the Ball1 drawer.

2. Select the Built-in > Math block. Then plug in the empty block to multiply two numbers or variables together.

As we explained earlier, velocity is made up of speed and direction. So in order to give the ball velocity to head off on its fling journey, you need to assign both a heading value and speed value to **Ball1**. To make the ball travel faster, you can drag out a Built-in > Math block and multiply its speed by 4.

3. Enabling the Dragged event

Create the following code block. In this event, you set the x and y coordinates of the new position of the block to be the "current" x and y—that is, where the user's finger leaves the screen.

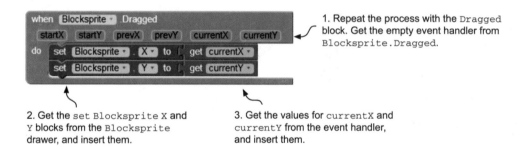

1. Repeat the process with the Dragged block. Get the empty event handler from Blocksprite.Dragged.

2. Get the set Blocksprite X and Y blocks from the Blocksprite drawer, and insert them.

3. Get the values for currentX and currentY from the event handler, and insert them.

4. Enabling the CollidedWith event

In this app, you want the block to look as though it has exploded when the ball hits it. So you need to use the **CollidedWith** block.

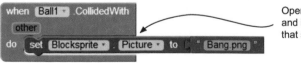

Open the Ball1.CollidedWith event, and insert a Blocksprite.Picture block that sets the picture to Bang.png.

Simple but effective, don't you think? The next app is a bit more interactive and, although still short, functions well as a game.

Fling It! app

PURPOSE OF THIS APP
This game is inspired by the audio game Bop It! In Fling It!, play consists of the user responding to a series of spoken commands on a rhythmic soundtrack by using the events **Touched**, **Flung**, and **Dragged**.

APP RATING

 2

ASSETS YOU'LL NEED
Images: Fling, Touch, Drag, and a Fling It! machine for the canvas background. Sounds: Fling, Touch, Drag, and Soundtrack.

Bop It! Is a game a bit like Simon Says. The Bop It! machine calls out instructions, and the player has to do different things such as twist a crank, pull a handle, and toggle a switch as quickly as they can.

Although Fling It! is an interactive app, the appearance of the screen doesn't change while the user is playing the game. The user is invited to use the **Touched**, **Dragged**, and **Flung** event on the sprites. Each sprite has a corresponding sound that plays when the player touches, drags, or flings it: the touch makes a "pop!" sound, the drag makes a "scrape" sound, and the fling goes "wheeeee!" You have to build the app to fully understand.

In the previous chapter, we suggested that you might want to start developing your independence by setting up the interface of your app using only the following table and a screen capture of the interface. The table contains the properties and files needed for the components.

Fling It!			
Screen1 properties	**AlignHorizontal**: Center **Scrollable**: No (unselected) **Icon**: Flingit_button.png (downloaded from our website) **AlignVertical**: Center **ScreenOrientation**: Portrait **Title**: Fling it! **BackgroundColor**: Orange		
Components	**What do I rename it?**	**What does it do?**	**What properties do I set?**
Canvas	Canvas	Allows you to position sprites	**Image**: Flingitmachine.png **BackgroundColor**: None **Width**: Fill Parent **Height**: Fill Parent
Horizontal-Arrangement	Horizontal-Arrangement1	Lets you place buttons next to each other horizontally	**AlignHorizontal**: Center **Width**: Fill Parent **Height**: Automatic
Image	Image1	Provides a spacer between the buttons	**Width**: 120
2 **Button**s	Have_a_go_button Stop_button	Start and stop the soundtrack	**Text**: "Have a Go!" and "Stop" **FontSize**: 20 **Width**: Automatic **Height**: Automatic
3 **Imagesprites** Palette group: Animation	TouchSprite1 DragSprite2 FlingSprite3	Stay still but respond by playing the corresponding sound when the user touches, drags, or flings the different sprites	**Picture**: Upload the matching image file for each **imagesprite** (such as Touchit1.png).
4 **Sound** objects	Touchsound1 Dragsound2 Flingsound3 Soundtrack	Sound objects you can play using the Blocks Editor, just as you played the baa sound in the Getting to Know Ewe app	**Source**: Upload the matching media file for each sound (such as Touchsound1.wav).
Media files			

4 sound files downloaded from our website:

Touchsound1.wav
Dragsound2.wav
Flingsound3.wav
Soundtrack.wav

Each **Sound** object's **Source** property is set to one of these matching files so that when you play the sound, you hear the correct file.

Media files

5 image files downloaded from our website:
   Flingit_button.png
   Flingitmachine.png
   Touchit1.png
   Dragit2.png
   Flingit3.png

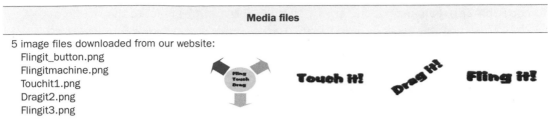

Each **Button**'s **Image** property is set to display one of these images.
The images are Portable Network Graphics (PNG) files, which enables them to have transparency so you can see the canvas image behind them.

The following diagram shows how the screen is designed.

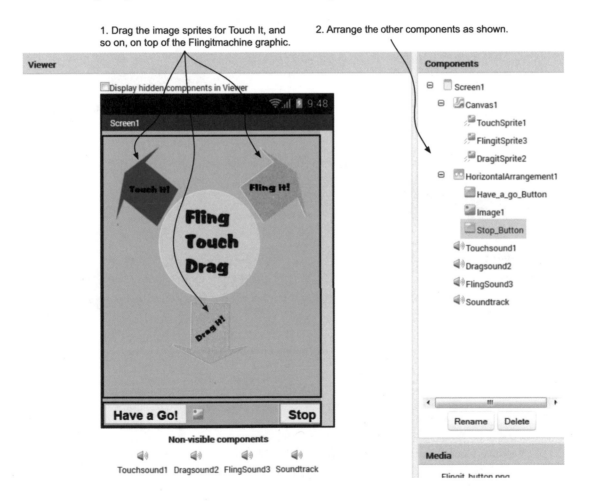

To code this app, you just need to ensure that the three sprites react to the **Flung**, **Dragged**, and **Touched** events and that the buttons start and stop the soundtrack. This app is effective, but coding it is relatively simple. Doing so can be broken down into five steps.

1. Making the touch sprite react to the user touching the sprite

Let's think about what is going on in App Inventor when the user uses a swiping motion to activate the **Flung** event. When you open the **FlingSprite1** drawer, for example, you see a number of different event handlers. The event handler "handles" the information (or arguments; see the next Learning Point) that you need if the event occurs. It can be helpful to give a voice to what is going on in the program. For the **Flung** event, for example, you can imagine the event handler is saying, "You know the user has just flung that sprite. Well, just in case you wanted to know, the sprite was in the bottom-left corner (x,y), the user flung it pretty fast (counted in pixels per millisecond), the direction the sprite was heading in was (0–360 degrees), the velocity of the x vector was this, and the velocity of the y vector was that."

The **Touched** event is a bit simpler and only reports the x and y values of the location on the screen where the user touched the sprite.

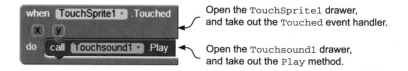

Open the `TouchSprite1` drawer, and take out the `Touched` event handler.

Open the `Touchsound1` drawer, and take out the `Play` method.

For this event, select **TouchSprite1** and select the **when Touched Flung do** event handler. The only thing you want to do in response to the **Flung** event is play the flung sound, so go to the **Touchsound1** drawer, select the **Touchsound1.Play** method, and slot it into the event handler.

Learning Point: Arguments

In computing, an *argument* is a value or piece of data that is passed between a function, procedure, or routine. In the case of the **Flung** routine, for example, when the user swipes their finger across the screen, the event handler collects the argument **speed**, which is then made available should you want to use it. In App Inventor, some event handlers report many arguments. You can, but don't have to, use all of them in the methods in the event handler. In fact, you can ignore them and do something completely different in response to an event—which is what you do in Fling It!

---

2. Making the drag sprite react to the user dragging the sprite

Again for this event, select the drag sprite and select the **when Dragged do** event handler. The only thing you want to do in response to the **Dragged** event is play the drag sound, so go to the **Dragsound2** drawer, select the **Dragsound2.Play** method, and slot it into the event handler.

Open the `DragSprite2` drawer, and take out the `Dragged` event handler.

Open the `Dragsound2` drawer, and take out the `Play` method.

3. Making the fling sprite react to the user flinging the sprite

Here, you'll follow essentially the same directions to get the fling sprite to react to a **Flung** event and play the fling sound.

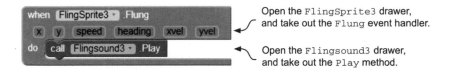

Open the `FlingSprite3` drawer, and take out the `Flung` event handler.

Open the `Flingsound3` drawer, and take out the `Play` method.

4. Playing the soundtrack

If you're reading this chapter and want to make your own soundtrack without downloading the resources, we'd better explain what the soundtrack is so you can record one yourself. It goes like this: "Fling it (clap-clap, clap-clap), touch it (clap-clap, clap-clap), drag it (clap-clap, clap-clap)." You can use a voice recorder to make a .wav file that is good-enough quality for this purpose. Then, to play the soundtrack (which lasts about 20 seconds), select the following blocks. To get an even rhythm, we recommend writing a varied combination of commands to read from: fling it, fling it, drag it, touch it, touch it, drag it, fling it, and so on.

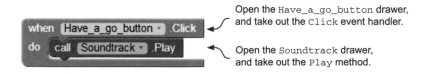

Open the `Have_a_go_button` drawer, and take out the `Click` event handler.

Open the `Soundtrack` drawer, and take out the `Play` method.

5. Stopping the soundtrack

Admittedly, a repeating soundtrack can be grating after a while, so we always recommend that you have a Stop button in an app that has a soundtrack.

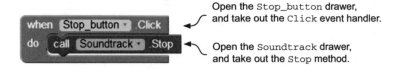

Open the `Stop_button` drawer, and take out the `Click` event handler.

Open the `Soundtrack` drawer, and take out the `Stop` method.

Taking it further

You've created this fun app using three user-interactive events. There are many more you can use to help customize your own creations. If you look at the following table, you'll recognize a few from your favorite phone apps. As you can see, some components can do more than others.

Event/Component	Button	Canvas	Ball	Sprite	Accelerometer
`Click`—Indicates that a user has clicked a button	✓				
`GotFocus`—Indicates that the cursor has moved over the button so the user can now click it	✓				
`LostFocus`—Indicates that the cursor has moved away from the button so it's no longer possible for the user to click it	✓				
`Dragged`—Collects coordinates related to the position of the user's finger when they have dragged it across the screen		✓	✓	✓	
`Flung`—Provides arguments such as the initial position and velocity of the swipe when a fling gesture (or a quick swipe) is made on the screen		✓	✓	✓	
`TouchDown`—Provides coordinates of the touch when the user begins touching the sprite		✓	✓	✓	
`TouchUp`—Provides coordinates of the position when the user stops touching the sprite		✓	✓	✓	
`Touched`—Provides position coordinates when touch-down and touch-up have occurred		✓	✓	✓	
`Shaking`—Called repeatedly when the Android device is physically shaken					✓

There are lots of creative ways you could change or rebuild the apps in this chapter. Here are a few ideas:

1 For Fling It!, provide an element of challenge by recording two soundtracks yourself, one fast and one slow. Incorporate level buttons for the user to choose their own level and have something to progress to.

2 In Fling It!, instead of a shape-based Fling Touch Drag machine, use images of percussive instruments that suggest those sound effects: for example, a drum for touch, a whistle for fling, and a washboard for drag.

3 In Flingflung, when the ball hits the block, change the image of the block to look like an exploded block.

What did you learn?

In this chapter, you learned the following:

- That different components do different things.
- That some event handlers come with information about the event, such as the speed of the sprite, called arguments.
- Once an event handler with arguments has been used, App Inventor creates value blocks for the arguments that are available from within the event handler.
- You can (but don't have to) use these arguments in the methods in the event handler. For example, the **Flung** event handler collects the speed of the sprite, which you can then use in combination with direction to fling the sprite across the screen.
- How to use arguments to produce **Dragged** and **Flung** events for actions.
- How to use the math functions to multiply a variable by a number.
- How to use the **CollidedWith** event.

Test your knowledge

1 Which event reports the **speed** argument?

2 Which event reports the **velocity** argument?

3 Once you have set up a **Dragged** event, if you wanted to use the **currentX** argument value, where would you find it?

4 What is a sprite?

5   What is the difference between a sprite and a ball?

6   What (in computing) is an argument?

Try it out

Your apps are starting to look more like games, which is great for now, but you may have noticed a few things that are still missing: a scoring system, levels, and animation. These will be addressed when we look at variables in chapter 5 and animation in chapter 6. Once you have those two things conquered, the world's your oyster (or eggplant, for the vegetarians)! So keep going, and enjoy inventing apps. When you understand those bits, you can come back and try these other projects:

1   Increase the difficulty of the Fling It! app in response to how the user is doing rather than letting them choose the difficulty level.

2   Rather than use the Flingitmachine.png graphic we have provided for the background image of the canvas, create your own. You can either hand-draw the machine or use drawing software to create a simple shape that becomes your Fling It! machine. The machine's three areas should be far enough away from each other that the user's flinging finger doesn't accidentally land on the Touch It sprite.

3   In the coming chapters, you'll learn how to keep score in a game. You can develop Fling It! to keep score and to use specific soundtracks that include known numbers of fling, drag, and touch mentions.

4   In Fling It!, instead of having static shapes responding to the user's touch, drag, or fling, you can have image sprites that perform an action (in addition to the sound) in response to the event. For example, in response to a touch, a tambourine could shake; or in response to a drag, a trombone could slide.

Variables, decisions, and procedures

In this chapter, we'll experiment with three powerful programming ideas. First we'll look at how programs can remember and use pieces of information using variables. You'll learn how programs can ask questions and make decisions using comparison operators and control blocks. Then we'll look at how you can split up programs into reusable chunks called procedures, and why you will want to do this. Along the way, we'll also look at some debugging and commenting tools that will help you troubleshoot pesky errors (programmers spend lots of their time doing this).

Remembering useful things

Often you'll want an app to remember something that just happened so it can do something else later. Here are some examples:

- *Keeping score*—How many coins have been collected? How many lives have been lost? In a fitness app, you might want to remember how many steps someone has taken during a run.
- *Tracking other game events*—For example, a player may have picked up a magnifying glass; if they have it later, they can use it to examine a fingerprint.
- *Storing a list of contacts*—A text message uses contacts in a communications app.
- *Using the start and end destination in a navigation app*—This way, you know how far you've travelled and how far you have to go.

Sometimes you only need to store information while the app is running (like a game score), so you use a variable stored in the phone's working memory (see the next Learning Point about RAM). Variables are *temporary*—if you restart the app or switch off the phone, you'll be starting with no memory of what happened before. Sometimes you want the app to remember information even after the phone is switched off, like a list of contacts or high scores—this is called *persistence*. To make data persistent, you can save the variables to a storage device and then load them back into the phone's working memory the next time the app runs (see chapter 11 for how to do this using the TinyDB database). Your phone is likely to have two places to store data permanently: internal storage (the phone's built-in memory that can't be removed) and a memory card.

Learning Point: Random access memory (RAM)

Variables are stored in your phone's working memory, called random access memory (RAM). It's *random access* because the computer in your phone can jump right in and retrieve data from any part of this memory without having to go through all the memory in sequence. When you use a dictionary, you use random access by jumping to the beginning letters of the word you're searching for.

When you stop an app or turn off the phone, the RAM you were using gets wiped. It's sometimes called *volatile memory*.

Total recall: naming and retrieving variables

Just storing information in the phone's memory isn't enough—you need some way to retrieve it, and for that you give each variable a name. You might have come across this idea in algebra, where you say something like x = 100: that means whenever you write x, you mean 100. Computer variables are similar to algebra variables, but they can store lots of types of information (not just numbers). They can also have labels that mean something (instead of just x). Can you work out what these variables might be used for?

- **Score** = 120
- **Sex** = "F"
- **Surname** = "Moriarty"
- **ArrivedAtDestination** = False

These examples show that variables can be different types. **Score** is a number. **Sex** and **Surname** are text variables (sometimes called *strings*). **ArrivedAtDestination** is a Boolean variable that can be either true or false.

You'll start out using variables by making a simple Flattery app that remembers and uses somebody's name. Then we'll look at how variables help you write flexible programs.

Flattery app

PURPOSE OF THIS APP
This is an app to make you feel good by telling you how wonderful you are! Inputting your name and clicking each of the four buttons gives you different personalized messages. The app works because it remembers your name in a variable you'll call **UsersName**.

APP RATING

ASSETS YOU'LL NEED
Four button images.

Flattery			
Screen1 properties	**AlignHorizontal**: Center **Title**: Flattery App **BackgroundColor**: Pink **ScreenOrientation**: Portrait **Icon**: happy.png (downloaded from our website)		
Components	**What do I rename it?**	**What does it do?**	**What properties do I set?**
Button	**StartButton**	Activates **AskNameNotifier**	**FontSize**: 20 **Text**: "Start"
Notifier Palette group: User Interface	**AskNameNotifier**	Asks the user to enter their name	None
TableArrangement	**MainTable**	A two-column by two-row grid to contain your four flattery buttons	**Columns**: 2 **Rows**: 2 **Width**: Automatic **Height**: Automatic **Visible**: hidden
4 **Buttons**	**HappyButton** **SingButton** **FriendsButton** **DanceButton**	The buttons the user clicks to see each message	**Image**: Upload the matching media file for each button (for example, **HappyButton**: happy.png). **Text**: Nothing—delete the text. **Width**: Automatic **Height**: Automatic

Components	What do I rename it?	What does it do?	What properties do I set?
`Label`	`FlatteryLabel`	Message that changes depending on which button has been clicked	`FontSize`: 20 `Text`: "You are brilliant!" Note: Position this label under `MainTable`.

Media files

4 image files downloaded from our website:
  happy.png
  sing.png
  friends.png
  dance.png

Set each button's **Image** property to display its image.

You'll stage what happens in this app so the user can't click a flattery button (Happy, Sing, Friends, or Dance) until they have entered their name and you've stored it in a variable to use later. Here's how the entire app will look when you're finished:

  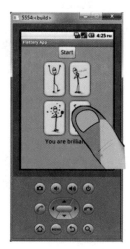 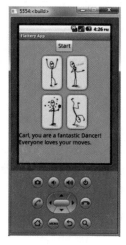

1. The app starts with just the Start button and `FlatteryLabel` showing. The `MainTable` component containing all your buttons is hidden.

2. Clicking Start pops up a notifier asking for a name. Clicking OK
a. Stores the user's name in a variable
b. Reveals the `MainTable` of buttons.

3. Whenever the user clicks a button …

4. … a message personalized with their name appears.

1. Setting up the screen

When the app starts, only the Start button and **FlatteryLabel** are showing. To do this, set **MainTable**'s **Visible** property to Hidden in the App Inventor Designer (see the previous Flattery app setup table). Hiding any screen arrangement also hides everything inside it, so all the buttons are hidden, too. Next, use the setup table to set up your screen. Don't forget that you can continue to work on hidden elements in App Inventor by checking DIsplay Hidden Components in Viewer.

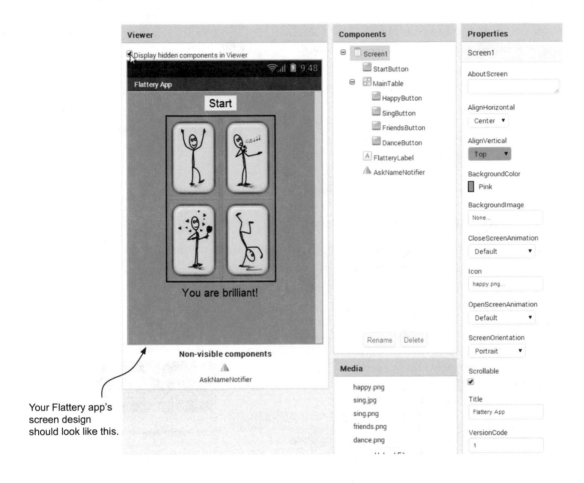

Your Flattery app's screen design should look like this.

2. Coding the blocks: creating a UsersName variable

Creating a variable means you tell App Inventor its name (or label) and what kind of thing it is (text, number, Boolean, list, and so on). Switch to Blocks, click Variables in the Built-in list, and choose the top orange block that says `initialize global [name] to`. *Initialize* means to create a new variable. The variable is *global* because you can use it in any block anywhere in the app. *Name* is the name or label—

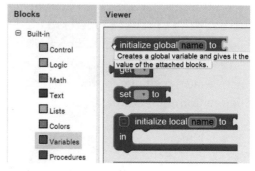

you don't want it to say `name`, you want to call it `UsersName`—so change this now (click the word *name*, and type over it).

To tell the app that this variable will hold text, plug an empty text block into it. The final result should look like this.

You've created a variable called `UsersName` that can store some text.

3. Getting and storing UsersName

When the user clicks the Start button, you want to pop up a notifier. This takes you all the way back to the Hello World! app—can you remember how to do it? There is a small difference, though: in Hello World!, you just had a message and button, but you want this notifier to show an input text box. You'll need to use the `ShowTextDialog` notification function block.

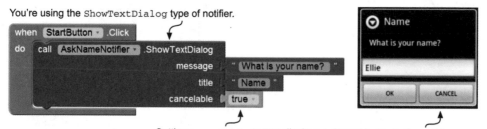

Setting `cancelable` to true displays a Cancel button in the notifier.

When the user clicks the button and the notifier pops up, you can't store the user's name immediately—they haven't had time to type it in yet! The time to store their name is when they have clicked the OK button—and in your `AskNameNotifier` blocks, there's a notifier event handler for that called `AfterTextInput`. Add it to your workspace now.

Did you notice that an extra orange **response** argument came along with your **After-TextInput** block? This argument can tell you what someone typed into the notifier. So if I type **Carl** and click OK, the value of **response** is "Carl"—and that's exactly what you want to store in your variable. Changing a variable's stored value means you need to create a **set** block—in this case, **set global UsersName**. Then you plug in the value of the **response** argument like this:

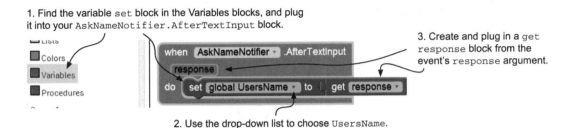

1. Find the variable set block in the Variables blocks, and plug it into your AskNameNotifier.AfterTextInput block.

3. Create and plug in a get response block from the event's response argument.

2. Use the drop-down list to choose UsersName.

4. Revealing the buttons

There's one other vital thing to do after the user enters their text and clicks OK: you need to display the four buttons in the hidden **MainTable**. You did something like this in chapter 2's Ewe Scared Her! app by setting a component's **Visible** property to True for visible and False for hidden. It's the same again here, so the final block looks like this:

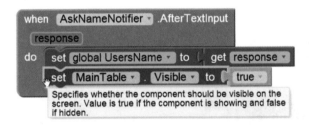

5. Stringing it all together: making the flattery messages

When the user clicks the Happy, Sing, Friends, or Dance button, the app changes **Flattery-Label** to display a related personalized message with the user's name in it. It does this by retrieving the user's name, which you just stored, and sticking it onto a premade sentence. As an example, if you join together **UsersName** and the sentence ", just seeing you makes me smile!" you will see "Carl, just seeing you makes me smile!" To do this joining, you'll use a Built-in > Text block called **join**.

The event handler triggers are straightforward: one **Button.Click** event for each button. Let's do the **HappyButton.Click** block first. Select and join these blocks:

Changing the FlatteryLabel.Text property changes the message at the bottom of the screen.

For this app, two sockets are perfect. If you want more, you can click the blue square and drag String blocks into the join block.

The join block is found in the Built-in Text blocks. The blue square shows that it's a *mutator* block: you can change the number of sockets it has.

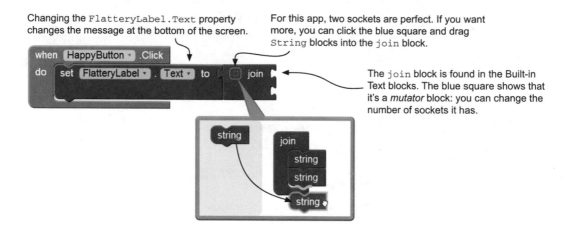

You use the **join** block to put the two parts of your message (**UsersName** and flattery text) together like so:

The quickest way to create these blocks is to create the HappyButton code, right-click it, and choose Duplicate three times. Then change

- The button name, using the drop-down list
- The blocks attached to the text join block

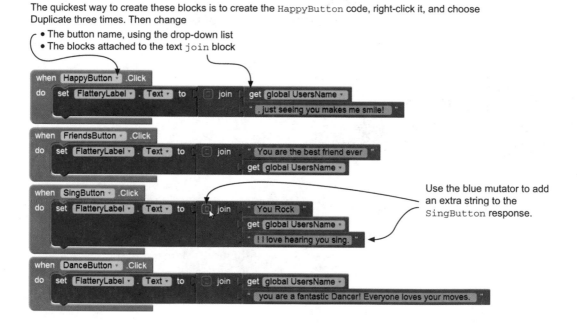

Use the blue mutator to add an extra string to the SingButton response.

You can change the messages, if you like, and you can play around with whether the name is included at the beginning, end, or middle of the message. One thing to bear in mind is that if you join **UsersName** Carl to the message "is an App Inventor", the result will be "Carlis an App Inventor"—so you'll have to make sure the message part always has spaces or punctuation marks in the right places.

That's it—you should have a fully functioning Flattery app. Fire it up, enter your name, and click the buttons to see how great you truly are! You'll adapt this app in a sneaky way in the next section so that you can play a prank on your friends.

Taking it further

1   Skip ahead to chapter 11 to look at the **TexttoSpeech** component. Then have the app also speak the flattery messages. We find the robotic voice telling us what good dancers we are hilarious!

2   Once the user has entered their name, either hide the Start button or, even better, change its text to say "Click to Change Name".

Learning Point: Variables vs. text boxes

In the Flattery app, you could have achieved a similar effect by putting a **TextBox** on screen for the user to type their name. Then the app could use something like **Textbox1.Text** instead of needing a variable. In fact, text boxes and other components that let you input information can be thought of as kinds of variables—they let you store data, and they have names. So why don't you use them instead of variables? Because text boxes are often useful, but

- They take up space and can quickly clutter the screen. Imagine if you needed 5 or even 10 pieces of information from the user.
- You can't predict when a user may choose to click and change the text box. This may cause the program to crash if it was expecting a piece of data that the user just deleted.
- A variable name like **UsersName** is easier to read and understand than something like **UsersNameTextbox.Text**.
- A text box is a relatively large area that users may accidentally click.
- For notifiers, you have to store the result in a variable. The notifier's response is wiped once the notifier has finished its work.

We aren't saying that you always need to store data in a variable. Sometimes a text box is fine. But usually, setting up a variable makes more sense.

Decisions, decisions: using variables to choose an action

You now know how to create a variable like **UsersName**, store a piece of information like "Carl", and retrieve it later. Variables become even more useful when you know how to use them to make decisions in your apps. To do this, you need to understand how to get apps to

1 Ask a question.
2 Make a decision based on the answer.

Let's deal with asking questions first. These aren't big, complex questions like, "How big is the universe?" "What's the meaning of life, the universe, and everything?" and "What color underpants should I wear?" (The answers, of course, are infinite, 42, and any except mustard yellow.) They're much simpler questions, like "Is 5 bigger than 4?" "Are you a girl or a boy?" "Does this word begin with *z*?" "Has the app repeated the same action 5 times?" and "Has the spaceship collided with the asteroid?" All these simple questions use *comparison*, where you ask whether things are the same or different.

Comparison operators

Computer programs do comparison by using comparison operators. You probably recognize most of them from mathematics lessons. The following tables shows the most useful comparison operators; each comparison block gives (or returns) either a True or False answer. The tables include comparison operators that can be used for text or numbers, and the first table applies to both. In each case, we have listed when each block returns True; for all other cases, it will automatically report False.

Text and number comparison operators		
Comparison operator	**Block**	**What does it do?**
Equals		Answers True if the two numbers or pieces of text plugged into the sockets are the same
Does not equal		The opposite of equals—answers True if two numbers or pieces of text aren't the same

Number comparison operators		
Comparison operator	**Block**	**What does it do?**
Greater than		Answers True if the number in the left socket is larger than the number in the right socket
Less than		Answers True if the number in the left socket is smaller than the number in the right socket
Greater than or equal to		Answers True if the number in the left socket is larger than *or* the same as the number in the right socket
Less than or equal to		Answers True if the number in the left socket is smaller than *or* the same as the number in the right socket
Is a number?	is a number?	Answers True if the item in the socket is a number

Text comparison operators		
Comparison operator	**Block**	**What does it do?**
Text less than	compare texts <	Answers True if text 1 is alphabetically smaller than text 2 (meaning it's earlier in the alphabet). For example "Apple" < "Bumblebee" is True.
Text greater than	compare texts >	Answers True if text 1 is alphabetically greater than text 2. For example, "Inventor" > "App" is True.
Text contains	contains text piece	Answers True if the text in the top socket contains the text in the bottom socket anywhere in it. For example, [text "AppInventor" contains piece "Inventor"] is True.
Is text empty?	is empty	Answers True if the text is empty—for example, if a user hasn't entered any text in a notifier box.

These comparison blocks are the basis of all questions. To make a question, you plug values or variables into the

comparison block sockets. Let's take a simple example. If you want to take the Flattery app and check whether the user is called Carl, you can make an **equals** block as shown here.

Here we have plugged in the variable **UsersName** on the left side and the value **Carl** on the right side. You could also plug in the value directly from a text box's **text** property.

Now you have a question that will return True or False depending on what the user types in—but what do you do with this information? What does it plug into? For that you have to understand how App Inventor uses control blocks to make decisions.

How can a dumb machine make a decision?

Computers (including phones) are pretty dumb at present—they can just follow simple rules fast—so how do you get them to do things like make decisions? When human beings make decisions, they often start with an "If" statement like these:

> *If* the price is less than $20, *then* buy the t-shirt.

> *If* the movie review is good, *then* get tickets.

> *If* the alarm sounds, *then* leave the building immediately.

Sometimes decisions have several outcomes:

> *If* the light is green, *then* go, *otherwise* stop.

> *If* the pasta is cooked, *then* drain it, *otherwise* cook it for another minute.

Most programming languages have a version of the basic "If … then do …" statement, including App Inventor—we'll call this an `if` block. The second set of "If … then, otherwise …" statements are also found in App Inventor using `if  ...  else` blocks. All `if` statements live in the Built-in > Control drawer. Here's an example of how a couple of the previous statements would look if you wrote them using App Inventor blocks:

You can also combine decisions using the logical operators **and** and **or**. The first example that follows states, "If the t-shirt is orange **or** purple, then buy it." The second example states, "If the movie reviews in **both** *Empire* **and** *Total Film* have five stars, then buy a ticket."

You're going to use `if  ...  else` blocks now to build a prank version of the Flattery app.

Prankster Flattery app (Personality Judge app)

 Let's Invent!

PURPOSE OF THIS APP

This app looks exactly like the Flattery app, but it only says nice things about you if it recognizes your name—otherwise it says something rude! The app pretends that it's judging your personality by reading bio-signs from your thumb (we made this up).

APP RATING

3

ASSETS YOU'LL NEED

A working version of the Flattery app.

The user will enter their name in a notifier box in exactly the same way as in the Flattery app. But you'll change the code blocks for each **Button.Click** event so that before displaying a message, the app makes a decision about whether it recognizes your name. If your name is Carl, then the decision looks something like this:

1 *If* **UsersName** = Carl (or whatever name you choose when you write the app) …

2 *Then* display the usual flattery message …

3 *Else* display an alternative rude message.

1. Setting up the app

1 Make a copy of the Flattery app by opening it and clicking Save As. Call it **PersonalityJudge**.

2 Change the **Title** property of **Screen1** to "Personality Judge".

3 Change the **Text** property of **FlatteryLabel** to "Enter your name and press your thumb onto any button - so that I can read your bio-signals."

4 Change the **Width** property of **FlatteryLabel** to Fill Parent so the whole message fits onscreen.

2. Coding the if ... else blocks

Look at the words that begin the three decision points for this app: *if, then, else.* That tells you you'll need some `if ... else` blocks. In App Inventor 2, you make an `if ... else` block by getting an `if` block from Built-in > Control and then using the mutator (blue square) to add an `else`, like this:

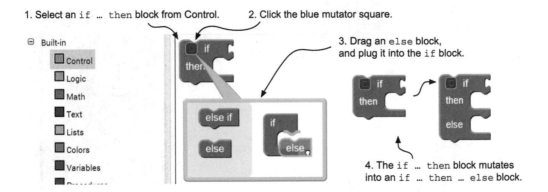

1. Select an `if ... then` block from Control.   2. Click the blue mutator square.

3. Drag an `else` block, and plug it into the `if` block.

4. The `if ... then` block mutates into an `if ... then ... else` block.

In the Blocks Editor, you need to alter the code for each of your four **Button.Click** events (Happy, Sing, Friends, and Dance). For each button, here's what to do:

1 Create four `if ... else` blocks (as just explained).

2 Make a comparison block out of the equals comparison, the variable **UsersName**, and a text block containing the name you want to recognize, and plug it into the `if ... else` block like this:

3 Now you have to say what to do if the test is true (top socket) or false (bottom socket). If the test is true, you want to display your usual flattery message; so, you can steal/drag this block from the existing flattery **Button.Click** code and click it into the top socket of `if ... else`.

4 For the bottom socket, you want to display a joke message (nothing that will offend the user, though—after all, they might be holding your phone when they read it!). The easiest way to do this is to copy and paste the text block from the top socket into the bottom socket and then change the message.

5   Plug the whole `if ... else` block you've just made into your (now empty) **Button.Click** event. The end result should look like this:

Now repeat these steps for each of the other three buttons. Make up your own rude messages, or you can use ours:

- **HappyButton**—"It's not often a chimpanzee presses that button! Hi "**UsersName** " oo, ooo, ooo, oook!"
- **SingButton**—"Wow, I'm detecting you can sing like a bird "**UsersName** " - you honk like a goose."
- **FriendsButton**—**UsersName** ", you are the most popular of all your friends. (Shame they're all imaginary.)"
- **DanceButton**—"You are a WILD dancer "**UsersName**". That's a Weirdly Inelegant Ludicrous Diva!"

Using creative comparison conditions

The Personality Judge app isn't terribly practical because every time you want it to recognize and respond to a different name, you have to reprogram the blocks and repackage it for your phone. It would be possible to make it a bit more flexible by combining a number of name check tests using the **or** condition, say **If UsersName = 'Carl' or UsersName = 'Lynne' or UsersName = 'Ellie' or UsersName = 'Daniel'**. But that would be a long block onscreen; and if you want to include Susanna in your group, you still need to go back to the app, add the new **or**, and repackage the app.

Wouldn't it be more fun if you could directly control whether the app says something nice or rude? It would confuse your friends—they might even believe the app was reading their biosigns. In this section, you'll change just the test part of the `if ... else` blocks to do that.

There are a number of sneaky ways you could tell the phone to do one thing or another. For example:

- *Timing events*—For example, if you enter a name and wait 5 seconds before clicking OK, the phone gives the nice message; otherwise it displays the rude version.

- *Orientation events*—The message depends on you tipping the phone in a certain direction after typing the name.
- *Voice recognition*—For example, the phone listens for a keyword that you say after entering the name (this is probably unreliable, though).

You're going to do something much simpler, but equally sneaky. You'll detect whether the user types a space at the beginning of their name (we said it was sneaky). That way, you (and anyone you tell the secret) will get a nice message, and your other friends and family won't be able to work out the trick. To get started, save a new version of the Personality Judge app with a name like PersonalityJudge2.

Learning Point: Characters and bytes

In programming, a *character* is usually a number, a letter, or a punctuation mark. It can also mean a control character like Enter or Tab. The easiest way to think about a character is as a key press. Incidentally, have you ever wondered what a *byte* is? Well, a byte is a way to measure memory; and, conveniently, this is true:

1 byte = 1 character = 1 key press

If you have a device that can store 16 GB (gigabytes), that means you could open a word processor and type 16 billion letters or numbers and save them on your device. That's because a gigabyte is roughly equal to 1 billion bytes!

App Inventor has lots of text blocks that can search for a piece of text or split up a text block. Take a look at them now, and see which one you think would be best for isolating the first character of **UsersName**.

Hey—we said to stop reading and go look at the text blocks in App Inventor! Have you done that yet? Really? OK, we believe you.

If you said that the **segment** block is the one to choose, then level up—you're thinking like a programmer! The **segment** block isn't the only way to do it, but it's the simplest. Here's an example of **segment** in action: the command **segment "Apples", start = 1, length = 3** returns the text string "App". Have you figured out what's going on? Try these for practice:

```
segment "grind", start=1, length = 4
segment "slaughter", start=2, length = 8
```

Hopefully you've worked out that the **segment** block takes some text and extracts a block of characters from it. It knows what to extract because you tell it where to begin (**start**) and how many characters to extract (**length**).

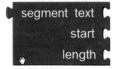

Question: What **segment** command could extract "ink" from "think"?

The text you want **segment** to work on is **UsersName**, and you want to look only at the first character, so **start = 1** and **length =1**. The final test looks like this:

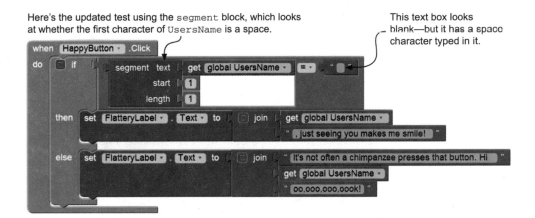

Here's the updated test using the segment block, which looks at whether the first character of UsersName is a space.

This text box looks blank—but it has a space character typed in it.

Duplicate the **if ... else** block, and insert it into the other three buttons. Now you have a prankster app that should make people scratch their heads puzzling over how it works.

Taking it further

1 Play a positive sound (like a fanfare) for the first part of each **if ... else** and a rude sound (use your imagination) for the second part. To do this, you'll need to add sound objects and media in the Designer and then add two **Sound.Play** blocks in each **if ... else** block.

2 Change the test in each **if ... else** block so that it just tests for a number of names. You'll need to read ahead and find out how lists and **for each** blocks work in chapter 6.

3 Use lists (chapter 6) and random numbers (keep reading this chapter) to pick a random response (positive or rude) from a list of statements.

Keeping track with comments

Before we move on from the Personality Judge app, there's one last thing we suggest you do: add comments to your blocks. *Comments* are notes made by programmers that help them remember how the program works; they're also useful to other people with whom you share your app code. In addition, writing comments as you go along can help you remember what needs to be done and clarify your own problem solving. Programmers often spend lots of time solving different parts of a problem at the same time, and it's hard to keep track and easy to get confused or forget something. In summary, comments

- Help clarify your thinking and problem solving
- Help you remember how the program works
- Help people understand and build on your program

You can write anything in a comment, and you can add a separate comment to every single block if you want to. To add a comment to a block, right-click the block and select Add Comment. You'll see a blue question-mark icon appear on the block to indicate a comment has been created. Click it, and a yellow text box opens that you can type in (the cursor doesn't always flash, but you can still type). You can move the position of the comment by clicking and dragging, you can collapse or minimize a comment by clicking the question mark. Here are some examples:

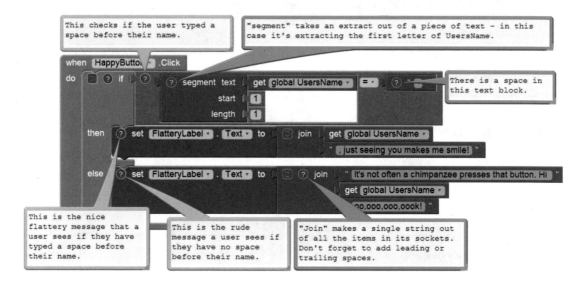

From now on, we suggest you use comments whenever you want to remember something for the future, you have questions, or you want to clarify your thinking about how a program works. Keep your comments short (the ones we used are a little wordy)—this helps make your programs easy for others to understand.

Changing variables

You know how to make variables, assign values to them, and use them to make decisions. The final thing you'll do in this chapter is look at how to change the value of a variable in an app. You're going to combine all this a little later in the chapter to make a Guessing Game app in which the user has to guess a number that the app has chosen at random. But first, you need to understand random numbers.

Dice Roll app

PURPOSE OF THIS APP
There are many times when you want an app to behave in a random or irregular way. For example, you might want a character in a game to move in an unpredictable way. In this simple example, you'll simulate a dice roll on your phone—the user shakes the phone to see a new random number. At this stage, you'll just display a number; later you'll make the result look more like an actual dice.

APP RATING

3

ASSETS YOU'LL NEED
Optional: six dice images (dice_1.png–dice_6.png). See "Taking it further."

Dice Roll			
Screen1 properties	`AlignHorizontal`: Center `Title`: Dice Roll App `Icon`: dice_6.png (downloaded from our website) `ScreenOrientation`: Portrait `BackgroundColor`: Black		
Components	**What do I rename it?**	**What does it do?**	**What properties do I set?**
`AccelerometerSensor` Palette group: Sensors	`Accelerometer-Sensor1`	Detects if the user has shaken the phone	Enabled (selected)
`Label`	`InstructionLabel`	Tells the user what to do	`FontBold`: selected `Text`: "Shake the Phone to Roll the Dice" `TextColor`: White `TextAlignment`: Center
`Label`	`DiceLabel`	Displays the number that has been rolled	`FontBold`: selected `Text`: "6" `FontSize`: 100 `TextColor`: Green

1. Programming the blocks

This is a simple app because App Inventor has a block called `random integer` that generates random whole numbers (integers). You'll find it in the Built-in > Math drawer. Plug two numbers into it, and it generates a random number between them (inclusive). So, plugging in 5 and 10 means it will pick 5, 6, 7, 8, 9, or 10. In your app, you'll choose from 1 to 6 as your lowest and highest numbers, because you're simulating a dice roll.

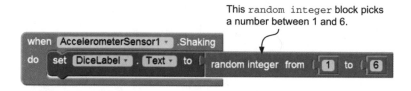

This `random integer` block picks a number between 1 and 6.

As you can see, you plug the `random integer` block into a `set DiceLabel.Text` block and then plug it all into an `AccelerometerSensor1.Shaking` event trigger (just like you did with the sheep button in chapter 2).

There you have it—the simplest app you've made since Hello World!—and now you know how to make a random whole number. If you ever need a random fraction for something, there's a sister block to `random integer` called `random fraction` that doesn't need a high and low value—it generates a random number between 0 and 1.

2. Taking it further

We've provided some dice-face images on the website so that instead of just a label showing the number, you can display a random dice face after each shake. Here are the essential parts of the task:

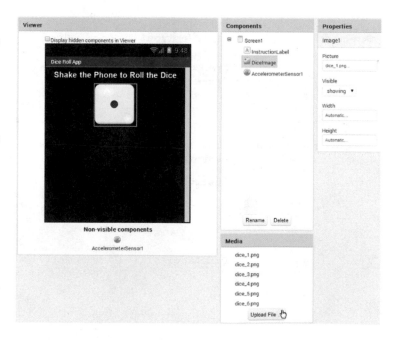

1 Load all six dice images using the Upload New button in the Media pane at the bottom of Designer. (You need to do this one image at a time.)

2 Delete `DiceLabel`, and add an `Image` called `DiceImage`. Set its `image` property to dice_1.png (a dice with one spot).

The interface changes are done. There are two ways to tackle the programming of the blocks. One is straightforward but long winded; the second isn't as obvious but is efficient. Programmers find this kind of thing in lots of situations: they're always searching for an efficient way of doing things because it saves them time, makes code easier to maintain, and usually makes apps run faster. Let's look at the two options.

THE LONG WAY AROUND: USING IF ... THEN
In this block, you use a variable called `DiceNumberRoll`. When the phone is shaken, you set `DiceNumberRoll` to be a random number (1–6).

To decide which image to show, you have six `if` decisions (three of which are shown here). These show a different `DiceImage` if their number is chosen.

This is straightforward, but look at all those `if` statements. The app will process all six of these, even if the first one is true. The only thing that changes each time is the `Dice-NumberRoll` test and the picture that is displayed. These two things match (if the random number is 2, you want Dice_2.png to appear), so wouldn't it make sense to say, "Pick a number from 1 to 6" and then load the image with that number in its filename? That's exactly what you'll do in your super-duper efficient version of the app.

THE SHORTCUT: CONCATENATING AN IMAGE FILENAME
Concatenating means joining things together (usually text), just like the `join` block you used earlier. In this case, you're going to set `DiceImage.Picture` to be a filename that joins (concatenates) the text "dice_", then a random number from 1 to 6, and finally ".png". Put them all together, and you have an efficient way to display a random dice image whenever the phone is shaken.

When the phone is shaken, `DiceImage.Picture` is set to a file with the following name: "dice_" + random number (1 to 6) + ".png".

Of course, it doesn't have to be dice images you display, and you aren't limited to six—as long as your image filenames all had the same format and contained a unique sequential number, you could have hundreds of images displayed at random this way. Imagine if you had to make hundreds of `if` blocks!

The Dice Roll app is one of the simplest in the book. The next app is the most complex you've made so far. It brings together everything you've learned about variables and random numbers, plus we'll add some new ideas like using procedures that make your code more efficient and explore the idea of validation. You'll also learn how to watch variables while the app is running to make sure they're doing what you expected.

Guess What I Am Thinking app

PURPOSE OF THIS APP
This is a simple guessing game in which the app thinks of a random number that the player has to guess. After each guess, the app tells you whether its number is higher or lower than the guess. Each guess you make reduces your score; and if you take more than 10 guesses, it's game over. To make things more interesting, you'll set three levels of difficulty. Easy uses numbers from 1 to 100, Medium from 1 to 200, and Hard 1 to 300.

APP RATING

3 ◀

ASSETS YOU'LL NEED
None, but you might want to add your own sounds for Higher and Lower guesses and also for when the player wins or loses.

Guess What I Am Thinking			
Screen1 properties	**AlignHorizontal**: Center **Scrollable**: Yes (selected) **Icon**= questionmark.png (downloaded from our website) **BackgroundColor**: Your choice **ScreenOrientation**: Portrait **Title**: Guess What I Am Thinking…		
Components	**What do I rename it?**	**What does it do?**	**What properties do I set?**
Vertical-Arrangement Palette group: Layout	**SelectDifficultyArr** (We've shortened **Arrangement** to **Arr** to save typing and to make you talk like a pirate.)	Contains the difficulty label and buttons	**Width** and **Height**: Automatic **Visible**: Showing
Label	**PickDifficultyLabel**	Asks the player to pick a difficulty setting	**FontSize**: 20 **Text**: "Pick your difficulty setting"
3 Buttons	**HardButton** **MediumButton** **EasyButton**	The buttons the user clicks to choose difficulty	**BackgroundColor** **Hard**: Red, **Medium**: Orange, **Easy**: Green **Text**: "Hard - 300", "Medium - 200", "Easy - 100" **FontSize**: 16 **TextAlignment**: center **Width**: Fill Parent **Height**: Automatic
Vertical-Arrangement	**GuessArr**	Contains **ScoreLabel**, **GuessButton**, **LastGuessLabel**, and **ResetButton**	**Width** and **Height**: Automatic **Visible**: hidden
Label	**ScoreLabel**	Displays the score at the beginning of the game and after every guess	**FontSize**: 20 **Text**: "Your score is 100"
Button	**GuessButton**	Button the player clicks to make a guess	**Text**: "Click to Guess" **FontSize**: 20 **TextAlignment**: Center
Label	**LastGuessLabel**	Displays the last guess and whether it's higher, lower, or correct.	**FontSize**: 20 **Text**: None (leave it blank)
Button	**ResetButton**	Resets the game	**Text**: "Restart Game" **FontSize**: 14 **TextAlignment**: Center
Notifier Palette group: User Interface	**HaveAGuessNotifier**	A pop-up notifier where the player inputs their guess	None
Notifier	**NotANumberNotifier**	Asks the player to try again if they type letters instead of numbers	None

1. Setting up the screen

Once you have all your components laid out, your screen should look as shown. Make sure the two vertical arrangements contain the right components. This is because you want the app to show different things at different times, just like in the Flattery, Personality Judge, and Ewe Scared Her! apps. That's why the `Guess-Arr` arrangement's `Visible` property is set to Hidden.

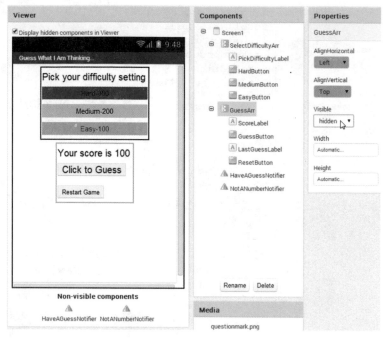

To begin with, you'll display the screen in step 1, shown next. Once the user clicks a difficulty setting, you'll hide the `SelectDifficultyArr` arrangement and show the `GuessArr` arrangement that contains all the components shown in step 2. If the user clicks the Reset Game button, you'll reverse the process to go back to step 1.

1. The player chooses a difficulty level.

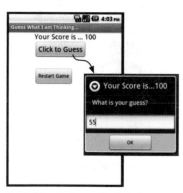

2. Clicking the top button lets the user enter a guess in a pop-up notifier.

3. The app tells the user how they're doing (including whether they win or lose).

4. Clicking Restart at any time takes the player back to the first screen (step 1).

Think about the app in three stages:

- *Initialization*—Where you'll set up the variables and figure out how step 1 works
- *Game play*—When the user makes their guesses (steps 2 and 3)
- *Reset*—When the player clicks the Reset Game button to restart the game (step 4)

2. Initializing

Think about what variables you'll need in the app. There are four—can you guess what they will be? One good way to figure this out is to look at steps 1–4. Three of the variables appear on the phone screen:

- *The difficulty setting*—Changes the highest number the computer might randomly choose, called **HighestNumber**
- *The score*—**Score**
- *The player's last guess*—**PlayerGuess**

Have you figured out the fourth variable? You use it all the time, but it only appears on screen at the end of the game:

- *The secret number that the player has to guess*—**SecretNumber**

In the Blocks Editor, set up these variables with the starting values shown:

```
initialize global HighestNumber to  100    initialize global Score to  100
initialize global PlayerGuess to  0        initialize global SecretNumber to  0
```

Next, think about what happens when the player clicks one of the three difficulty buttons. First you want to set the **HighestNumber** variable to match the difficulty level: 100, 200, or 300. Here's the code block for **HardButton**.

Duplicate this for **EasyButton** and **MediumButton**, but obviously change the values to 100 and 200.

```
when HardButton .Click
do  set global HighestNumber  to  300
```

What else does clicking a difficulty button do? It needs to start playing the game by hiding everything in the **SelectDifficultyArr** arrangement and showing the **GuessArr** arrangement. Finally, it needs to choose the secret number. Here are the code blocks; you can make them now:

```
set SelectDifficultyArr . Visible  to  false
set GuessArr . Visible  to  true
set global SecretNumber  to  random integer from  1  to  get global HighestNumber
```

Now here's a vital programming trick: *all three difficulty buttons do exactly these same steps.* That's important, because it means rather than copying and pasting the blocks of code three times, you can instead use a programming idea called *procedures* that will save you lots of time and make your code easier to understand.

Learning Point: Creating procedures

In chapter 2, you used the **Sound.Play** *procedure*—a block of code that has a name. You can create your own procedures and call them whenever you like. But it's possible to write all the programs in this book without creating procedures—so why use them?

Procedures help programmers save time and make apps that are more understandable and efficient. Procedures are also reusable:

- *Saving time*—Procedures are used in the real world all the time. When a doctor says "Take his temperature" or a chef says "Fry the sausages," they're using a shortcut that saves them having to issue lots of detailed instructions. Even "Tidy your room" is a kind of procedure. Procedures save programmers time because once they have defined a procedure in detail, they can call that procedure whenever they need it. Also, if a programmer makes a mistake in a procedure, they only have to correct it once—whereas if those blocks were copied and pasted into many different places, the mistake would take much longer to fix.
- *Understandable apps*—Procedures can be given helpful names (just like variables), and that makes understanding someone else's code much easier. This is a form of abstraction (see chapter 1).
- *Efficient apps*—Apps that call procedures are smaller, are more efficient, and generally run faster than apps that use lots of repeated code.
- *Reusable procedures*—If you've written a great procedure that could be used in lots of apps, then it's a simple matter to copy and paste it whenever you need it.

Creating and using procedures is similar to creating and using variables. You find them in the Built-in > Procedures section. Drag out a new **to procedure do** block now.

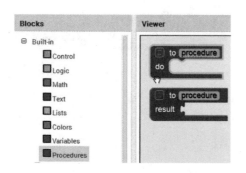

Just like with variables, you want to change the name of the procedure to something meaningful—in this case, **StartPlaying**. Click the word **procedure** in your new block and change it now.

Now that you've created and named a procedure, you'll find a new block named **call StartPlaying** in the Built-in > Procedures section of the Palette. Add it to your workspace.

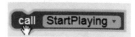

Time to put all the blocks onscreen together now.

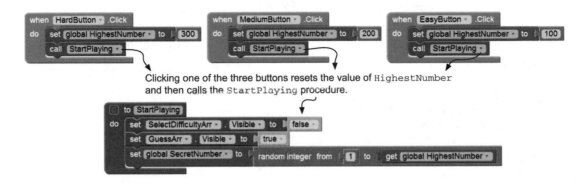

Clicking one of the three buttons resets the value of `HighestNumber` and then calls the `StartPlaying` procedure.

Just Do It!

At this point, it would be useful to check that the app is doing what you expect. If you run it on the phone or the emulator and click a button, you should see that the buttons disappear and the game screen appears with buttons and a score. The problem is, you don't know whether the app has set **HighestNumber** correctly and chosen an appropriate **SecretNumber**. App Inventor has a feature that lets you activate individual blocks to test them and also to see what variables are doing while the app is running—it's called *Do It*.

Right-clicking any block and choosing Do It executes that block on the phone. Let's say you want to check whether **EasyButton** is working. Right-click the **set global HighestNumber** block and choose Do It, and then repeat this on the **call Start-Playing** block. You'll see that the phone displays the game screen.

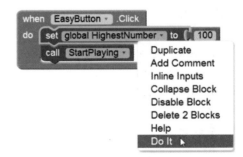

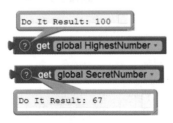

Many blocks also give you a pop-up comment that tells you their value. You can check that the value of **HighestNumber** is still 100 and find out what the secret number is by creating temporary **get variable** blocks and clicking Do It on them. It's important to realize that these results only update when you click Do It, like a snapshot. If the user clicks a button that changes the values, you won't see the change until you click Do It again.

In this example, it looks like everything is working as expected—I clicked Easy, and the app has set **HighestNumber** to 100; it has chosen a random number of 67, which is in the range from 1–100.

Watching variables like this is a useful way to debug programs—if you can't figure out what's happening in a program, add some **get** blocks, activate Do It, and check that blocks and variables are doing what was expected. Remember to delete any temporary **get** blocks once you're done. This means that your app isn't doing unnecessary steps and is easier for others to read.

3. Gameplay

Clicking **GuessButton** should open a notifier to enter a guess—you did this kind of thing already at the start of the chapter. I thought it might be good to always have the score on screen, so you add a concatenated `join` text block for the title of the notifier that says something like "Your Score is … 100."

When a guess has been made and the player clicks OK, the notifier's **AfterTextInput** event fires. You can store their response in the **PlayerGuess** variable like this.

You could move straight to checking whether they're correct, too low, or too high. Before we get to that, let's consider another possibility—what if they type some text like "eighty eight" or "banana"? Unlikely, but how about if they accidentally click OK without entering text? In all these cases, your program will behave strangely, because asking a question like "Does **SecretNumber** = "**banana**"?" doesn't make any sense! If the text isn't valid, then it must not be processed, and the user must be given an error message and asked to input a different value. You need a way of checking that the player has put in something reasonable or valid—that's called *validation*.

Learning Point: Validation (and verification)

There are lots of ways of checking whether a user has entered valid input. They include these:

- *Presence check*—Has the user typed anything?
- *Data-type check*—Has the user typed letters, numbers, symbols, or a combination? For example, people's names can only contain letters, and their dates of birth can only contain numbers.
- *Range check*—Has the user typed a value in a certain range? For example, the month of birth must be between 1 and 12.
- *Format check*—For example, date of birth must use the format mm/dd/yyyy.
- *Table-lookup check*—For example, the user can only choose an item from a list.

All of these will tell you whether input is reasonable or valid—but they won't tell you whether it's correct or true. For instance, I could tell you my date of birth is 12/12/1971—a perfectly valid date, but completely untrue. Checking facts by, for example, asking a user to enter data twice is a different kind of check called *verification*.

For your validation, you're going to use a combined presence and data-type check—that means the user *must* enter a number as their guess. The test you'll use is a Math comparison block called `is number`. If the player's answer is a number, that's fine—you'll call a new procedure that you'll create called `CheckPlayersGuess`. But if the user didn't enter a number, you'll pop up a notifier asking them to try again. Here's the final block:

(Note that you'll need to define a new procedure called `CheckPlayersGuess` so you can plug in the `call CheckPlayersGuess` block.)

Try typing **banana**—what happens? How about if you enter no data and just click OK? Finally, try typing a number like 55. You have a way of entering a valid guess—now you need to do something with that information. There are three possibilities: the user has entered a guess that is too high, too low, or exactly right. You can check these possibilities with three `if ... then` blocks. If the user is wrong, you'll reduce their score—and so you also need to keep track of whether their score is less than zero, at which point they lose and have to start again. You'll split out this bit into two procedures: `CheckPlayersGuess` works out which one of the three conditions is true and tells the user whether they're too high, too low, or correct. Then a new procedure you'll create called `DisplayScore` will update the score onscreen and check whether the player has lost.

HAVE I WON YET? CHECKPLAYERSGUESS
Here are the `if ... then` questions and actions in English:

- If `PlayersGuess` is greater than `SecretNumber`, output "Too High". Reduce the player's score by 10.
- If `PlayersGuess` is less than `SecretNumber`, output "Too Low". Reduce the player's score by 10.
- If `PlayersGuess` is equal to `SecretNumber`, output "You win!"

You should be able to work out how to turn these three questions into blocks. You'll tell the player the result of these questions by setting `LastGuessLabel.Text`.

You'll also need to know how to reduce the score by 10—here's the block. It says to set `Score` to itself minus 10; so, for example, a score of 50 becomes 40.

Try creating the three `if` blocks for the procedure `CheckPlayersGuess`. Then check what you come up with against the blocks shown next. You use `Text` blocks to provide the user with a reminder of what they guessed and whether it was high, low, or correct. Then you update their score by subtracting 10 points for a wrong answer (too high or too low).

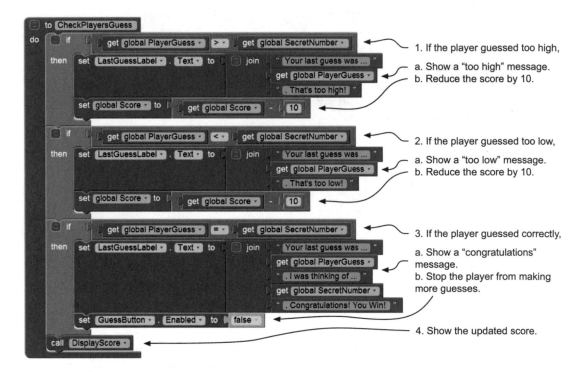

If the player guesses correctly (the bottom `if` test) then you probably want to stop them from guessing again (what would be the point?). There are lots of ways to achieve this, but the simplest is to disable `GuessButton` by setting `GuessButton.Enabled` to false. This means the button text is greyed out and nothing happens until the app reenables the button, which you'll do when the player clicks `ResetButton`. You'll do the same thing if the player loses, so their score can never be less than zero.

Test the app now—it won't display the score yet, but everything else should work.

DISPLAYSCORE

Games change scores for lots of different reasons. For example, in Temple Run, you get points both for running along a track and for collecting gems. In your game, having a separate procedure for updating the score and checking whether the user has lost is useful because it makes it easy to extend the game if you want to give points for actions other than guessing. For example, you could add a timer so that if the user spends too long between guesses, points are deducted—and at that point, you could also call **DisplayScore**.

Create a new procedure called **DisplayScore** now. It will check that **Score** is greater than zero. If it is, then **DisplayScore** will set **ScoreLabel.Text** to the current score; otherwise it will say that the player lost, reveal **SecretNumber**, and stop the player from guessing again. Remember that "otherwise" questions are usually **if ... then ... else** blocks, and that's the case here:

Initialization and gameplay are finished! The final piece of the puzzle is what to do when **ResetButton** is clicked.

4. Resetting the game

To put the game back to its starting state, you'll need to reverse your show and hide of the two arrangements. You also need to remember to

- Set **Score** back to 100
- Re-enable **GuessButton**
- Clear **LastGuessLabel.text**

In the block, you can see that to clear **Last-GuessLabel.Text**, you plug in an empty text block.

You should now have a fully functioning guessing game. Of course, if it's too easy or hard, you can always adjust the **HighestNumber** settings on the difficulty buttons (don't forget to change the button labels too).

Taking it further

1   You could add considerable pizzazz to this game by adding sound effects for higher, lower, won, and lost conditions.

2   Change the scoring system so that harder levels give the player more points.

3   Add a Grand Total Score that keeps a running total of all the scores the player has achieved over several games.

4   Add notifiers so the player can enter the starting **Score** and **HighestNumber** values instead of clicking a preset difficulty button.

5   Add a timer (see chapter 7) so the player's score decreases, the longer they take.

What did you learn?

In this chapter, you learned the following:

- How to create, name, set, change, and use variables
- How to join text and variables together into one text string, and how to use a segment block to pull out a piece of text
- How to ask questions and make decisions using comparison operators and **if** . . . **then** control blocks
- How to generate a random number
- How to use debugging tools, comments, and the Do It function to manually activate a block and use these debugging tools with a **get** variable block to watch variable values.
- Why procedures are important and how to create and use them
- How to validate data

Test your knowledge

1   Using the block above, decide whether these T-shirts would be bought:

a   A 20$ yellow t-shirt

b   A 15$ green t-shirt

c   A 1$ red t-shirt

d   A $20 red t-shirt

2   Which validation tests could you choose in the following situations: presence check, data-type check, or range check? (You can choose more than one.)

   a   Checking whether someone's age is between 8 and 16

   b   Checking whether a telephone number is valid

   c   Checking whether a user has entered their name

   d   Checking whether a price has been entered on an item for sale

3   Write a segment command like this example **`Segment "Apples", Start = 1 Length = 3`** to extract the following text:

   a   *grin* from *grinch*

   b   *itch* from *stitch*

   c   *tent* from *ostentatious*

Try it out

1   Add a dice roll sound and/or animation to the Dice Roll app.

2   Make a percentage discount calculator that lets you input a percentage and then applies it as a discount to any amount you type in. This is handy for checking stores that offer "15% off all marked prices" type deals.

3   Add a stats counter to the Spooky Sound FX app that keeps track of how often each sound is played by displaying a counter under each button. Add a label that states the most popular sound and updates after each button click (use a procedure).

4   Create an area calculator for rectangles. Extend it to work for other shapes like circles and triangles.

5   Change the size of dots and lines in the Graffiti Artist app from chapter 3. Start with a copy of the app and add two buttons that call notifiers to let you set **`LineSize`** and **`DotSize`** variables. (Hint: Use **`Dotsize`** to set the radius of **`WallCanvas.Circle`**, instead of using the value 5. Use **`LineSize`** to change the width of the line—you'll need to add a **`set WallCanvas.LineWidth`** block from **`WallCanvas`**.)

CHAPTER 6

Lists and loops

Chapter 5 showed you how apps can remember things. In this chapter, we'll build on that idea to make apps that remember and use collections of things using a special type of variable: the *list*. You'll also find out how to make apps that repeat an action several times using *loops*.

Lists are all around you—especially in the technology you use. If you think about it, we bet you can think of at least five lists you've used today. Here are some examples:

- Choosing a person to send a message to from your contacts list
- Choosing a ring tone from a list of sound files
- Reading a list of updates from your friends on social media
- Choosing a TV program to record from a TV planner list
- Selecting a way to pay from a list of options when internet shopping

These are all visible lists, where you choose one or more items. Computers also use invisible lists like these to track activities:

- *Your internet history*—A list of which pages you've visited.
- *Actions you've taken in a program*—They're saved in a list so they can be undone using the Undo button.
- *Game saves*—When you quit a game, your PC or console saves a list of parameters like your score, your current location or level, which objectives you've achieved, and so on.

In the first part of this chapter, you'll learn how to create visible lists to help users choose items. Then we'll move on to invisible lists, which are a flexible way to store lots of data items without having to create a bunch of separate variables.

Readymade lists

Your phone already contains lists of useful information, and App Inventor can access and use a few of them. You access these lists using *list pickers*.

Let's do a quick experiment to see how two of the readymade pickers work:

- **ImagePicker** opens the phone's gallery so you can pick an image. Click an image, and a copy is saved on your SD card. The pathname is automatically stored in the **Image-Picker Selection** property.
- **PhoneNumberPicker** lets you pick one of your phone contacts. App Inventor can access and use the contact's name, phone number, and picture.

For this experiment, you'll need a real phone (not the emulator) that already has some images saved, and some phone contacts to choose from—if you don't have any, add some before you begin. Because this example isn't a full app and has just a few simple components, we'll go ahead and tell you how to build it without presenting the usual app table. You'll put the two pickers on a screen, and whenever the user clicks one to make a choice, you'll show them the gallery picture or contact picture they selected, along with some additional information.

Start a new project called **ListExperiments**, and lay out the screen as follows:

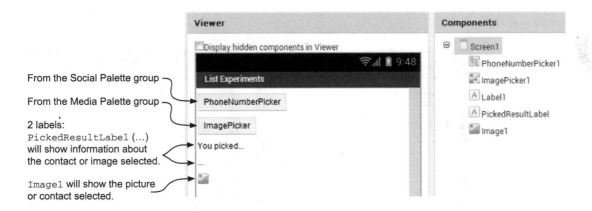

These pickers will work (to display the list) even before you code any blocks—try clicking the list-picker buttons. You can choose a contact (if you click the top button) or an image from the gallery (bottom button). So far, App Inventor isn't doing anything with that information. But each time you click a picker button and make a choice, you're generating an **AfterPicking** event. It's called **AfterPicking** because it fires only after you've chosen an item from the list. There's also a **BeforePicking** event that fires when you first click the list-picker button. You'll use the **AfterPicking** event to trigger your blocks (you saw something similar with the **AfterTextInput Notifier** event in chapter 5's Flattery app).

For the **PhoneNumberPicker**, you'll grab the contact's name and phone number and display them as a joined text string with "Tel:" in the middle, like this: "Martin Cooper Tel:555-12345678". You'll also change Image1 to a picture of the contact. Here are the blocks:

The **ImagePicker** saves a temporary copy of the image you select and provides you with the path and filename. You'll use these to display the file information and picture like so:

Here you can see the results of the two pickers.

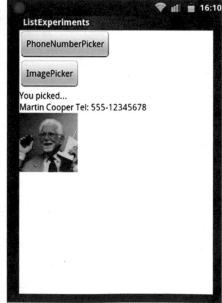

Of course, now that you've grabbed this information, you could do something much more interesting with it. For example, you could send an automatic text message to the contact or dial their number using the **PhoneCall** or **Texting** component (in the Social group of the Palette). Here are a couple other ideas:

- **ContactPicker**—Lets you pick one of your contacts. App Inventor can access and use their name, email address, and picture.
- **EmailPicker**—Like the ContactPicker, but lets you type the beginning of a name rather than choose from a list of people.

Later in this chapter, you'll use the in-built list pickers to select a new background for the Graffiti app you made way back in chapter 3. You'll also use the **ContactPicker** and **Texting** to send encrypted messages. Before that, let's take a look at how you can make your own list picker from scratch.

Making your own list picker

You can use a list picker whenever you want to give the user a choice of options: for example, choosing a drawing color from a palette of options or even something simple like whether they're male or female. This is a lot more efficient than creating lots of separate buttons or check boxes. List pickers are expandable, so you can create a long, scrollable list with more options than can fit on a single screen. But list pickers only let you pick a single option at a time—just like a multiple-choice quiz.

At right are some keywords we'll use when talking about list pickers.

We hope it's obvious why you need *elements* (so the list has something in it) and a *selection* (so you know what was chosen), but why do you need a *selection index*? For some simple lists like choosing Male or Female, the position of each element doesn't matter. But there are lots of times when it's useful:

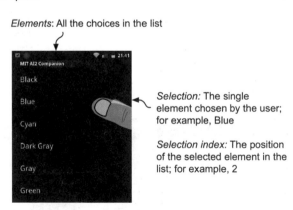

Elements: All the choices in the list

Selection: The single element chosen by the user; for example, Blue

Selection index: The position of the selected element in the list; for example, 2

- *When you're sorting lists into order.* For example, it's important to know where to put each name in a telephone directory.
- *When you're searching or processing a list of elements.* It's useful to know which position you're up to and whether you've reached the last element, so you know it's time to stop the search.
- *When you're working with parallel lists.* Sometimes you'll have several lists that all correspond to one person or thing. For example, if you know the First Name list is in the

same order as the Eye Color list, you can work out that Ellie (in Search Index position 6) has blue eyes (because the eye color found at Search Index position 6 is Blue).

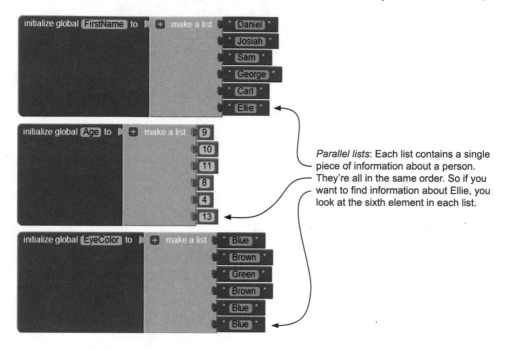

Parallel lists: Each list contains a single piece of information about a person. They're all in the same order. So if you want to find information about Ellie, you look at the sixth element in each list.

Ready for ice cream?

Let's experiment with a custom list picker by making a simple list of ice cream flavors. When the user picks one, you'll output a message that says "Out of these flavors [list of the flavors] you chose [chosen flavor] which was at position [number] in the list". The app works as follows:

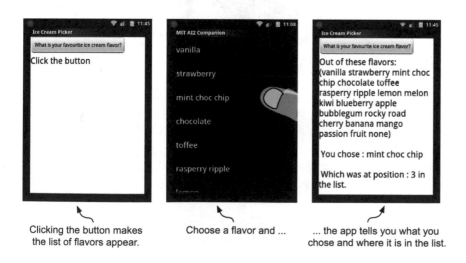

Clicking the button makes the list of flavors appear.

Choose a flavor and ...

... the app tells you what you chose and where it is in the list.

Again, this is a really simple experiment, so no app table for this one. Jump right in and set up your screen like this:

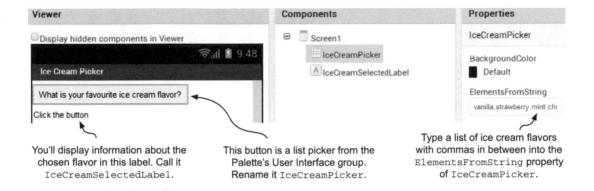

You'll display information about the chosen flavor in this label. Call it `IceCreamSelectedLabel`.

This button is a list picker from the Palette's User Interface group. Rename it `IceCreamPicker`.

Type a list of ice cream flavors with commas in between into the `ElementsFromString` property of `IceCreamPicker`.

You can type in your own list of flavors, or use ours: vanilla, strawberry, mint choc chip, chocolate, toffee, raspberry ripple, lemon, melon, kiwi, blueberry, apple, bubblegum, rocky road, cherry, banana, mango, passion fruit, none (although we've never met anyone who doesn't like ice cream).

The block follows exactly the same format as the **PhoneNumberPicker**:

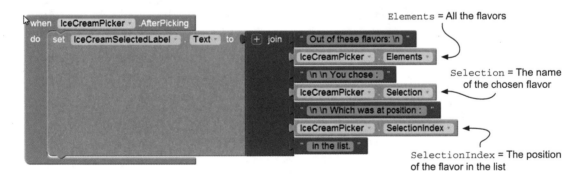

Elements = All the flavors

Selection = The name of the chosen flavor

SelectionIndex = The position of the flavor in the list

Have you noticed that you've typed **\n** several times in these text blocks? Run the app on your phone, choose an ice cream flavor, and see if you can work out what **\n** does. What happens if you remove **\n** from the text blocks?

Get yourself some ice cream if you worked out that typing **\n** in a text string inserts a new line at that point in the text (just like pressing Enter). This splits up the text neatly—each sentence starts its own line. If you want to add a blank line, you just add **\n** twice. Of course, you could have created three different labels in the Designer screen and then changed each of their `Text` properties to one of the sentences, but using `\n` is much simpler and keeps everything contained in a single label.

At the beginning of the chapter, we talked about visible and invisible lists. Everything you've done so far has been visible—now let's turn our attention to invisible lists that you program in blocks.

Excuse Generator app

PURPOSE OF THIS APP
This app generates a unique excuse if you forget to do your homework. It uses 4 hidden lists, each with 10 elements. There are 10,000 possible combinations of excuses. Some are sensible—but most are very silly!

APP RATING

 3

ASSETS YOU'LL NEED
keep-calm-and-make-excuses.png.

Excuse Generator			
Screen1 properties:	`Title`: Excuse Generator `AlignHorizontal`: Center `BackgroundColor`: Red `Screen Orientation`: Portrait		
Components	**What do I rename it?**	**What does it do?**	**What properties do I set?**
`Button`	`ExcuseButton`	Produces a new excuse each time it's clicked.	`Image`: keep-calm-and-make-excuses.png `Text`: None
`Label`	`ExcuseLabel`	This is where the excuse will appear.	`BackgroundColor`: Red `FontSize`: 28 `Text`: "Your Excuse:"

1. Setting up the screen

Here's the screen layout. Every time you click the button, a new excuse will appear at the bottom of the screen:

We've gone for a large `ExcuseButton` so that you can press it quickly in an emergency! Don't forget to erase the text in its `Text` property.

The random excuse will replace the text in this `ExcuseLabel`.

2. Coding the blocks: a slot-machine algorithm

The rules (or steps) that programmers think about and then turn into code are called an *algorithm*. In this case, you're going to use an algorithm that works like a slot machine. On a slot machine, symbols spin around on three wheels, and if all three match, you get a pay-out. In your algorithm, you'll have four wheels (lists); and instead of symbols, you'll write parts of a sentence that make up an excuse. As long as you write the sentence parts so that they follow the same structure and fit together when you read them, you can mix and match any combination of the four lists.

The sentence structure must always be the same. It starts with an apology, followed by a person who did some kind of action at a location, like so:

Sentence part list:	Apology	Person	Action	Location
Example:	I'm sorry,	my sister	set fire to my homework	at the swimming pool.
Example:	A thousand apologies,	my dog	ate my homework	in the Principal's office.

If you write 10 elements for each list (Apology, Person, Action, and Location), then the number of possible combinations is 10 x 10 x 10 x 10 = 10,000 sentences.

Learning Point: Algorithms

An *algorithm* is a precise set of instructions that solve a problem. Algorithms exist outside of the world of computer programs. You'll find them everywhere—in math, science, engineering, English, art, and even in your day-to-day life. Here are some examples of algorithms you've probably come across:

- A recipe to bake a cake
- Working out the area of a shape
- Folding a paper model like a bird or airplane
- Following the rules of a game

These algorithms might appear in lots of different ways: a recipe is usually written down; to work out a math problem, you might have written instructions or an example to follow; to fold a paper model, you'll probably follow a diagram or copy someone else; and to learn a game, you may listen to instructions. Computer scientists do all these things, too, when they want to figure out and share an algorithm—they may imagine it and talk it through, write down the steps, or draw a diagram like a flowchart.

One thing that is often very important in computer algorithms is that programmers want to build an *efficient* algorithm. This is because computers can do millions of operations every second, so even a small change in the time to complete some instructions can make a big difference in how quickly the overall program or app runs. Think about it like this: saving 5 seconds when you bake a cake is no big deal; but if you make a million cakes, the overall saving is about 58 days!

---

3. Setting up the lists

First set up the Apology list with 10 elements. This is almost the same as setting up any other variable. As with any other variable, you start with an `initialize global` block from the Variables group of the blocks. Change the name of the variable to something sensible: `Apology`. Now, instead of a number or text string, you use a `make a list` block from the Lists group. Your block will look like this.

In some apps, you may not know what the list will contain in the future—for example, if you're setting up lists to store users' contacts or high scores, you can only fill in the list elements once the user is running the app. In that case, you would stop here, leave this variable definition block as it is (with empty sockets after `make a list`), and move on to programming the rest of the app. But in this app, you're going to build the sentence elements right into the program—so you can add the 10 apologies to the list as text blocks, like so:

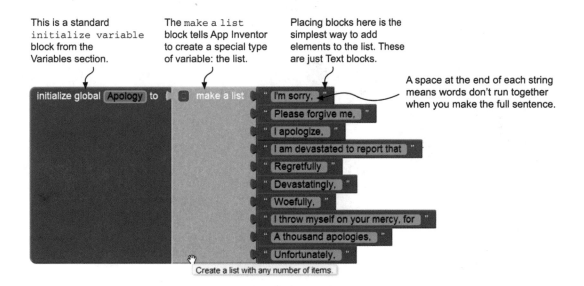

This is a standard `initialize variable` block from the Variables section.

The `make a list` block tells App Inventor to create a special type of variable: the list.

Placing blocks here is the simplest way to add elements to the list. These are just Text blocks.

A space at the end of each string means words don't run together when you make the full sentence.

Now add the other three lists to the blocks. The fastest way is to select, copy, and paste the previous block three times; change the variable names (to **Person**, **Action**, and **Location**); and then change the text blocks. Feel free to change these or add additional text blocks to any of the lists. Here's the way ours looked when we finished:

```
initialize global  Place  to    make a list   "  in my bedroom.  "
                                               "  on the bus.  "
                                               "  at the mall.  "
                                               "  at the fair.  "
                                               "  in the Principal's office.  "
                                               "  at the cinema.  "
                                               "  under a bridge.  "
                                               "  on a mountaintop.  "
                                               "  on my computer.  "
                                               "  at the swimming pool.  "
```

```
initialize global  Person  to    make a list   "  I  "
                                                "  my mother  "
                                                "  my father  "
                                                "  my brother  "
                                                "  my sister  "
                                                "  my dog  "
                                                "  my cat  "
                                                "  my goldfish  "
                                                "  my friend  "
                                                "  my neighbor  "
```

```
initialize global  Action  to    make a list   "  left my homework  "
                                                "  stole my homework and hid  "
                                                "  ate my homework  "
                                                "  set fire to my homework  "
                                                "  concealed my homework  "
                                                "  gave away my homework  "
                                                "  stopped me from doing my homework  "
                                                "  erased my memory of the homework  "
                                                "  copied my homework  "
                                                "  used my homework as a paper airplane  "
```

4. Building the sentence

You've finished all the hard work. When **ExcuseButton** is clicked, you need to choose a random element from each of the four lists. In some programming languages, you do this by picking a random number and then choosing the element at that position (or *index*) in the list. App Inventor makes things even simpler using a block called `pick a random item`. You tell it which list to use, and it randomly selects an item from that list. If you do that for the four lists and display the elements together in `ExcuseLabel`, your blocks look like this:

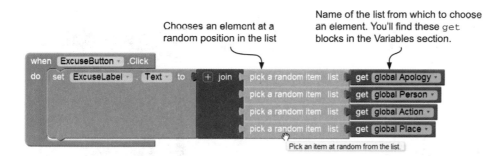

Try it—each time the button is clicked, you should see 1 of 10,000 possible excuses. You could use this as the basis for a game with friends where each player clicks the button and then has to explain what happened to their homework, starting with that sentence. The more plausible, creative, and imaginative they are, the more points you should give them.

You could enhance the app by having it play some sad music as you give your excuse—maybe it will sway your teachers. You could also have the text-to-speech component speak the excuse (we guarantee it will sound more plausible than you—because it won't snicker or laugh).

Learning Point: Lists can contain (almost) anything

In this example, your lists just contain text strings. But we wouldn't want you to think that lists have to be text. App Inventor lists are very flexible and can contain any variable types, including text strings, numbers, boolean (True/False), and color variable types.

You can even mix and match different types of variables in the same list.

In the next app, you'll combine everything you've learned about lists to improve the Graffiti Artist app you first made in chapter 3.

Graffiti Artist 2:
the spray-paint returns!

PURPOSE OF THIS APP

Now that you know how to create list pickers, you can go back and improve the chapter 3 Graffiti Artist app by making the following changes:

- Users can select a background image from their gallery instead of the wall.
- Users can choose the size of the lines and dots they draw.
- Users can select from a wider range of colors.
- The user interface is improved by using icon buttons at the top of the screen.

APP RATING

ASSETS YOU'LL NEED

Icon images: clear_icon.png, color_icon.png, size_icon.png, and background_img_icon.png.

1. Updating the screen layout

Load a copy of your Graffiti Artist app, and use Save As to save the project as GraffitiArtist2. You'll start by creating a new toolbar in the existing **ColorBar** horizontal arrangement. You'll do these things:

- Replace the five color-choice buttons with a single list-picker button.
- Move the wipe button (from the bottom of the screen) up into your new toolbar.
- Add new buttons to pick a background and change the line size.

Begin by deleting the five color buttons (ignore any warnings that appear—click OK). Then move the "Clean it off!" **WipeButton** from the bottom to the top of the screen.

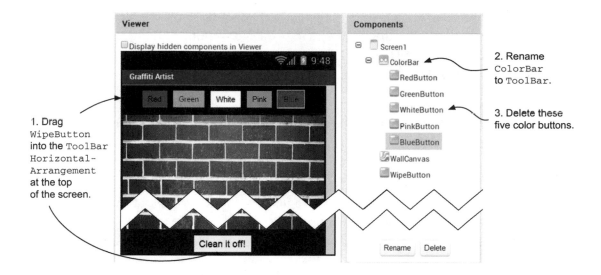

1. Drag `WipeButton` into the `ToolBar` Horizontal-Arrangement at the top of the screen.

2. Rename `ColorBar` to `ToolBar`.

3. Delete these five color buttons.

Now add three new buttons, and update **WipeButton** as follows:

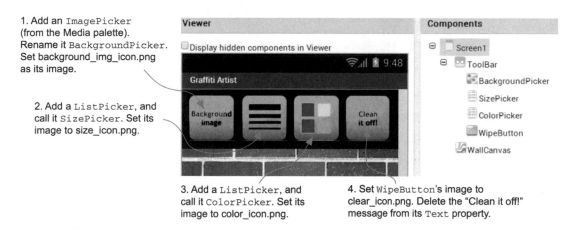

1. Add an `ImagePicker` (from the Media palette). Rename it `BackgroundPicker`. Set background_img_icon.png as its image.

2. Add a `ListPicker`, and call it `SizePicker`. Set its image to size_icon.png.

3. Add a `ListPicker`, and call it `ColorPicker`. Set its image to color_icon.png.

4. Set `WipeButton`'s image to clear_icon.png. Delete the "Clean it off!" message from its `Text` property.

BackgroundPicker is an image picker just like you used earlier in this chapter. It will take the user to their phone Gallery, and you'll code some blocks that make the image they choose appear on the **WallCanvas**.

SizePicker is a regular list picker that lets the user choose the size of the lines and dots they draw. A good range of sizes to give them is 1, 3, 5, 7, 9 (pixels)—enter these into the **Elements** property of **SizePicker**. You can experiment with some other choices if you like by adding to or changing this list of elements.

`ColorPicker` gives the user a range of color names to choose from—this means you can offer many more choices than the five they had in the old version of Graffiti Artist. Here's the full list of colors you need to type into the `Elements` property of `ColorPicker`: Black, Blue, Cyan, Dark Gray, Gray, Green, Light Gray, Magenta, Orange, Pink, Red, White, and Yellow.

`WipeButton` works exactly as before—you don't need to change anything other than its position and icon.

2. Coding the blocks: choosing a background image

You're using exactly the same sort of code here that you saw in the `ImagePicker` experiment earlier in this chapter. The only change is that you're setting the `WallCanvas` `BackgroundImage` property rather than changing an `Image` object's `Picture` property.

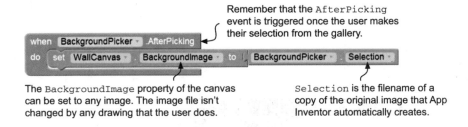

Remember that the `AfterPicking` event is triggered once the user makes their selection from the gallery.

The `BackgroundImage` property of the canvas can be set to any image. The image file isn't changed by any drawing that the user does.

`Selection` is the filename of a copy of the original image that App Inventor automatically creates.

3. Changing the line and dot sizes

You can set the line width of any lines drawn by using the canvas `LineWidth` property. So the first job is to set this property to whatever the user chose in the `SizePicker`. Here are the blocks:

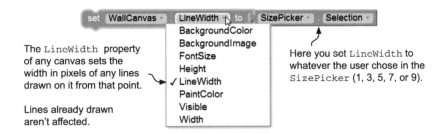

The `LineWidth` property of any canvas sets the width in pixels of any lines drawn on it from that point.

Lines already drawn aren't affected.

Here you set `LineWidth` to whatever the user chose in the `SizePicker` (1, 3, 5, 7, or 9).

You've finished the line size, but changing the size of the dots (which appear when the user taps the screen) is trickier. If you look at your original Graffiti Artist blocks, you'll see that you drew a circle for each dot and set the circle radius to 5 pixels. You need to change this so that instead of directly coding a value (5) into the blocks, you use a variable instead. You'll store the user's `SizePicker` choice in the variable; and whenever they dot the screen, you'll set the circle's radius to the variable's value. To do this, define a global variable called `DotRadius` with an initial value of 5, and then replace the number 5 block with the `DotRadius` variable block. Here are the before and after:

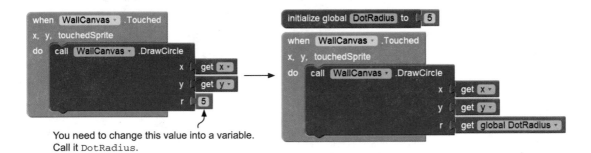

You need to change this value into a variable. Call it `DotRadius`.

Now you have a way to change the line size and the dot size—all that's left is to have the `SizePicker`'s `AfterPicking` event trigger the changes. Here are the `AfterPicking` event blocks:

Choosing a new size in `SizePicker` changes both the line width and the dot size of any new drawings.

Note that in this example we created just one list picker to set both the line and dot size, because they both use the same units (pixels). But you could have separate list-picker buttons and events—one for dots and one for lines. That would mean the user could set each property independently: if they clicked the line-size list picker and changed lines from fat to thin, their dot size wouldn't change until they clicked its list picker.

4. Offering a rainbow of colors

In the original Graffiti Artist, you gave a choice of colors by using five separate buttons that set the `WallCanvas PaintColor` property to five different premade color blocks like this one:

This red color block from the Colors section of the Blocks Editor is actually the number -65536.

In Graffiti Artist 2, you need an easy way to translate text color descriptions in the `Color-Picker` list into premade color blocks. If the user clicks the `ColorPicker` button and chooses Red, then you want to set `WallCanvas.PaintColor` to a red color block. You might think, "Why not plug color blocks into the `ColorPicker` list in the first place? Why type the names of all those colors?" If you try it, you'll see that the premade color blocks in App Inventor are just a bunch of numbers. Asking a user to choose between -65536 or -16776961 is a lot less helpful than saying Red or Blue. So the task becomes how to link the text *Blue* with the App Inventor blue color block (-16776961). The easiest way to do this is to set up a new list of color blocks that matches the order of the elements in the `Color-Picker`. Then you can use the `SelectionIndex` of a selected color name to look up the color value, like so:

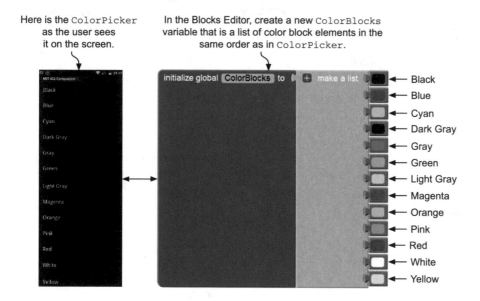

Here is the `ColorPicker` as the user sees it on the screen.

In the Blocks Editor, create a new `ColorBlocks` variable that is a list of color block elements in the same order as in `ColorPicker`.

When the user picks a color from the `ColorPicker` (left), you can use its index position to set the same `WallCanvas.PaintColor` from the matching `ColorBlocks` list (right). Here are the blocks that are triggered when the user chooses a color from the `ColorPicker`:

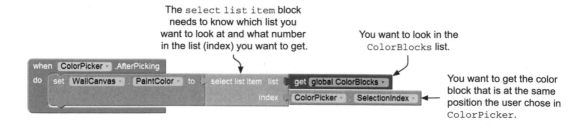

The `select list item` block needs to know which list you want to look at and what number in the list (index) you want to get.

You want to look in the `ColorBlocks` list.

You want to get the color block that is at the same position the user chose in `ColorPicker`.

An example will help explain this:

1 The user clicks the **ColorPicker** icon and chooses Blue, which is second in the list of colors (**index**=2).

2 The **AfterPicker** event is triggered.

3 **WallCanvas.PaintColor** is set to whichever color block is at position 2 in the **ColorBlocks** list.

Which is … Blue (phew!). We hope you can see why being able to use the index position of an item in a list is useful—in this case you have two lists, but because they're paired up (in the same order), you can translate from one to the other. The Graffiti Artist 2 app is complete, and at the end of this chapter we give you some suggestions for how you could take it even further.

We've covered a lot of ground so far in this chapter. We're about halfway through, so this is a good point to take a break if you need one. In the next section we'll look at how apps can repeat actions using loops, and how this can help you make and use lists efficiently.

Loop the loop

Computers (including smartphones) are really fast at carrying out instructions; they can perform literally millions of instructions in a second. This speed becomes most obvious and useful when we ask computers to repeat an action many times over—this is called a *loop*.

Loops are programmable blocks (rather than components), so you'll find them in the Blocks Editor under Control. There are three types of loop, as we'll show you next.

for range … do …

This block runs a set of blocks (in the **do** section) for a fixed number of times (the range).

EXAMPLE

i is a counter variable. It keeps track of how often you have gone around the loop. You could rename it something meaningful like LoopCounter.

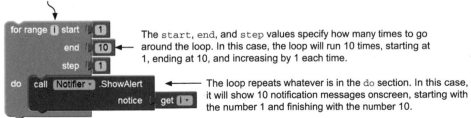

The start, end, and step values specify how many times to go around the loop. In this case, the loop will run 10 times, starting at 1, ending at 10, and increasing by 1 each time.

The loop repeats whatever is in the do section. In this case, it will show 10 notification messages onscreen, starting with the number 1 and finishing with the number 10.

You set the range by plugging in a **start** value, an **end** value, and a **step** value. The **start** and **end** values are straightforward—they say what number you want to start at and when the loop should stop. The **step** value is how quickly and in what direction you want to count. Usually you want to count up in single steps, so **step** will be 1. But you can change **step** to a larger value; for example, if you wanted to count up in fives, then you'd set **step** to 5. You can also count down instead of up: if **start** = 10, **end** = 0, and **step** = -1, then the loop will start at 10 and count down until it reaches 0. The **i** in the block is a counter variable that keeps track of how many times the app has gone around the loop. You don't always need to know this information, but sometimes it's very useful—as in the example we just showed you, where we output the value of **i** into a notifier to make a simple counting app (also see the next app for a further example).

You might wonder why the variable is called **i**. It's a habit programmers have developed because it's the first letter of the word *index*. Just like any variable, you can rename it something meaningful like **LoopCounter** by clicking the **i** and typing a new name. It's a *local* (rather than global) variable, which means you can only use it within the **do** part of the loop—other blocks can't "see" it.

WHEN YOU MIGHT CHOOSE IT

Use a **for range ... do ...** loop whenever you know in advance how many times you need to execute a loop. It's safer than a **while ... do ...** loop (explained in a minute) because you can be sure it will end after a specific number of times.

for each ... in list ... do ...

This block runs a set of blocks (in the **do** section) for every item in a specified list.

EXAMPLE

i is a list item variable. It starts with the same value as the first item in the list and then, with each loop, switches to the next value in the list.

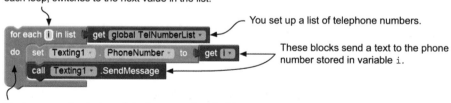

You set up a list of telephone numbers.

These blocks send a text to the phone number stored in variable **i**.

The loop repeats whatever is in the **do** section. In this case, it sends a text message to every phone number in **TelNumberList**.

The local variable **i** refers to the value of an item in the list. At first the value of **i** is the same as the value of the first item in the list. Once the **do** part of the loop has finished, the value of **i** is set to the next item in the list, and so on, until the last item of the list has been processed.

WHEN YOU MIGHT CHOOSE IT

Use a `for each ... in list ... do ...` loop whenever you want to work through a whole list of items. It's safer than a `while ... do ...` loop (discussed next) because you can be sure it will end once it reaches the end of the list.

while (test) do ...

This loop tests if something is true (just like an `If` block). If the test is true, all the blocks in the **do** section are run, and then the whole process starts again. The loop continues until the test is false. At that point the loop stops, and any blocks after the loop are run.

EXAMPLE

The test here is whether the variable `DiceThrow` does not equal 6.

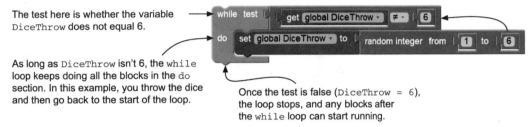

As long as `DiceThrow` isn't 6, the `while` loop keeps doing all the blocks in the `do` section. In this example, you throw the dice and then go back to the start of the loop.

Once the test is false (`DiceThrow = 6`), the loop stops, and any blocks after the `while` loop can start running.

WHEN YOU MIGHT CHOOSE IT

Use a `while (test) do ...` loop if you can't use one of the other loops—for example, because you don't know how many times the loop needs to run. You could use it to process a list if you didn't want to search through every element (`for each`) but instead wanted to stop when a particular element is found.

Learning Point: Infinite loops and loops that take too long!

INFINITE LOOPS

We suggested that the two `for ...` type loops might be better than the `while` loop because you can be sure they'll stop after a certain number of loops. This is important because you could accidentally make a `while` loop that never ends—an *infinite loop*. The only way to stop this kind of loop is to quit the app. As an example, if you change the `DiceThrow` blocks in the earlier `while (test) do ...` example to choose a random integer from 1 to 5, then you can never throw a 6—the loop would run forever!

LONG LOOPS

Sometimes loops can take a long time to finish, and the Android operating system worries that your app has crashed. At this point, it will ask the user if they want to wait a little longer or force the app to close. At the time of writing, you can't stop this from happening in App Inventor—so if a loop takes a long time when you test the app, make sure you use a pop-up notification or message onscreen to warn the user that they will need to click Wait.

Multiplication Table Generator app

PURPOSE OF THIS APP
This app generates a multiplication table. This is a good way to find out how a **for range** loop works, because you know how many times you want the loop to run: 12 times.

APP RATING

3

ASSETS YOU'LL NEED
None.

The user will type in a number. When they click the Generate Table button, the app will multiply their chosen number by 1, then 2, then 3, and so on, until it reaches 12. The output will look like what is shown above.

Notice that the first number (or factor) in each calculation starts at 1 and increases by 1 each time, all the way up to 12. The second factor is what the user typed in the text box: in this case, 5.

Multiplication Table Generator			
Screen1 properties:	**Title**: Multiplication Table Generator		
Components	**What do I rename it?**	**What does it do?**	**What properties do I set?**
Label	InstructionLabel	Tells the user what to do.	**Text**: "Which Multiplication Table would you like to generate?"
TextBox Palette group: User Interface	FactorTextBox	Lets the user input a number.	**NumbersOnly**: Yes (selected)
Button	GenerateButton	Produces the multiplication table.	**Text**: "Generate Table"
Label	ResultLabel	The multiplication table is displayed in this label.	**Text**: None

1. Setting up the screen

Here's the screen layout:

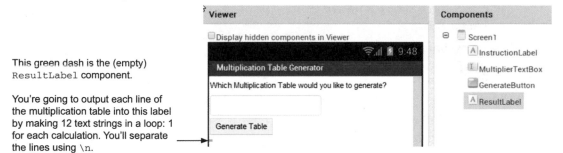

This green dash is the (empty) `ResultLabel` component.

You're going to output each line of the multiplication table into this label by making 12 text strings in a loop: 1 for each calculation. You'll separate the lines using `\n`.

2. Coding the blocks: defining the programming problems

You need to solve two programming "problems" for this app. The first problem is displaying a single calculation so that it looks something like "1 x 5 = 5". The second problem is repeating this process 12 times while changing the first number—so the next calculation says "2 x 5 = 10", then "3 x 5 = 15", and so on.

Without a loop, you would need to program 12 sets of blocks—one for each line. Even worse, what if the user wanted more flexibility—say, multiplication tables that go beyond 12 for the first factor? There are lots of ways to solve these problems. Stop reading now, and have a go at writing some step-by-step instructions before you read our suggested solution.

You may have a different solution than the one we present—it may be shorter or more efficient, or it may be longer and less efficient. Making these judgment calls is one of the ways in which programming is a creative (some would say artistic) process as well as a logical one. Try our solution app, and then try turning your ideas into an app, and see which works best.

Here's the step-by-step for the app:

1. Set up a variable for the user's multiplication factor. Call it **UserFactor**.
2. When the user clicks the Generate Table button …
   a. Set the value of **UserFactor** to whatever number they typed in the text box.
   b. Clear the **ResultLabel** (in case they already have an old table displayed there).
   c. Set up a loop that counts from 1 to 12. Keep track of how many times the loop has run using a local variable called **LoopCounter**.
   d. For each loop, add a line to the current **ResultLabel** with the following text joined together:
      - The value of **LoopCounter**
      - The letter *X* (to represent multiplying)

○ The value of `UserFactor`

○ The character `=`

○ The result of `LoopCounter * UserFactor` (`*` means "multiply" when using a computer)

○ A new line `\n`

e Repeat step d until you reach the 12th line.

We've chosen to loop 12 times because children commonly learn multiplication tables from 1–12. But you can experiment with higher values—why not try a 100X table? Also see "Taking it further" at the end of this chapter for a challenge to give the user control of this value.

Here are the finished blocks. One loop does all 12 calculations:

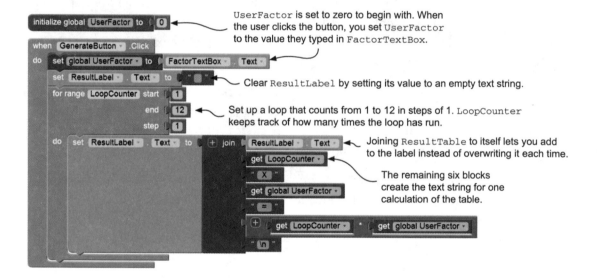

When you run the app, you may notice a slight delay between clicking the button and seeing the result (particularly if you try increasing the **end** range value in the loop). This is because App Inventor does one thing at a time, so it runs through the loop, prepares the label, and updates the display only once the loop has finished.

3. Looping the loop: nested loops

If you put one loop inside another, the inner loop will run as many times as the outer loop tells it to. This is a little like multiplying loops together. Putting one loop inside another is called *nesting*.

What's the point of nesting? Here's a simple example of the power of putting one loop inside another. At the moment, you have an app that can use a single loop to generate 12 calculations for a value the user types in. What if instead of just one multiplication table, you wanted to generate *all* the multiplication tables from 1 up to the value the user chose? In other words, if the user typed **3**, they would get three multiplication tables:

1X table	2X table	3X table
1 X 1 = 1	1 X 2 = 2	1 X 3 = 3
2 X 1 = 2	2 X 2 = 4	2 X 3 = 6
3 X 1 = 3	3 X 2 = 6	3 X 3 = 9
… (up to)	… (up to)	… (up to)
12 X 1 = 12	12 X 2 = 24	12 X 3 = 36

1 This extra power requires very little modification to the code: Save As your project with the name **AllMultiplicationTablesUpTo**.

2 Detach (but don't delete) the **for range** loop block you created previously (you're going to reuse it in a moment).

3 Add a new **for range** loop block that counts from 1 to **UserFactor** (this is your new outer loop). Call its index **Factor1**.

4 In the new loop, add a couple of blank lines to **ResultLabel** (this splits the tables so you can tell where each begins).

5 In the new loop, add the old **for range** block that you detached earlier (this is your new inner loop).

6 Change the multiplication calculation from **LoopCounter*UserFactor** to **LoopCounter*Factor1**.

7 The final result will look like this:

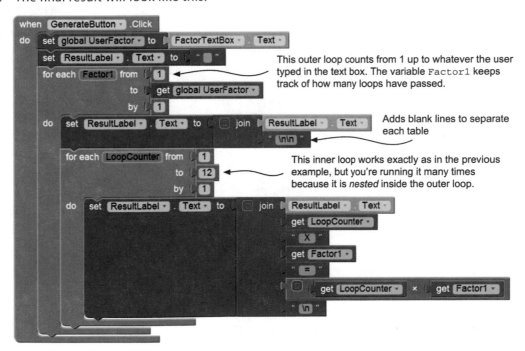

This outer loop counts from 1 up to whatever the user typed in the text box. The variable `Factor1` keeps track of how many loops have passed.

Adds blank lines to separate each table

This inner loop works exactly as in the previous example, but you're running it many times because it is *nested* inside the outer loop.

You can try this out with some large numbers—it will take a little while, but it's still much faster than a human could calculate all those multiplication tables.

Now that you know about lists and loops, this chapter's final app brings them together in a top-secret app we call …

Secret SMS Sender app

PURPOSE OF THIS APP
This app takes a message you type and turns it into a secret code. The app lets you send the coded message by SMS text to one or more of your agents (or friends) from your phone's Contacts list. Your fellow agents can decode the message by copying and pasting it into their own version of the app.

APP RATING

3

ASSETS YOU'LL NEED
Image: authkey.png. Sounds: coding_completed.mp3 and message_sent.mp3.

WARNING!
Before you start this app, you need to know that sending messages may cost money—and this app can send lots of messages all at once. Check with whoever pays your mobile phone bill to be sure this is OK. You can test the app without sending messages; we'll tell you how as you work through it.

Secret SMS Sender			
Screen1 properties	**Title**: Secret SMS Sender **BackgroundColor**: None **BackgroundImage**: authkey.png		
Components	**What do I rename it?**	**What does it do?**	**What properties do I set?**
Horizontal-Arrangement	HorizArr1	Contains **MsgTextBox** and **CodeButton**	None
TextBox Palette group: User Interface	MsgTextBox	Lets the user input a message	**FontSize**: 18 **Hint**: "Type your message here" **MultiLine**: Yes (selected)
Button	CodeButton	Turns the message into code (and back again)	**Text**: "Encode/Decode"
Horizontal-Arrangement	HorizArr2	Contains **AddTelPicker**, **DeletePicker**, and **SendButton**	None
PhoneNumber-Picker	AddTelPicker	Lets the user choose a contact to receive the message	**Text**: "Add Agent"
ListPicker Palette group: User Interface	DeletePicker	Lets the user remove a contact from the list of those who will receive the message	**Text**: "Remove Agent"
Button	SendButton	Sends the message to the agents	**FontBold**: Yes (selected) **FontSize**: 18 **Text**: "Send"
Label	Label1	Explains the list of agents	**Text**: "The message above will be sent to these agents:"
Label	AgentsLabel	Displays the current list of agents	**Text**: "No Agents selected"
Texting	TextSender	A non-visible component that lets you send a text	None
Notifier	MsgSentNotifier	Displays a pop-up confirming the message has been sent	None
Sound	CodeSound	Plays a confirmation sound when the message is coded	**Source**: coding_completed.mp3
Sound	SentSound	Plays a confirmation sound when the message is sent	**Source**: message_sent.mp3

1. Setting up the screen

Here's the screen layout:

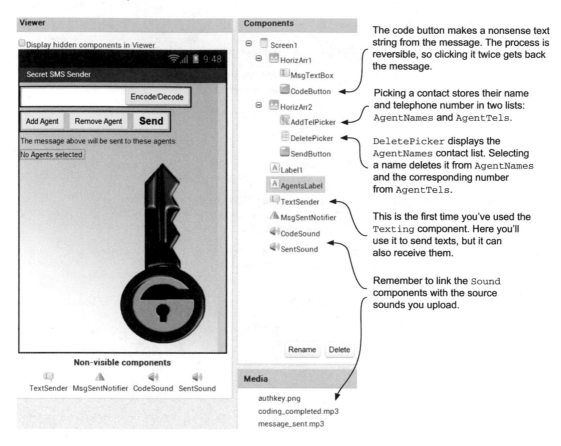

The code button makes a nonsense text string from the message. The process is reversible, so clicking it twice gets back the message.

Picking a contact stores their name and telephone number in two lists: AgentNames and AgentTels.

DeletePicker displays the AgentNames contact list. Selecting a name deletes it from AgentNames and the corresponding number from AgentTels.

This is the first time you've used the Texting component. Here you'll use it to send texts, but it can also receive them.

Remember to link the Sound components with the source sounds you upload.

Depending on your phone, you may find that the list of agents the user selects overlaps the image of the key (on the screen background). You can improve this by putting **AgentsLabel** into a **VerticalArrangement** so it's contained in a column on the left of the screen.

2. Coding the blocks: encrypting the message

Here's an encrypted message: *suineg a era uoy*. Can you tell what it says? Chances are you can crack this code very quickly (if not, we'll explain how to decode it in a minute). But the code is probably sufficient to stop someone from glancing over your shoulder and reading the message, and later we'll make some suggestions about how you can strengthen the encryption.

Learning Point: Cryptography in the real world

The science of secret codes is called *cryptography*. This word comes from parts of two ancient Greek words: *crypt*, meaning hidden; and *graph*, meaning writing. Turning a message into a code is called *encryption* (which rhymes with "description").

This app is for fun, and the code can be easily cracked; but real computer programmers are paid to figure out how to send secret messages that can't be read even if they're intercepted. This isn't just for secret agents—whenever you buy something online, you want to be sure that only you and the online shop have your personal payment details.

An algorithm that encrypts a message has a special name: a *cipher* (pronounced "syfer"). Our example cipher is incredibly simple—if you haven't guessed it yet, we just reversed the message. That's a simple idea for a human to understand, but how do you explain it to a computer? Try explaining the process step by step to a friend now. You could even write it down.

Did you come up with something like this?

1 Start at the last letter of the message.
2 Repeat the following for as many letters as are in the message:
   a Write down the current letter.
   b Move one letter towards the start of the message.

Look back at the three types of loops that we showed you earlier in the chapter. Which kind makes the most sense here? Before you run the loop, you do know how many times it should run: the same as the number of characters in the message. App Inventor can tell you the number of letters in any text string using a block called **length** in the text section. So, you can use a **for range** loop. Step 1 says you start at the end of the message and work backward, so you need the **for range start** value to be the length of the message. You're working back to the first letter, so the **end** value needs to be 1 and because you're working backward, you set the step value to -1, like this:

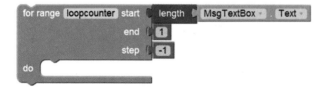

The **do** part of the loop needs to perform step 2a: "Write down the current letter." In programming terms, you set up a variable called **CodedMessage** and keep joining the current letter to it as you run through the loop. How do you look at just the current letter? You worked out the solution to that particular problem in the chapter 5 Prankster app—the **segment** block lets you extract any part of a text string. In this case, you want to extract a single letter at the current position or loop counter. Once the loop is complete, you'll change the **MsgTextBox** to show the new encrypted message, and you'll also play a sound so the user notices that the coding has finished. Here are the final blocks:

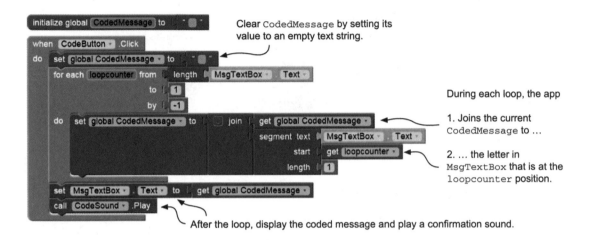

Clear CodedMessage by setting its value to an empty text string.

During each loop, the app

1. Joins the current CodedMessage to …

2. … the letter in MsgTextBox that is at the loopcounter position.

After the loop, display the coded message and play a confirmation sound.

Try it now. A single button click encrypts the message; clicking the button a second time decrypts the message. Next you need to figure out how to send the message to a list of contacts.

3. Adding agent contacts

The idea here is that you can add a list of agents to receive the message. The user can keep clicking and adding agents until they're happy. You'll put the names and numbers of all the selected agents in two lists called **AgentNames** and **AgentTels**. You'll also display their names onscreen so the user can be sure they're sending the coded message to the right people. You set up the two lists just like any other variables (in this case, you want them to be empty lists).

To choose an agent, you use your telephone picker (called **AddTelPicker**), processing the agent's details using the **AfterPicking** event. Add two new list blocks: one for **Agent-Names** and one for **AgentTels**. Finally, you want to output the names of all the agents chosen so far into the **AgentsLabel**. Here are the completed blocks to select an agent:

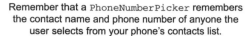

Remember that a `PhoneNumberPicker` remembers the contact name and phone number of anyone the user selects from your phone's contacts list.

You store the name and telephone number in two lists: `AgentNames` and `AgentTels`.

You output all the names the user has selected so far into `AgentsLabel`.

You're using a quick option here—outputting all the **AgentNames** elements into the label, as you did in the ice cream example earlier. This means the names appear one after another with no breaks in between. You could make this better by having a **for each** loop output each name on a separate line (using **\n**).

4. Deleting agent contacts

Letting the user delete an agent from the lists is a two-step process. First you need to fill the **DeletePicker** list picker with all the agents the user has selected so far, to give them a choice of whom to delete. Then, when they pick an agent, you need to delete that agent's name from **AgentNames** and their telephone number from **AgentTels**.

When the user clicks a list picker, they trigger a **BeforePicking** event. At that point, you can set the list picker's elements. Even though the list picker is empty when the user clicks it, the app immediately fills it. Because you already have all the chosen agents' names in the **AgentNames** list, you just need to set the **DeletePicker Elements** property to the **Agent-Names** list. A diagram of this process might help:

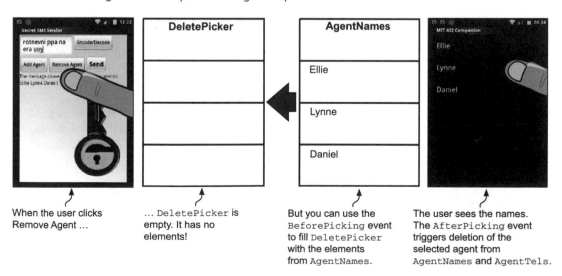

When the user clicks Remove Agent …

… `DeletePicker` is empty. It has no elements!

But you can use the `BeforePicking` event to fill `DeletePicker` with the elements from `AgentNames`.

The user sees the names. The `AfterPicking` event triggers deletion of the selected agent from `AgentNames` and `AgentTels`.

The blocks to do this are actually simpler than the explanation! Here's the block to fill (or *populate*) the `DeletePicker` list picker:

Then, to delete the agent from the two lists, you can use the `SelectionIndex` of the agent the user chose from the onscreen list. You also need to update the onscreen label so the user knows the agent is no longer selected:

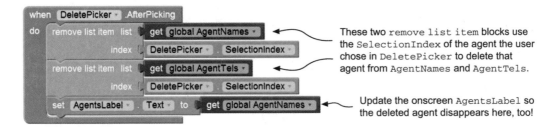

These two `remove list item` blocks use the `SelectionIndex` of the agent the user chose in `DeletePicker` to delete that agent from `AgentNames` and `AgentTels`.

Update the onscreen `AgentsLabel` so the deleted agent disappears here, too!

5. Sending the message

To send an SMS text message, you'll use a new **Texting** component that includes blocks to send a text messages to a phone number. You'll call this block once for each agent in the **AgentTels** list, sending the same coded message to each agent.

Learning Point: Short Message Service text messages

What is SMS? SMS means *Short Message Service*. It's a system that lets mobile phone users send and receive texts. The messages are limited to 160 characters (letters, numbers, or symbols). Longer text messages are sent as multiple messages and are put back together by the receiving phone service.

REMINDER!

Before you start this section, remember that sending messages may cost money—and this app can send lots of messages all at once! Check with whoever pays your mobile phone bill to be sure this is OK. You can test the app by leaving out the texting block `call   TextSender.SendMessage` until you're sure the rest of the app is working perfectly.

1 Here's the basic idea broken into steps. When the user clicks **SendButton** ...
2 Set the text message to be whatever the coded message says (we have this stored already in the variable **CodedMessage**).

3   For each agent in the **AgentTels** list:

   a   Set the texting phone number to that agent's number.

   b   Send the SMS text message.

4   Once all the SMS texts have been sent, play a confirmation sound and display a notification message.

Turning these ideas into blocks gives you the following:

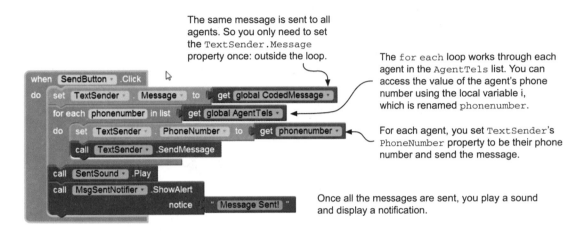

The same message is sent to all agents. So you only need to set the `TextSender.Message` property once: outside the loop.

The `for each` loop works through each agent in the `AgentTels` list. You can access the value of the agent's phone number using the local variable i, which is renamed `phonenumber`.

For each agent, you set `TextSender`'s `PhoneNumber` property to be their phone number and send the message.

Once all the messages are sent, you play a sound and display a notification.

This is a complex app. You could make it simpler, especially if you only wanted to send a message to a single agent at a time. And it's by no means perfect—we've given you some suggestions for improvement in the "Try it out" section. But we hope you can see how mastering lists and loops gives you a great deal of programming power to create apps that do things humans would take a long time to do manually.

What did you learn?

In this chapter, you learned a huge amount, including the following:

- Apps can contain visible lists that users can select from, called *list pickers*; and invisible lists you can create that hold data, in the form of **List** blocks.
- App Inventor gives you access to ready-made lists for selecting images from your gallery and choosing contact details and photos of people you've added to your phone.
- The items in a list picker are called *elements*.

- The position of an item in a list is called its index.
- You make a data list by declaring a variable with a **make a list** block.
- You can select an item from a data list using its index or randomly.
- Lists can contain any data types (text string, number, or Boolean).
- The **BeforePicking** event fires when a user clicks a list picker, and the **After-Picking** event fires when they select an item from a list.
- There are three types of loops in App Inventor: **for range**, **for each**, and **while**.
- Loops can be nested inside each other.
- _Encryption_ is the process of turning a message into code.
- _Decryption_ is the process of decoding a message.
- The **Texting** component provides methods for sending and receiving text messages.
- Inserting **\n** into a string causes a line break in the text.
- A step-by-step plan in computing is called an _algorithm_.

Test your knowledge

1 Which loop (**for range**, **for each**, or **while**) would you choose in the following cases?

   a Working through a list (called **Haystack**) of one million items of data to find the first time the word _needle_ appears

   b Adding up all the numbers from 1 to 100

   c Counting the number of times the name Smith appears in a list of 1,000 surnames

   d Guessing numbers at random until three lottery numbers are matched

2 What are the two properties of a **Texting** component that need to be set in order to send a text message?

3 How many elements are in this list, and what data is contained at index 6?

`[bright, smart, clever, intelligent, talented, genius, wise]`

4 Is each of these statements true or false?

   a Lists always have to contain elements.

   b A **for range** loop can have **start**, **end**, and **step** values set by variables.

   c Lists must contain only one sort of data.

   d Users can select only one item of data at a time from a list picker.

Try it out

1 Add the ability to select a contact's picture in the Graffiti 2 app.

2 Find out how App Inventor lets you create custom colors, and add three new colors to the Graffiti 2 app (see http://mng.bz/58mP.

3 Create a slot-machine game using three lists of kinds of fruit. Award points and play a sound when three matching fruits are selected. Take it further by adding delays and animation sprites (see chapters 7 and 8).

4 Super Challenge: Write a nested-loop app that makes a list of every possible excuse from the Excuse Generator app.

5 Make the Multiplication Tables Generator display the tables in reverse order, from highest to lowest.

6 The Secret SMS Sender app generates errors if the user tries to delete an agent or send a message when no agents have been selected. Add validation rules to stop this from happening.

7 Improve the encryption of the Secret SMS Sender app. Here are some ideas:

   a Add a fixed number of random characters to the beginning and end of the coded message.

   b Create a list of all the keyboard letters and a corresponding list of substitute letters. For example, the first list might read "abcdefg" and the second "rfzyabpl". Make sure the second list contains no duplicates. Then create a loop that works through the message one letter at a time, substituting each letter by finding its index position in list 1 and creating a string from the letter with that index position in list 2.

NOTE
When you change the way the encryption works, you'll probably have to split the Code/Decode functions into two separate buttons in the app. You may find creating separate procedures for each function helps.

Clocks and timers

Take a look at the clock on a microwave oven. If you had to tell an alien what it was for, what would you say? Does it just provide information about the time?

Normally, this kind of clock does two useful things:

1 It tells you what time of day it is in hours and minutes.

2 When the oven is cooking, it shows a countdown of how long is left and does something useful when the timer gets to zero: stops the oven and goes "Ping!"

It might also do other cool (or hot) stuff, like starting the oven at a preset time or changing cooking programs halfway through. Why all this talk about microwaves? Well, the `Clock` component in App Inventor is similar to an oven clock. It can

- Tell you information about the current time (and the date)
- Count down and do something useful after a set time has passed

One important difference between an App Inventor clock and a microwave oven clock is that an App Inventor `Clock` timer automatically restarts over and over again until you turn it off. Try that with a microwave, and you'll quickly have burned food and a house on fire!

What time is it?

We're writing this chapter at exactly 1402295407271—at least, that's what time my Android phone thinks it is. What on Earth does that mean? Well, it's exactly 1402295407271 milliseconds since midnight on January 1, 1970. This date and time were chosen as a standard fixed starting point for lots of different computers and devices and means they can all refer to time in the same way. Having a standard way of writing about times and dates is sensible for several reasons:

- Humans write dates and times differently across the world. For example, writing this in the UK, today's date is 09/06/2014, but in the United States it's 06/09/2014.
- Computers deal in milliseconds, whereas human beings mostly deal in hours, minutes, and seconds.
- Storing information like today's date in text form (Mon Jun 9 2014 07:30:07 GMT+0100) takes more memory and processing time than just saying 1402295407271 milliseconds—especially when you want to start running calculations involving time.

Time to experiment

There are a couple of ways to tell the time in App Inventor, so before you build some fully fledged apps, let's experiment with the blocks. This is the kind of thing programmers do in the real world, especially if the systems they're working with don't have a good instruction book (documentation). Even better—trying things out helps ideas stick in your head. You're going to set up a basic app and then change a block or two to see what happens when you run it. Because this isn't a full app, and it has a few simple components, you'll build it without the usual app table describing all the components.

Start with a new app called **ClockExperiments1**. You might find it useful to save each experiment as a checkpoint with a helpful name so you can remember what you found out. Don't forget to add comments to your blocks, too.

Add three components: a **Label** (**ClockOutputLabel**), a **Button** (**ExperimentButton**), and a non-visible **Clock** (**MyClock**), all from the User Interface section of the Palette (don't forget to rename them and set their text as shown):

Turning to the blocks, you have a simple setup with a button `Click` event resulting in a change to the label. Here's the basic test rig.

You'll plug in different blocks here to see what happens to the output.

Outputting the system time

To start off, let's see how many milliseconds it's been since midnight on 1/1/1970. Plug the `MyClock.SystemTime` block (from `MyClock`) into the test blocks, and then run the program on your phone or emulator. Click the button a few times, and you'll see those milliseconds whooshing by! From the milliseconds you can work out all kinds of useful things like what the date and time are right now or even what day of the week it is. Luckily, App Inventor has a lot of built-in blocks that can do the conversion for you. Before you can use them, you need to know about `Instant`s.

Instant answers

In chapter 5, you found out that variables can be different data types like numbers, strings, or Booleans. App Inventor stores times (and dates) using a data type called `Instant-InTime`, or `Instant` for short. The `MyClock.SystemTime` block in the example converts a time `Instant` (at the moment you clicked the button) into a number so you can see the number of milliseconds. Let's take an `Instant` in time right now and convert it into something a little more useful than milliseconds. Here are the blocks:

This block formats an `Instant` into a date and time.

The `Now` block makes an `Instant` from the phone's current system time.

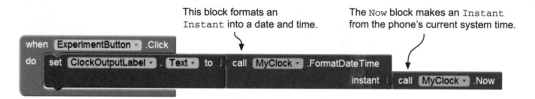

Run the program on your phone, and you should see the date and time formatted something like Aug 29, 2014 9:19:34 PM. Now do some experimentation—switch out the middle `MyClock.FormatDateTime` block for some of the other clock format functions. Try each of the following blocks, clicking the button on your phone each time to see the result:

`MyClock.Second`	`MyClock.Month`
`MyClock.Minute`	`MyClock.MonthName`
`MyClock.Hour`	`MyClock.Year`
`MyClock.DayOfMonth`	`MyClock.FormatDate`
`MyClock.Weekday`	`MyClock.FormatTime`
`MyClock.WeekdayName`	

1 What's the difference between **MyClock.Month** and **MyClock.MonthName**?
2 What's the difference between **MyClock.Weekday** and **MyClock.WeekdayName**?
3 If **MyClock.Weekday** = 7, what day of the week is it?

Making time

You can output the date/time in a dozen different ways, but how do you use dates and times in the past or future? Let's try calculating the weekday of a date such as your next birthday. Rather than start from scratch, save your current project with the name **Weekday-Calculator** (choose Save As on the Designer screen). Make these changes to the UI so the user has somewhere to type a date:

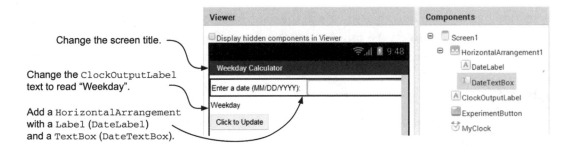

In the last section, you used **MyClock.Now** as your **Instant**. Now you want to make a new **Instant** based on the date the user types in. You'll then format that **Instant** as a **Week-dayName** such as Friday. The end result is that when you enter a date and click the button, the app tells you the weekday. Here are the blocks:

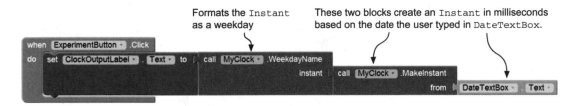

Taking it further: validation

If the date is invalid or in the wrong format, the app generates an error message and exits. You can catch some of these errors using validation, because months can only be from 1–12 and days can only be from 1–31. By making separate text boxes for the MM, DD, and YYYY parts, you can then use **if** statements to check whether the range of MM and DD is sensible before running the app (for example, MM must be a number greater than 0 and less than 13). If you're feeling really clever, you can also say things like "If the month is 2, then the days must be 29 or less" (because February can never have more than 29 days).

Learning Point: App Inventor time formats

In this example, you ask the user to type using United States date format (MM/DD/YYYY) because that's what App Inventor expects. In fact, App Inventor can automatically convert a date/time to an `Instant` as long as it's in one of the following forms. Try each of them in your text box now to see the results:

- *Date only*—MM/DD/YYYY, like 12/19/1971.
- *Time only*—hh:mm, like 22:10. App Inventor assumes you're referring to today's date, but you can also type a time beyond 24 hours. For example, 24:10 is the same as saying "One day plus 10 minutes from now."
- *Date and time (with seconds) combined*—MM/DD/YYYY hh:mm:ss, like 12/19/1971 22:10:15.

This section has covered how to use some of the date and time functions of the `Clock` component. Now we'll look at the other `Clock` functions, using timers to trigger events at regular times called *intervals*.

Using timers

Almost everything you've done in the book so far relies on the user doing something to make the app respond; it might be clicking a button, or dragging their finger on the screen, or shaking the phone. Timers mean you can get the app to do useful things at regular intervals, even if the user isn't touching the phone. You'll start by making a simple app that beeps at regular intervals.

Beeper app

PURPOSE OF THIS APP
This app demonstrates how the timer works by beeping at regular intervals. The beeper begins by beeping every second; the user can change this interval by typing a number of milliseconds and clicking a button. You'll also see how this app can be adapted to play a simple game called Where Are Ewe Hiding?

APP RATING

ASSETS YOU'LL NEED
Audio file: beep.wav.

Start a new project called **Beeper** (you'll use components similar to those in Weekday Calculator, so you can choose Save Project As > Beeper).

Beeper			
Screen1 properties	`Title`: Beeper		
Components	**What do I rename it?**	**What does it do?**	**What properties do I set?**
`Label`	`IntervalLabel`	Instructs the user	`Text`: "How long between beeps (milliseconds)?"
`TextBox`	`IntervalTextBox`	Where the user enters the time to wait between beeps	`Hint`: "1000 = 1 sec" `NumbersOnly` = Yes (selected) `Text`: "1000"
`Button`	`IntervalButton`	Sets the time between beeps to the value typed in `IntervalTextBox`	`Text`: "Change Interval"
`Sound`	`BeepSound`	Plays the beep.wav sound	`MinimumInterval`: 1 `Source`: beep.wav
`Clock` Palette group: User Interface	`BeepTimerClock`	When the timer fires, plays a beep sound	`TimerAlwaysFires`: Yes (selected) `TimerEnabled`: Yes (selected) `TimerInterval`: 1000
Media files			
1 sound file downloaded from our website: beep.wav			

1. Setting up the screen

Here's the screen layout. It's one of the simplest in the book: just the five components, ordered as shown.

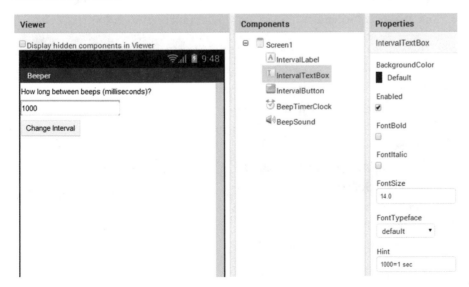

A clock like `BeepTimerClock` has three important timer properties:

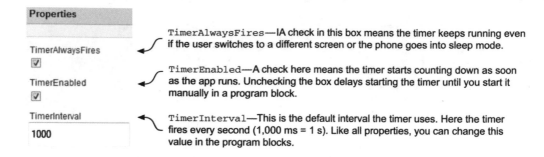

Properties

TimerAlwaysFires
☑

TimerEnabled
☑

TimerInterval
1000

`TimerAlwaysFires`—IA check in this box means the timer keeps running even if the user switches to a different screen or the phone goes into sleep mode.

`TimerEnabled`—A check here means the timer starts counting down as soon as the app runs. Unchecking the box delays starting the timer until you start it manually in a program block.

`TimerInterval`—This is the default interval the timer uses. Here the timer fires every second (1,000 ms = 1 s). Like all properties, you can change this value in the program blocks.

Let's think about why you might choose these options:

- **TimerAlwaysFires**—In an application like an alarm clock, you want the timer to keep checking whether it's time to sound an alarm, even if the phone receives a call or goes to sleep. But for something like a game, you probably want the game to pause if the phone receives a call or sleeps. So for an alarm you set **TimerAlwaysFires** to True, but for a game you might set it to False.

- **TimerEnabled**—The decision here is, do you want the clock to start firing right away or only if the user switches on the clock through some action? For example, a bedside clock app that displays the current time probably needs the timer enabled right away, but a stopwatch app only needs its clock to be enabled when the user clicks a Go button.

- **TimerInterval**—This is how often the clock fires. For something like a stopwatch, you probably want it to fire lots of times every second (maybe every 100 ms) so you can capture at least tenths of a second. But if you want a chime to sound every 60 seconds, then **TimerInterval** can be much slower (such as 60,000 ms).

The other new property you've come across here is setting **BeepSound**'s **MinimumInterval** to 1 (millisecond). By default, this is set to 1,000 ms (1 second), and for most apps that's fine. But in this case, if the user wants to play a sound really often (say, every 20 milliseconds), you want them to be able to hear the difference.

2. Coding the blocks

When a timer fires (reaches zero), it generates a **Timer** event—just like a button click. Select the **BeepTimer-Clock.Timer** event block, and plug in the **BeepSound.Play**

block. If you run the app, you'll hear a beep once a second after the app starts running.

At the moment, entering a number of milliseconds in **IntervalTextBox** and clicking the button does nothing. You want the **BeepTimerClock** interval to change to whatever the user typed in—so if they type **10000**, it will beep every 10 seconds. You need to add a button **Click** event and change the **BeepTimerClock Interval** property to whatever the user typed:

The basic app is finished—try some different values to see how the timer responds. If you try small intervals, you may hear the beep overlapping itself and therefore increasing in volume.

In the next app, you'll turn this simple idea into a hide-and-seek game for your phone. Along the way, you'll learn how to turn timers on and off.

Where Are Ewe Hiding? app

PURPOSE OF THIS APP
This game makes a noise (in this case, a baa) at random intervals. The user can choose a maximum time between bleats and a time delay before the game starts. Touching the sheep starts the game, and the Stop button ends it. Here are some ideas for how you could use this with friends who all have phones that run the app:

- *Playing Hide and Seek*—Everyone has to turn their phone volume up and run this app before they go hide. You never know when the sound might give away your position.
- *Playing Blind Man's Bluff*—Everyone except a blindfolded player runs this app on their phone. The blindfolded player hunts for them while they move around the room. If your phone makes a sound, you must freeze for 5 seconds.
- *Playing Hunt the Thimble*—Everyone runs the app and hides their phone. The seeker then has 60 seconds to find as many phones as possible.

APP RATING

ASSETS YOU'LL NEED
Sound file, baa.wav; and image file, sheep.png.

Where Are Ewe Hiding			
Screen1 properties	**Title**: Where Are Ewe Hiding? **BackgroundColor**: Black		
Components	**What do I rename it?**	**What does it do?**	**What properties do I set?**
`Label`	`IntervalLabel`	Instructs the user	**Text**: "How long between Bleats (seconds)?" **TextColor**: White
`Label`	`DelayLabel`	Instruct the user	**Text**: "Delay before the game starts?" **TextColor**: White
2 **TextBox**es	`IntervalTextBox` `DelayTextBox`	Where the user enters the times for the interval between beeps and the delay before the game starts	For both text boxes: **Hint**: "Seconds" **NumbersOnly** = Yes (selected) **Text**: "20"
`Button`	`GoButton`	Starts the game	**Text**: None **Image**: sheep.png **Width** and **Height**: 200 pixels
`Button`	`StopButton`	Stops the game	**FontSize**: 28 **Text**: "STOP" **Width** and **Height**: 200 pixels
`Sound`	`BaaSound`	Plays the baa.wav sound	**MinimumInterval**: 500 **Source**: baa.wav
`Clock` Palette group: User Interface	`BaaTimerClock`		**TimerAlwaysFires**: Yes (selected) **TimerEnabled**: No (unselected) **TimerInterval**: 1000
Media files			

2 files downloaded from our website:
  baa.wav
  sheep.png

1. Setting up the screen

Here we've kept the layout simple; you might like to use some screen-arrangement components to tidy things up a little. Notice that you set **TimerEnabled** to False—that means the timer won't fire until you're ready. When you make your own apps, it's easy to forget this, so get into the habit now of disabling timers unless you definitely want them to start as soon as the app runs.

Also, in this app you're letting the user enter seconds rather than milliseconds, so you have to remember to convert their input by multiplying the number of seconds in the text boxes by 1,000. Here's the layout.

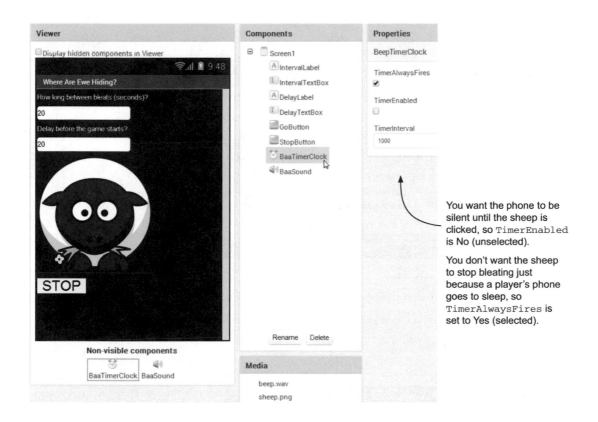

You want the phone to be silent until the sheep is clicked, so `TimerEnabled` is No (unselected).

You don't want the sheep to stop bleating just because a player's phone goes to sleep, so `TimerAlwaysFires` is set to Yes (selected).

2. Coding the blocks

When the user touches the sheep to start the game, you want to do the following:

1 Convert the value in **DelayTextbox** to milliseconds by multiplying it by 1,000.
2 Set the timer interval to be the same as the value in step 1 so the sheep doesn't start baaing until the user is ready.
3 Activate the timer.

Here are the blocks:

This means when **GoButton** is clicked, the timer starts counting down and then fires.

Each time **BaaTimerClock** fires, you want to change the timer interval to a random time between, say, half a second up to the user's maximum time (from **IntervalTextBox**) and then play the "baa" sound. The app will continue baaing at random intervals until the user clicks. For example if you set the maximum time (**IntervalTextBox**) to 15 seconds, your sheep might baa at 6 and a half seconds, then 10 seconds later, then 2 seconds later, and any time in that range of half a second up to 15 seconds. You might get 2 baas in a row and then wait for 15 seconds. The larger the maximum time, the more likely you'll have long periods of silence. You could use this to even up differences in players—so if big kids and little kids are playing together, the big kids could have a maximum of 10 seconds and the little kids might get, say, a 30-second maximum between baas. Here are the blocks:

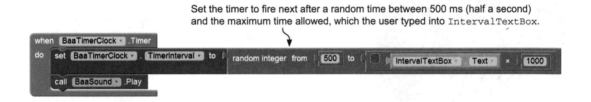

The last really easy bit of code says that when the user clicks **StopButton**, the game no longer plays "baa" sounds. To do this, you switch off (disable) **BaaTimerClock**:

Multiple timers

Complex apps like games often need lots of events to be timed at the same time. For example, in a game like Pac-Man, you need timers to

- Control the animations, like Pac-Man chomping and the ghosts flashing
- Insert pauses in the game between levels
- Count down when Pac-Man eats a power pill

It would be impossible to do this with just one clock, but luckily clocks are free—so you can add as many as you like! Also, using multiple clocks with specific names helps other people understand your program and saves you from getting in a confused tangle when you're programming. In the next simple example, you'll learn how to use three timers in one app.

Splat the Rat app

PURPOSE OF THIS APP

This game shows a rat at random intervals. Touch the rat quickly as many times as you can before it disappears, to splat it. Each splat adds 1 to your score. Games are limited to 30 seconds total time.

APP RATING

3

ASSETS YOU'LL NEED

Sound and image files: splat.wav, squeek.wav, rat.png, and storm_drain_cover.png.

Splat the Rat			
Screen1 properties	**Title**: Splat The Rat **AlignHorizontal**: Center **BackgroundColor**: White		
Components	**What do I rename it?**	**What does it do?**	**What properties do I set?**
Label	**ScoreLabel**	Shows the game score	**Text**: "Score: 0" **FontSize**: 28
Label	**TimeLabel**	Shows the time remaining	**Text**: "Time Remaining: 30" **FontSize**: 28
Button	**RestartButton**	Restarts the game	**Text**: Restart
Horizontal-Arrangement	**HorizArr**	Contains **TimeLabel** and **RestartButton** at the bottom of the screen	None
2 **Sound**s	**SqueakSound** **SplatSound**	Play a "squeak" sound when the rat appears and a "splat" sound when you touch it	**Source**: squeak.wav and splat.wav (one for each **Sound**)
Canvas Palette group: Drawing and Animation	**Canvas1**	The game play area	**BackgroundImage**: storm_drain_cover.png **Width** and **Height**: 350 pixels

Components	What do I rename it?	What does it do?	What properties do I set?
ImageSprite Palette group: Drawing and Animation	**RatSprite**	Displays an image of a rat	**Picture**: rat.png **Rotates**: Yes (selected) **Visible**: No (deselected) **Width**: 75 pixels **Height**: 50 pixels
Clock Palette group: User Interface	**WaitRatTimer**	Counts down a random time between 1 and 5 seconds; when it fires, the rat appears.	**TimerAlwaysFires**: Yes (selected) **TimerEnabled**: Yes (selected) **TimerInterval**: 5000
Clock Palette group: User Interface	**HideRatTimer**	Starts when the rat appears, counts down 2 seconds, and then hides the rat	**TimerAlwaysFires**: Yes (selected) **TimerEnabled**: No (unselected) **TimerInterval**: 2000
Clock Palette group: User Interface	**GameTimer**	Fires once a second; when it fires, it reduces the time remaining by 1 second and checks to see whether the game is over	**TimerAlwaysFires**: Yes (selected) **TimerEnabled**: Yes (selected) **TimerInterval**: 1000

Media files

2 sound files downloaded from our website: splat.wav and squeak.wav
2 image files downloaded from our website: rat.png and
storm_drain_cover.png

1. Setting up the screen

Set up the screen as shown here.

At the moment you can sit **RatSprite** anywhere on the drain cover. Once you have the basic game working, you'll set it whizzing around the screen.

You might be wondering why you need three timers. There are lots of ways to approach this game, just as when you're writing a story there are lots of different words and phrasings you might choose. Part of being a programmer is choosing the way you think is best; you can probably

improve the game further. In fact, you could make a simple version of the game with one timer and an `if ... else` block—you might want to try this first. The logic behind the blocks would be as follows, when the timer fires:

1 Set the timer's interval to a random number between, say, 1 and 10 seconds.

2 If the rat is visible, then hide it. If the rat is hidden, then show it:

```
IF RatSprite.Visible = True THEN RatSprite.Visible = False
ELSE RatSprite.Visible = True
```

That would work, but the gameplay wouldn't be right because there would be no end point—the rat would keep appearing and disappearing forever. The rat would also spend about the same amount of time hidden as it did onscreen, but you want it to stay hidden more and only flash onscreen for short bursts to make the game challenging. There are all kinds of ways to solve this problem, and we had to think hard about how the timers should be set up at the start of the app. Here's what we came up with:

1 To make sure the game ends, **GameTimer** fires once a second. When it has fired 30 times (30 seconds), the game is over.

2 To make the rat hide and appear for different amounts of time, you use **WaitRatTimer** and **HideRatTimer** to work like a relay team:

a **WaitRatTimer** controls when the rat appears. It fires at a random time between 1 to 5 seconds, shows the rat, and passes control to **HideRatTimer**.

b **HideRatTimer** lets the rat appear for just 2 seconds. Then it hides the rat and passes control back to **WaitRatTimer**.

Learning Point: The tortoise and the hare—timers that start other timers

Getting one timer to start another is a useful trick to remember that is used in lots of apps. But a confusing thing can happen when you have a fast timer (the hare) starting a slow timer (the tortoise). Here's what happens if the hare fires every second and the tortoise fires every 2 seconds:

Time	0s	1s	2s	3s
Action	Hare timer starts	Hare fires and starts the tortoise timer	Hare fires and *restarts* the tortoise timer	Hare fires and *restarts* the tortoise timer

This will keep happening, with the result that the tortoise timer never fires. That can be frustrating and stops the program from working.

You can have a similar problem if part of your app takes longer to run than the timer that starts it—weird things happen, like only part of the app working.

The solution is that when the hare fires, it switches off (disables) itself and starts the tortoise. Then, when the tortoise has finished, it disables itself and restarts the hare. ➤

Here's the new sequence:

Time	0s	1s	2s	3s
Action	Hare timer starts	Hare fires, disables itself, and starts the tortoise timer		Tortoise fires, disables itself, and starts the hare timer

That sequence will keep repeating, with the hare and tortoise working together.

2. Coding the blocks: showing and hiding the rat

You'll sort out the scoring and gameplay mechanism in a moment, but first let's get the rat working. When `WaitRatTimer` fires after 5 seconds, you want it to choose a new timer interval for itself so the rat isn't too predictable. You can do this in exactly the same way as in Where Are Ewe Hiding? earlier in this chapter. Then you need to show the rat for 2 seconds and play a "squeak" sound. That means

1   Show `RatSprite`.

2   Play a "squeak" sound.

3   Switch off `WaitRatTimer`.

4   Switch on `HideRatTimer`.

Here are the blocks:

At this point the rat is onscreen and squeaking. You only want it there for 2 seconds, though, so as soon as `HideRatTimer` fires you reverse what just happened as shown here.

The rat is hidden, and `WaitRatTimer` is again counting down a random amount of time before you restart the whole process of showing the rat.

This app always has the rat onscreen for 2 seconds, so you don't change its `Timer-Interval`. But once you have it working, try a random time like with the `WaitRatTimer`, and see how that affects gameplay.

Run the app on your phone, and you should see the rat appearing and disappearing. Now let's figure out how to splat it!

3. Splat that rat! Changing the score

This should look familiar—you need a variable to store the score, set to 0. You detect that the rat is touched using the `RatSprite.Touched` event. When it's triggered, you increase the score by 1, change the score onscreen, and play a satisfying splat sound.

```
initialize global score to 0

when RatSprite .Touched
 x  y
do  set global score to     get global score  +  1
    set ScoreLabel . Text to  join  " Score: "
                                    get global score
    call SplatSound .Play
```

4. Timing, ending, and restarting the game

The concepts here (variables and `if` statements) were all covered in chapter 5. The only difference is that you're triggering the events using the `GameTimer.Timer` event, which fires once a second.

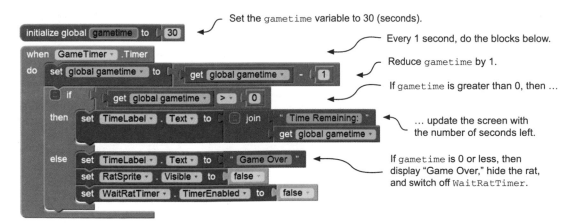

Set the `gametime` variable to 30 (seconds).

Every 1 second, do the blocks below.

Reduce `gametime` by 1.

If `gametime` is greater than 0, then …

… update the screen with the number of seconds left.

If `gametime` is 0 or less, then display "Game Over," hide the rat, and switch off `WaitRatTimer`.

Learning Point: Comparing values—equals vs. greater/less than

You might think it's a little strange that you test to see whether `gametime` is greater than 0 to decide whether to continue with the game. Why not just use `If gametime = 0` ...?

Less-than and greater-than are good catch-all operators in case something goes wrong in your program. In this case, if at some point `gametime` got set to -1 (maybe `GameTimer` fired erratically), testing to see if it equaled 0 would result in the game going on forever. But checking to see if it's greater than 0 means any time it's 0 *or less*, the game will stop.

If you run the game on your phone now, you'll find that the countdown timer works, splatting the rat increases your score, and the game ends after 30 seconds.

Starting a new game is super-simple. Reset the `GameTime` and `Score` variables and `ScoreLabel`. Hide the rat, and switch the timers back to their start states—you already have a procedure to do that called `HideRat` (that's the beauty of procedures). Here are the blocks.

The game is pretty much finished—but you might find it less than exciting. Hitting a stationary rat isn't much of a challenge. Let's introduce some craziness!

5. Setting the rat free

In chapter 4, you saw how to move a sprite. You'll do the same thing here by giving the `RatSprite` a heading and speed in its properties. Switch to the App Inventor Designer window, and set these properties for `RatSprite`: **Heading** 25, **Interval** 100, **Speed** 20. This starts the rat running in one direction, but when it reaches the canvas edge, it will stop. You can bounce the rat by adding the blocks shown here. Note that the `get edge` block is an event argument (see chapter 5). We'll explain these animation settings and blocks in the next chapter.

Run the app, and you'll find the game much more challenging.

Taking it further

Here are some ideas to change the difficulty:

1 Try making the rat smaller or larger, faster or slower. You can do this using properties in the App Inventor Designer, but you could also change these properties randomly

each time a timer fires. If you used `GameTimer`, they would even change every second—an incredible growing and shrinking rat, perhaps?!

2 Read the next chapter, and then animate the splat so the rat changes to a splat symbol for 1 second when touched.

3 Try making multiple rats—and give bonus scores for splatting more than one. You could even add a Rat King who only appears very briefly but is worth mega points.

What did you learn?

In this chapter, you learned the following:

- That many computers store times and dates in a standard format that we humans would find hard to work with: milliseconds from midnight on 1/1/1970
- How to use clocks to find out and display the current date and time
- How to make and use an `Instant` in milliseconds for some point in the past or future
- How timers can trigger events
- How to work with multiple timers, and how to enable and disable timers

In chapter 14, we'll take these ideas further in an app called Zombie Alarm! that uses timers, lists, and animation to make an alarm clock. You might want to take a sneak peek now while these ideas are fresh in your head.

Test your knowledge

1 Which one of these examples would generate an error?

  a `MyClock.MakeInstant` from 19/12/1971

  b `MyClock.MakeInstant` from 02/28/2013

  c `MyClock.MakeInstant` from 04/02/1989

2 For an `Instant` made from 04/02/1989, what would each of the following be?

  a `MyClock.DayOfMonth`

  b `MyClock.Month`

  c `MyClock.MonthName`

3 Is each one of these statements True or False?

  a A timer fires once and then stops.

  b More than one timer can fire at the same time.

c When a timer is enabled, it continues counting down from the point when it was disabled.

d All timers start when the app starts.

Try it out

1 Experiment with the "Taking it further" ideas for Splat the Rat.

2 Try making a stopwatch. Can you add lap times?

3 Make a clock that displays the time and a different image depending on the time of day: for example, a Sun from 7 a.m. to 7 p.m. and a Moon from 7 p.m. to 7 a.m.

4 Make a season clock that tells you what the season is today. Can it also tell you how long until the season changes?

5 Make a kitchen timer: the user puts in a number of minutes and the timer beeps when dinner is ready.

Animation

As we've explained in previous chapters, Android devices can do many things. But when learning to program, one of the first things young people usually want to do is create a game, and this often involves animation. Have you ever used or made a flip book—you know, the ones with a stick person walking along the bottom of the page or slam-dunking a basketball? When you see something moving smoothly across a screen, whether it's a cartoon or a game, what you're really seeing is a sequence of quickly changing pictures, like in a flip book. Imagine animating a walking zombie. Its position needs to change, which

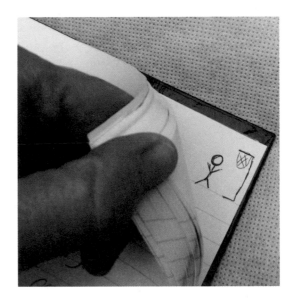

can be achieved by adjusting the zombie's speed, the direction it's heading in, and how often it moves (heading and interval properties) in the App Inventor Designer or by letting the user interact with the zombie by clicking buttons, dragging the sprite, tipping the phone, and so on. But if you don't change the position of the zombie's legs, it appears to be frozen or floating. To do this in App Inventor, you use a clock timer and lists of images that change each time the zombie moves, giving the appearance of walking rather than floating.

In chapter 3, we briefly explained the coordinate system; in chapter 4, you had a go at designing apps with user interaction; and in chapter 6, you saw the clock in action. In this chapter, we'll show you how to create short animations and exciting games using these things and more.

NOTE
Full games can be long, involved programs, so while you're at the learning stage we're providing short projects rather than full games.

Animation type 1: moving sprites using properties

Without using the clock timer or any intervention from the user, you can create the illusion of movement by using the properties `Heading`, `Speed`, and `Interval`. These properties can be set in the App Inventor Designer before you even reach the Blocks Editor. The following mini app demonstrates something that could be used as part of a bigger game. Give it a try: it's quick to put together and good fun. (Ballybally is what my [Paula's] nephew used to call pool when he was 4 years old.)

Ballybally app

PURPOSE OF THIS APP
This mini app demonstrates the use of properties in the Designer to make a ball appear to bounce from one corner to another, changing the canvas color as it does so.

APP RATING

 2

ASSETS YOU'LL NEED
None!

Ballybally			
Screen1 properties	`AlignHorizontal`: Center `AlignVertical`: Center `Scrollable`: No `ScreenOrientation`: Portrait `Title`: Ballybally		
Components	**What do I rename it?**	**What does it do?**	**What properties do I set?**
`Canvas`	`Canvas1`	Allows you to position the ball	`Color`: Green (to look like the baize on a pool table) `Width`: Fill Parent `Height`: Fill Parent
`Ball` Palette group: Drawing and Animation	`Ball1`	Travels diagonally across the canvas, and bounces when it reaches the edge	`Heading`: 315 `Interval`: 10 `PaintColor` Red `Radius` 10 `Speed` 5 Initial **X** and **Y**: Physically drag to the top-left corner so **X** and **Y** are low numbers.

1. The properties explained

Because most of the work is done in the Designer we'll give an explanation of each of the properties. We encourage you to tinker with the properties once you've completed the app and have the emulator open to see what difference your changes make to the app's behavior. Sprites and balls default to **Heading** 0 (heading east), **Interval** 100 (moving every 1/10 of a second), and—the important part—**Speed** 0.0. We know **Heading** 0 being east is a bit peculiar, but as a default it makes sense to go from left to right. In order for your sprite to move, you need to give it some speed (explained further in a moment).

Learning Point:
Reminder about setting properties!

You should think of properties as a jumping-off point for components. You might start with a ball that has a **Radius** property of 10 and change the property in your coding. But every time you restart (or initialize) the app, all properties go back to those set in the Designer.

HEADING

The **Heading** property in App Inventor can be set to anything between 0 degrees and 360 degrees.

The **Heading** numbering system is a little peculiar in App Inventor, with 0 being to the right and 180 being to the left. But as long as you use this diagram as a guide, you'll be fine. The **Heading** property means the direction of travel the ball or sprite is "heading" in when the app initializes. For this app, we advise you to set the **Heading** property of the ball to 315 degrees. This means if you've positioned the ball in the top-left

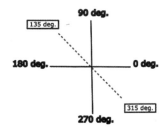

corner of the screen, it will head southeast, roughly toward the bottom-right corner of the screen. Later, in the Blocks Editor, you'll change the heading to 135, which is the opposite direction of 315 degrees and makes the ball head northwest (in this case, back to the top-left corner).

INTERVAL

The **Interval** property lets the app know how frequently (in milliseconds) you want the ball or sprite to move. The smaller the interval, the smoother the animation appears. For Ballybally, you set **Interval** to 5 milliseconds, which means the ball moves once every 5/1000 of a second. The default interval for a ball is 100 milliseconds, which is 1/10 of a second.

SPEED

The speed is measured in pixels: that is, how many pixels do you want the ball to travel per interval? The default speed is 0.0 (stationary); in this app you set it to 5 pixels per 5/1000 of a second, which gives a fast, smooth action.

2. Coding the blocks: identifying that the edge has been reached, and testing which way the ball is heading

When sprites collide with the edge of the screen or each other, they trigger an event. In this case, you're using the event **Ball1.EdgeReached**. In response to these blocks, when the edge of the screen is reached, the app asks, "Is the ball heading in the direction 315?"

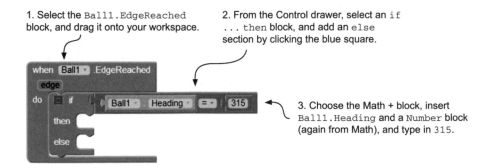

1. Select the Ball1.EdgeReached block, and drag it onto your workspace.

2. From the Control drawer, select an if ... then block, and add an else section by clicking the blue square.

3. Choose the Math + block, insert Ball1.Heading and a Number block (again from Math), and type in 315.

3. Responding to the direction of travel

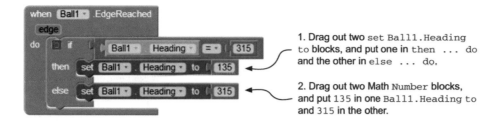

1. Drag out two set Ball1.Heading to blocks, and put one in then ... do and the other in else ... do.

2. Drag out two Math Number blocks, and put 135 in one Ball1.Heading to and 315 in the other.

The control block is needed to determine which way the ball is heading when it hits the edge. If it's heading 315, you make it head to 135; and if it's heading 135, you make it head to 315, so it boings back and forth!

4. Changing the color of the canvas when the edge is reached

Once you've set up the coding for an **if ... else ... then ... do** block, you can make a number of things happen when the conditions are satisfied. Just for fun, in this app you make the canvas background color change each time the ball reaches the edge of the screen.

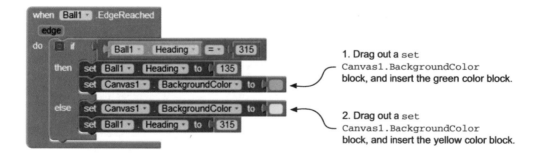

1. Drag out a set Canvas1.BackgroundColor block, and insert the green color block.

2. Drag out a set Canvas1.BackgroundColor block, and insert the yellow color block.

Animation type 2: Creating movement with a clock timer and user interaction

The previous app showed how you can create the illusion of movement by giving the sprite properties of speed and a heading direction, and then making it appear to bounce off the screen edges. In this type of animation, you use an internal clock to remind the app to do something every so often, thereby making it appear to be animated. You also let the user tap the screen to enable movement.

Cheeky Hamster app

PURPOSE OF THIS APP

In this mini game, a bored hamster empties its pouch back into its randomly moving bowl by shooting seeds out of its mouth. When tapped by the user, the hamster shoots the seeds toward the food bowl and only gets to keep them if the seeds hit the moving target.

APP RATING

ASSETS YOU'LL NEED

Image sprites: Cheekyhamster.png, Bowl.png, Hamstericon.png.

Cheeky Hamster			
Screen1 properties	`AlignHorizontal`: Center `AlignVertical`: Top `ScreenOrientation`: Portrait `Scrollable`: No `Title`: Cheeky Hamster `BackgroundColor`: Blue `Icon`: Hamstericon.png		
Components	**What do I rename it?**	**What does it do?**	**What properties do I set?**
`Canvas`	`Canvas1`	Allows you to position sprites	`BackgroundColor`: White `Width`: Fill Parent `Height`: Fill Parent
`ImageSprite`	`BowlSprite`	In response to the `BowlClock`, appears in random locations across the top of the screen	`Picture`: Bowl.png `X`: 100 `Y`: 0
`Ball`	`Seed`	Is shot out of the hamster's mouth toward the bowl	`Heading`: 90 `Interval`: 10 `PaintColor`: Orange `Radius`: 5 `Speed`: 20 `Visible`: Yes (selected) `X`: 152 `Y`: 276 (drag **Seed** to near the hamster's mouth)

Components	What do I rename it?	What does it do?	What properties do I set?
ImageSprite	HamsterSprite	Moves back and forth across screen, and appears to spit out seeds	**Heading**: 0 **Picture**: Cheekyhamster.png **X**: 100 **Y**: 270 (approximately: drag to the bottom of the screen)
Horizontal-Arrangement	Horizontal-Arrangement1	Allows the buttons to be placed together	
2 Buttons	RightButton LeftButton	When clicked, move the hamster back and forth across the screen	**BackgroundColor**: Light Gray **Font**: Bold **FontSize**: 20 **Text**: "<=" (for left) and "=>" (for right) **TextColor**: Red
Label	Scorelabel	Provides the text for the score	**Font**: Bold **FontSize**: 20 **Text**: "Score:" **TextColor**: Red
Label	Scorelabelcount	Counts the number of seeds that hit the bowl	**Font**: Bold **FontSize**: 20 **Text**: "0" **TextColor**: Red
Button	Resetbutton	When clicked, returns the score to 0	**BackgroundColor**: Light Gray **FontSize**: 20 **Text**: "Reset" **TextColor**: Red
Clock	BowlClock	Sends a reminder every 2 seconds for the bowl to move randomly across the top of the screen	**TimerInterval**: 2000

Media files

3 files downloaded from our website:

Bowl.png
Cheekyhamster.png
Hamstericon.png

In this app, you use the clock timer to provide animation, and you also get the user to interact with the sprite via buttons to move the sprite around on the screen. In the previous chapter, you were particular about the ball's **Interval** and **Speed** properties. It's important to note that when you're using a clock timer with a sprite or ball, the timer's **Interval** number effectively overrides the sprite's or ball's **Interval** property—but it's still important to set the correct initial heading for the sprite or ball in the Designer.

> **TIP**
> Don't forget that although there are up to 12 properties to set for each component, you should leave them at the default values unless we specify that you should change them.

The coding for Cheeky Hamster isn't too difficult and gives some great results. The three things that happen in the app—shooting, random sprite movement, and moving sprites with buttons—can be used in lots of other games. So once you've used them, you'll know how to do these things for your own game design.

1. Coding the blocks: setting the BowlClock timer

`BowlClock.Timer` does the job of making the bowl move to random locations across the top of the screen every two seconds. Only the X coordinate of the bowl changes, because the bowl stays in the same vertical position throughout. Drag out the `BowlClock.Timer` block, and put in the blocks as shown. You want the bowl to appear at a random position, so choose **random integer** and Number blocks between 0 and 300.

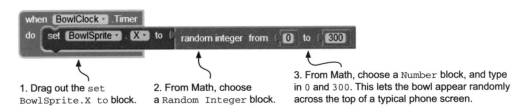

1. Drag out the `set BowlSprite.X to` block.

2. From Math, choose a `Random Integer` block.

3. From Math, choose a `Number` block, and type in `0` and `300`. This lets the bowl appear randomly across the top of a typical phone screen.

2. Moving the hamster

The coding for the left and right buttons is the same, except one uses the subtraction Math block and the other uses addition. After accessing the **LeftButton.Click** block, insert blocks to move the hamster 20 pixels for each click. We chose 20 pixels because the moves are big enough for the user to see but small enough for the user to be accurate with placing the hamster.

1. From the `LeftButton` drawer, select the `when LeftButton.Click do` event handler.

2. From the `HamsterSprite` drawer, choose the `set HamsterSprite.X` block.

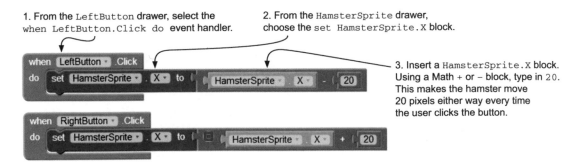

3. Insert a `HamsterSprite.X` block. Using a Math + or – block, type in `20`. This makes the hamster move 20 pixels either way every time the user clicks the button.

3. Shooting seeds

This step is a little more complicated, because you need to position the seed so it appears to be coming out of the hamster's mouth. If you reproduce this app and use your own image, you'll have to do this by trial and error, relative to the position of the hamster. Some people post screencast tutorials on the web, and it's hilarious to watch them trying to position things in the right spot. One guy I watched took 15 minutes of his airtime positioning a sprite and kept forgetting partway through whether the X coordinate was too big or too small. Anyway, we (in the privacy of an office, un-videoed) have discovered that if you position the seed at **HamsterSpriteX** + 58 and **HamsterSpriteY** + 22, it looks about right. You can see in the screenshots that you adjust these settings in the **call Seed.MoveTo** event handler.

It may seem unusual to be setting the timer to **Enabled** and the seed to **Visible**. You do so because once the user shoots the seed, it has to disappear off the screen in order to start again from the hamster: at that point, you'll disable the timer and make the seed not visible. In summary, when the user touches the hamster, these things happen:

1 App Inventor detects the touch.

2 The seed appears, enabled and visible, at the hamster's mouth.

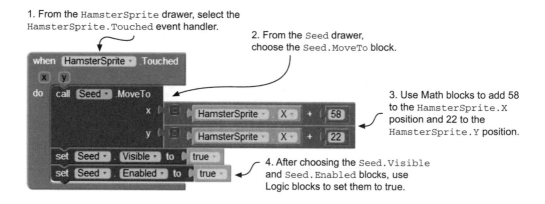

1. From the HamsterSprite drawer, select the HamsterSprite.Touched event handler.

2. From the Seed drawer, choose the Seed.MoveTo block.

3. Use Math blocks to add 58 to the HamsterSprite.X position and 22 to the HamsterSprite.Y position.

4. After choosing the Seed.Visible and Seed.Enabled blocks, use Logic blocks to set them to true.

3 The seed immediately (moved by its own **Interval**, **Heading**, and **Speed** properties) moves up the screen.

4. Making the seed disappear at the edge of the screen

If you don't tell the app what to do with the seed once it has been shot, the seed will sit at the top of the screen going nowhere. The following bit of code instructs it to stop moving and disappear when it reaches the edge.

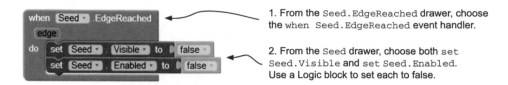

1. From the `Seed.EdgeReached` drawer, choose the `when Seed.EdgeReached` event handler.

2. From the `Seed` drawer, choose both `set Seed.Visible` and `set Seed.Enabled`. Use a Logic block to set each to false.

5. Scoring when the seed hits the bowl

In order for the player to score, a seed needs to hit the bowl. App Inventor has provided a great event handler for this called **CollidedWith**, which you'll use in lots of games.

1. From My Blocks > My Definitions, choose Value Other (which has been generated by your choosing this event handler).

3. From the Variables drawer, choose a `get` block, and select `other`.

4. Select a Math = block. From the `BowlSprite` drawer, choose the component block.

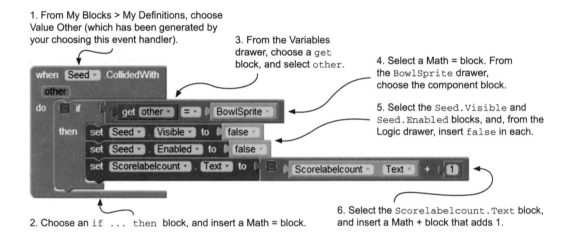

5. Select the `Seed.Visible` and `Seed.Enabled` blocks, and, from the Logic drawer, insert `false` in each.

2. Choose an `if ... then` block, and insert a Math = block.

6. Select the `Scorelabelcount.Text` block, and insert a Math + block that adds 1.

The event handler **Seed.CollidedWith** automatically produces a variable named **other**. This means it's reporting when the seed collides with any component (which could include the hamster). In this case, you want a score to occur when the seed collides with **BowlSprite**, so you use an `if ... then ... do` test to check that in this case the score increases only if the seed collides with the component **BowlSprite**.

6. Resetting the score

The score automatically resets each time you start the app. But if you want to reset it while playing, it's simple to reset the **Scorelabelcount.Text** back to 0:

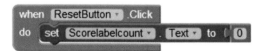

Taking it further

1 The Cheeky Hamster app could involve a scoring and levelling system by making the bowl smaller or faster-moving.

2 You may have noticed that if you press the hamster again before the seed reaches the top of the screen, another seed appears and the original one disappears. To enable the user to shoot lots of seeds in quick succession, you could try having five seed sprites that fire one after the other. Then, tapping five times will release five separate seeds; by the time the fifth one reaches the top, the first one will be ready to go again.

Animation type 3: creating movement using lists and a clock timer

To create the genuine illusion (is that an oxymoron?!) of animation, you need to combine a change in position with a change of image. To make professional-looking animations, you need many different frames. In this chapter, we'll teach you how to pick images from lists and move them around the screen. Then, if you want to go further, you'll have the skills to do so.

The app you'll work on shortly uses 10 images of a spider in motion. Remember that at the beginning of the chapter, we talked about animation actually being a quick succession of pictures changing. Well, first you have to ensure that you have the right pictures to begin with. The crawling motion of a spider is produced by its odd-numbered legs moving together, followed by its even-numbered legs moving.

After about 50 rubbish attempts at cutting up one spider picture and reattaching the legs to look like a crawling spider, we threw in the towel. Our animated spider looked more like one that had been chewed by a cat! Bleuggh. So we did what all sensible people do: we borrowed from somebody who is a lot better at this side of things. We took an existing animated GIF of a crawling spider and exploded the file to reveal the 10 frames that produce the illusion of crawling. These images are from http://heathersanimations.com/, which is a great website that provides fantastic free images.

Creepy Spider app

PURPOSE OF THIS APP
This mini app demonstrates the use of the clock and lists to produce an animated creeping spider. The spider continually crawls across some rotting leaves. When the user touches the spider, it makes a convincing chomping sound, vibrates, and stops moving. When the user takes their finger off the spider, it sets off again.

APP RATING

ASSETS YOU'LL NEED
Image sprite: Spider1frame.gif (10 images, 1–10). **Canvas** image: leavesbackground.jpg. Sound: spiderbitesound.wav. Image: creepyspider.png.

Creepy Spider			
Screen1 properties	`AlignHorizontal`: Center `AlignVertical`: Center `ScreenOrientation`: Portrait `Scrollable`: No `Icon`: creepyspider.png `Title`: Creepy Spider		
Components	**What do I rename it?**	**What does it do?**	**What properties do I set?**
Canvas	`Canvas1`	Allows you to position sprites	`BackgroundImage`: leavesbackground.jpg `Width`: Fill Parent `Height`: Fill Parent
ImageSprite	`SpiderImagesprite`	Crawls diagonally down the screen	`Heading`: 225 `Interval`: 100 `Picture`: Spider1frame.gif `Rotates`: No (unselected) `Speed`: 5 `X`: 190 `Y`: 10

Components	What do I rename it?	What does it do?	What properties do I set?
Sound	Spiderbitesound	Provides a biting sound that is activated when the user touches the spider	**Source**: spiderbitesound.wav
Clock	Clock1	Reminds the spider sprite to change its image each time it moves	**Interval**: 100

Media files

13 files downloaded from our website:

    spiderbitesound.wav
    leavesbackground.jpg
    creepyspider.png

Spider1frame.gif (and nine more files labelled Spider2frame.gif, and so on, up to Spider10frame.gif)

1. Coding the blocks: making the spider appear to crawl

Despite looking simple, this app involves quite a lot of coding. The first thing you need to do is download the 10 images and upload them into your App Inventor Media area in the Designer. You only use Spider1Frame.gif for **SpiderImageSprite**, but you need the rest available for later.

Learning Point: Exploding GIFs

An animated Graphics Interchange Format (GIF) file is a graphic image that's usually shown on a web page and that appears to move. To create this illusion of movement, the GIF contains any number of images that loop endlessly in succession. If you want to look at the separate images of the animated GIF, you have to "explode" it, like a flipbook! A useful website to achieve this quickly is http://gif-explode.com/.

In App Inventor, you make a list by defining two essential elements: a variable, and an index that enables you to refer to the items in the list by number and progress through them in order. The following diagram shows the **List** block you need to assemble.

1. From Variables, choose the `initialize global name to` block. Drag this onto the workspace, and replace the word `name` with `Spiderimage`.

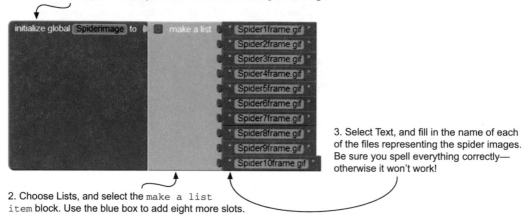

3. Select Text, and fill in the name of each of the files representing the spider images. Be sure you spell everything correctly—otherwise it won't work!

2. Choose Lists, and select the `make a list item` block. Use the blue box to add eight more slots.

To make App Inventor count through a list, you need an index to go with it. All the index does is say to App Inventor, "The first item in the list is called 1, the second is called 2, and so on." This means you can easily identify where the end of the list is, using the length of the list.

1. From Variables, choose the `initialize global name to` block. Drag this onto the workspace, and replace the word `name` with `Index`.

2. From Math, insert the number 1 into the `Index` variable block.

The blocks that follow enable the spider to change images every tenth of a second. How frequently you change the image depends on the effect you're trying to produce. The changes in image are handled by **Clock1.Timer**.

You may remember that in chapter 3 we discussed giving the program a voice to help understand what is going on. Well, the clock definitely has a nagging, persistent voice. In this capacity, the timer is more like a reminder bell going off every tenth of a second, saying "Don't forget to show the next image!" Of course, the program doesn't understand "next image"; but because you've given the list an index, it does understand that every time the timer reminder goes off, the index number has 1 added to it. The app effectively counts through the list, displaying first Spider1frame, then Spider2frame, and so on.

1. Select the when `Clock1.Timer do` block, and drag it onto your workspace.

2. From Variables, drag out the `set to` block, and select `global Index` from the drop-down list.

3. Drag out a `get` block from Variables, and again select `global Index`. Add this to a Math `Number 1` block using a Math + block.

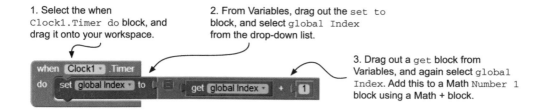

We experimented for a while before settling on changing the image every tenth of a second (100 milliseconds) to give a smooth and scarily quick look to the crawl!

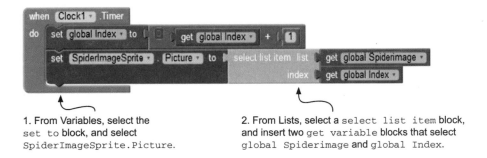

1. From Variables, select the set to block, and select SpiderImageSprite.Picture.

2. From Lists, select a select list item block, and insert two get variable blocks that select global Spiderimage and global Index.

Next you need to make the link between the index and the image change by inserting a **Clock1.Timer** event hander. It counts through the index and changes the spider picture each time the index calls the next picture in the list.

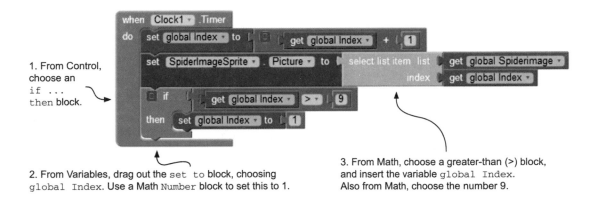

1. From Control, choose an if ... then block.

2. From Variables, drag out the set to block, choosing global Index. Use a Math Number block to set this to 1.

3. From Math, choose a greater-than (>) block, and insert the variable global Index. Also from Math, choose the number 9.

The last thing you do in this section is return the count to the beginning of the list so Spider1frame is shown again, enabling you to loop through the crawl. You tell the program that when the index has reached more than 9 (that is, 10), it's at the end of the list of images, so it should go back to the beginning and start again.

Don't be disheartened by how much goes into changing the costume of the spider. You may be thinking that it's much easier in a program like Scratch. But once you understand this listing sequence, you can use almost identical coding any time you want to run through a list, be it of images or quiz questions, for example.

Learning Point: Scratch

Scratch is a super-fun programming language that is looked after by the same people as App Inventor (Massachusetts Institute of Technology [MIT]). It is a bit like the App Inventor Designer and Blocks Editor rolled into one, and it lets you put animations and games together quickly on a computer. Have a look: http://scratch.mit.edu/.

2. Making the spider move repeatedly

The settings you've given the spider in the App Inventor Designer will make it head diagonally down the screen without you doing anything else. Just as a reminder, the settings for **SpiderImageSprite** are as follows:

Setting	In English!
Heading: 225	Moves toward the bottom-left corner of the screen
Interval: 100	Moves every 1/10 of a second
Speed: 5	Moves 5 pixels each time
X: 190 **Y**: 10	Starts in the top-right corner of the screen

If you left these settings alone, the spider would head down the screen and stay there. But you want her (him or her—how can you tell?) to hit the edge of the screen and then appear again in the top-right corner. In order to do this, you need to tell the spider, "If you reach the edge of the screen, get yourself back up to X = 190 and Y = 10." Then the spider is free to do it all again.

1. From `SpiderImageSprite`, choose the `EdgeReached` block.

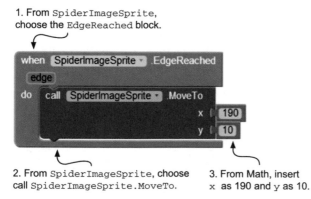

2. From `SpiderImageSprite`, choose call `SpiderImageSprite.MoveTo`.

3. From Math, insert `x` as 190 and `y` as 10.

3. Making the spider bite and stay still

Now you can use a new set of events called **TouchDown** and **TouchUp**. When the user touches the spider and holds their finger still, the spider responds by making a biting noise, vibrating, and staying still. As soon as the user takes their finger off the spider, it carries on crawling. You want the spider to appear to bite at the moment the user puts their finger on the spider image. The blocks to achieve this are shown next.

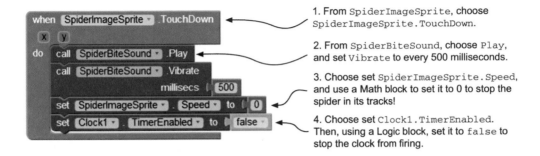

1. From `SpiderImageSprite`, choose `SpiderImageSprite.TouchDown`.

2. From `SpiderBiteSound`, choose `Play`, and set `Vibrate` to every 500 milliseconds.

3. Choose set `SpiderImageSprite.Speed`, and use a Math block to set it to 0 to stop the spider in its tracks!

4. Choose set `Clock1.TimerEnabled`. Then, using a Logic block, set it to `false` to stop the clock from firing.

4. Making the spider start moving again

You know already that to stop the spider, you set **SpiderImageSprite.Enabled** to **false**. What do you think you need to do to make it walk again? That's right: set **enabled** to **true**. You also want to restore the spider's speed to 5 for the speedy, scary crawl. But in this event, you don't want the spider to bite, so you don't mention the sound or vibration.

Taking it further

1 In Creepy Spider, you could provide some variety by changing the background every time the spider is touched. This would involve adding an extra action in the **Touch-Down** event handler to change the background image of the canvas.

2 You could introduce levels of difficulty by making the background more and more difficult to find the spider on, or by making the spider smaller. The user could score depending on how quickly they touch the spider. Taking inspiration from the "Where's Waldo?" illustrations, you could make the boss level lots of pictures of stationary spiders among which to find the moving one.

3   Rotate the spider, and have it head the other way across the screen rather than reappear at the top.

What did you learn?

In this chapter, you learned the following:

- How to create movement without a clock timer or any user interaction
- How to create random movement with a clock timer
- How to create movement with a clock timer and lists
- How to apply your list and index knowledge to animation
- How to explode GIFs so you can use the images in your own animations
- How to use the **EdgeReached** event handler
- How to use built-in Logic blocks

Test your knowledge

1   What are the three ways of producing animation in an app?
2   What are the default settings for **Heading**, **Speed**, and **Interval** for a sprite or ball?
3   What is an animated GIF, and what do you have to do to one to use it in your app?
4   If you want a ball to head straight down the screen, what **Heading** value do you assign it?
5   What does a speed of 5 mean?
6   What does an interval of 100 mean?
7   Which event-handling block would you use to make a sprite change in some way when it reached the edge of the screen?
8   In which block drawer do you always find the block that should be used when you want to refer to a sprite?
9   How do you switch off a **Clock.Timer**?
10   When you've defined a list, what else do you always need to define if you want to count through the list?
11   Is Carl scared of spiders?

CHAPTER 9

Position sensors

In chapter 2, you shook your phone and made a sheep disappear
using the phone's accelerometer sensor. Most phones have sensors
that can detect much smaller motions than a strong shake. You can
see this when you tilt the phone to one side and the display rotates,
or if you've played a driving game where you steer left and right by
gently tilting the phone. Phones can tell which way up they're facing—for instance, some people set their phone's ringer to be silent

automatically if the phone is face down on a desk. Your phone can also tell which direction
is north by using its own built-in compass.

All the apps in this chapter rely on you using an actual
phone, because the emulator doesn't have any position
sensors. Most phones will work with the apps in this
chapter because the sensors you're using are common.
You can double-check exactly which sensors your
phone has by downloading a free app from the Google Play
Store such as the excellent Android Sensor Box from iMobLife
(shown at right). You might find that your phone has some
sensors that App Inventor can't access yet (like a proximity or
light sensor), but these features may be added to App Inventor
as the sensors become common in more phones.

By the end of the chapter, you'll have made apps that are controlled not by clicking buttons, but by altering the phone's position in space. You'll create an amazing magic trick and a simple motion-controlled game.

We'll start by looking at how the phone knows which direction you're facing by looking at the compass sensor. Or, as you can call it if you want to impress your friends, the *magnetometer*.

  # Compass app

PURPOSE OF THIS APP

This app is a simple compass. When you move the phone, the compass rotates so that N always lines up with the Earth's magnetic North Pole (as long as there are no strong magnets near the phone). That means the compass direction that is at the top of the phone is the direction you're currently facing. There's also a heading label at the top of the screen that tells you your current direction in degrees from north. So, for example, if you face south, the letter S will be at the top of your phone and the heading will be 180 degrees.

APP RATING

 2

ASSETS YOU'LL NEED

Compass.png.

Compass			
Screen1 properties	**Title**: Compass **AlignHorizontal**: Center **ScreenOrientation**: Portrait **Scrollable**: No (unselected)		
Components	**What do I rename it?**	**What does it do?**	**What properties do I set?**
`Label`	`HeadingLabel`	Displays the direction in which the top of the phone is pointing (in degrees)	**FontBold**: Yes (selected) **FontSize**: 28 **Text**: "Heading"
`Canvas`	`Canvas`	Holds the compass face	**Width** and **Height**: Fill Parent

Components	What do I rename it?	What does it do?	What properties do I set?
ImageSprite	CompassSprite	Displays the compass face	**BackgroundImage**: compass.png **Rotates**: Yes (selected) **Width** and **Height**: Automatic
OrientationSensor Palette group: Sensors	OrientationSensor1	Tells you the azimuth—the phone's current heading based on the Earth's magnetic field	**Enabled**: Yes (selected)

1. Setting up the screen

The screen layout for this app is simple: a heading label plus a compass face. One new idea we're including for this app is that the compass face automatically resizes to any screen size; so whether you're using a tiny 2-inch smartphone screen or a 10-inch tablet, the compass should fill the screen. You do this by setting up a basic screen layout and then programming some blocks to resize the compass face depending on the size of the screen. Here's the basic layout.

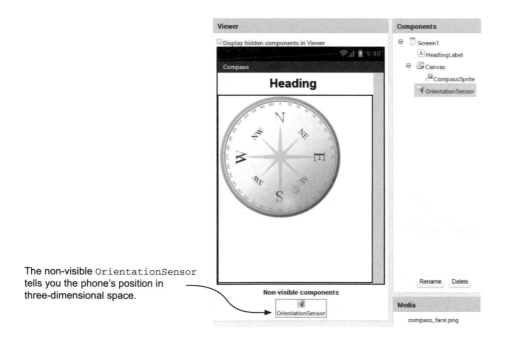

The non-visible OrientationSensor tells you the phone's position in three-dimensional space.

The canvas's height and width are set to Fill Parent so that when the app starts, the canvas automatically resizes to the width and height of your phone's screen. This would make the compass a strange-looking ellipse. You want **CompassSprite** to have the same height and width as the canvas width—then it will fill the screen horizontally. Here are the blocks to resize the compass:

Setting both the CompassSprite's height and width to be the same as the Canvas's width means the compass remains a perfect circle that fills the screen horizontally.

Notice that you're using the **Screen1.Initialize** event to trigger this change so it will happen as soon as the app runs. The user probably won't even notice that the compass is being resized.

2. Coding the blocks: where are you heading?

You need to know what direction the phone is pointing; then you can update your heading label and rotate the compass face to match that direction. The orientation sensor you added in Design view gives you lots of information about the position of the phone (see the "Defying gravity" Learning Point, later in the chapter, for details). You'll use the **Azimuth** property of the sensor to tell you which compass direction the top of the phone is pointing toward. The azimuth gives you a reading from 0 to 360 degrees. For example, the azimuth is 0 degrees when the top of the device is pointing north, 90 degrees when it's pointing east, 180 degrees when it's pointing south, 270 degrees when it's pointing west, and so on.

The azimuth reading gives you lots of decimal points of accuracy. That's great if you have a highly accurate device and need to steer a ship around the globe, but most of us only need a rough navigation guide—say, to the nearest degree. So you'll round off the **Azimuth** value using a Math block called **round**. Here's the block that outputs the heading at the top of the screen:

Round up the azimuth (compass heading) to the nearest whole degree.

That takes care of the Heading label at the top of the screen. Now you need to rotate the compass to the same heading—and this is surprisingly easy! You've set **CompassSprite**'s **Rotates** property to **yes**, so if you set **CompassSprite**'s **Heading** property to match **Azimuth**, the sprite will rotate to point in the right direction. Here's the block:

The reason this works is complicated and is probably easiest to understand from a diagram—see the "Compass and sprite headings" Learning Point.

The final piece of the puzzle is how and when you should trigger the previous two blocks. You know from chapter 7 that you could set up a clock that triggers, say, every tenth of a second to run these blocks and update the screen. But the orientation sensor has one more trick up its sleeve: it can trigger an event whenever the position of the phone changes. The event is called `OrientationSensor.OrientationChanged`. If you drag out that event block and insert the two blocks you just saw, you have the finished program:

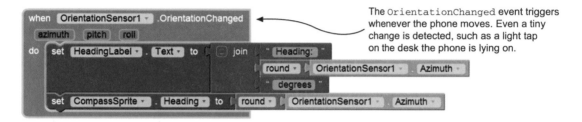

The `OrientationChanged` event triggers whenever the phone moves. Even a tiny change is detected, such as a light tap on the desk the phone is lying on.

Learning Point: Compass and sprite headings

Compass headings start at 0 degrees (north) pointing up and increase as you move around the compass clockwise. You found out in chapter 8 that App Inventor sprite headings start at 0 degrees pointing to the right side of the screen and increase as you travel counterclockwise. If that's so, how does the Compass app work without converting from one system to another?

We hope this diagram will explain. We have superimposed a running man onto the compass so you can see the direction the compass sprite would travel if we gave it some speed (remember, in reality it stays in one place and rotates around its center):

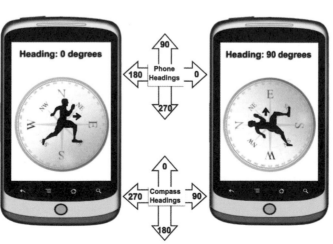

When the phone is pointed north, the azimuth heading is 0 degrees. A moving sprite with a heading of 0 moves right. App Inventor assumes sprites are drawn facing right, so the sprite won't rotate.

When the phone is pointed east, the azimuth heading is 90 degrees. A moving sprite with a heading of 90 moves up. App Inventor rotates the sprite so it looks like it's facing up on the screen, and your compass now has east at the top.

Before we move on to look at some of the other orientation sensors in your phone, you're going to use the magnetometer (or compass) once more to perform an astonishing magic trick.

Astonishing Prediction! app

PURPOSE OF THIS APP

This app turns you into a master illusionist. You deal four playing cards face up on the desk and place your phone face down. You ask a member of the audience to point to any one of the cards. Announcing that you've already predicted their choice, you flip over your phone to reveal a matching card on its screen. The audience can examine the phone as much as they like, and then you can repeat the trick with another audience member.

APP RATING

 3

ASSETS YOU'LL NEED

Images of four playing cards (2 to 5 of clubs).

Astonishing Prediction			
Screen1 properties	**Title**: Astonishing Prediction! **AlignHorizontal**: Center **ScreenOrientation**: Portrait **Scrollable**: No (unselected)		
Components	**What do I rename it?**	**What does it do?**	**What properties do I set?**
Button	PredictionButton	Lets you switch the **OrientationSensor** on/off. Also displays an image of the chosen card via its **Image** property.	**Text**: Blank **Width** and **Height**: Fill Parent
Orientation-Sensor Palette group: Sensors	Orientation-Sensor1	Tells you the azimuth—the phone's current heading based on the Earth's magnetic field	**Enabled**: No (unselected)

Understanding the secret of the app

Have you guessed how such a simple app knows which card has been chosen? Cunningly, you'll use the phone's compass to work out which direction the phone is facing when it's flipped over. If it's pointing roughly northeast, you'll display the 2 of clubs; southeast, and it's the 3 of clubs; southwest, the 4 of clubs; and northwest, the 5 of clubs.

How do you stop the image from changing whenever the phone is being waved around? You'll use a *long click* of a button (which fills the screen) to activate the orientation sensor—a long click means you leave your finger on the button for a couple of seconds. A short click (regular click) disables the orientation sensor. So any time you show the screen to your audience, a quick touch of the screen freezes the image until you long-click the button again. The following sequence should make the trick clear from start to finish:

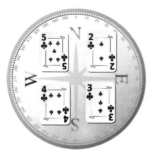

1. Before you start, locate a memorable item in the room that is directly north of where you'll perform the trick. Memorize the positions of the cards shown above.

2. Run the app. Keeping the phone screen private, long-click the grey button to activate the orientation sensor. Flip the phone face down on the desk.

3. Invite an audience member to point to a card. While asking them, "Are you sure that was a free choice?" casually spin the phone (keeping it face down) to point in whichever compass direction you memorized for that card in step 1.

4. Carefully flip the phone, keeping it pointing in the correct direction. At the same time …

5. … short-click the button (which now displays the selected card). This disables the orientation sensor and "locks" the card so it doesn't change.

6. After the applause dies down, you can restart the trick by secretly long-clicking the card and flipping the phone face down.

Here are some performance top tips:

- Make up a story to explain your powers. Perhaps you have mind control and have already selected the card that you'll insert into the audience member's brain!
- Always point the phone either NE, NW, SE, or SW. Pointing directly N, S, E, or W will mean you're never sure whether you have it in the right direction. A little less than north, and the card will be the 5 of clubs, whereas a little more than north and it will be the 2 of clubs.
- If you're struggling to remember which compass direction you need to point the phone, you could lay out the cards in their compass positions. So, place the 2 of clubs in the northeast position on the table, the 3 of clubs southeast, and so on, in a circle with the phone face down in the center—but don't be surprised if your audience guesses the secret.
- If you've set your phone to go into sleep mode when it's not being used, you'll find that it keeps sleeping because you aren't touching the screen when the phone is face down on the desk. Flipping over a blank screen isn't impressive, so adjust or disable the screen-timeout duration in your phone's system settings.

1. Setting up the screen

You use a straightforward layout here: just a blank button that fills the screen, an orientation sensor, and four images of the four cards. You could substitute different images if you wanted to. For example, you could take pictures of four objects to put in the app, and then place those objects on the table for the spectator to choose from. Another idea might be to use pictures of four friends you know will be watching the trick, and have one of them selected as the prediction. Use your imagination to create a magical, memorable illusion.

Note that you start the app with the orientation sensor disabled because you use the **OrientationChanged** event to trigger the card change.

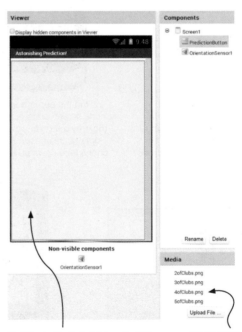

Set the button's height and width to Fill Parent to fill the screen. This makes it easy to click even if you aren't looking. Also, the card will appear here—nice and large for the spectators to see.

Don't forget to add the four card images by clicking Upload File.

You don't want that to happen until the phone is face down and the screen is out of sight.

2. Coding the blocks: abracadabra!

Let's deal with switching the orientation sensor on and off first. Remember that a long click of the button activates the sensor and a short click deactivates it, like so:

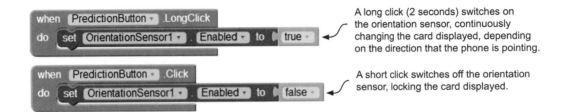

A long click (2 seconds) switches on the orientation sensor, continuously changing the card displayed, depending on the direction that the phone is pointing.

A short click switches off the orientation sensor, locking the card displayed.

Whenever the phone moves, you want to update the picture of the card that is displayed:

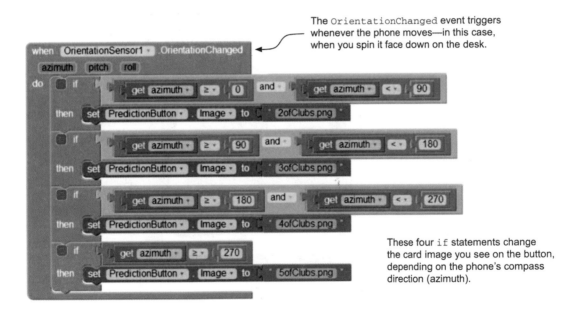

The `OrientationChanged` event triggers whenever the phone moves—in this case, when you spin it face down on the desk.

These four `if` statements change the card image you see on the button, depending on the phone's compass direction (azimuth).

To avoid errors and unpredictable behavior, it's important that you make sure all values from 0 to 360 can be true for only one of the `if` statements. For example, if the phone is pointing 90 degrees from north, it will only display the 3 of clubs—because the previous `if` statement covers from greater than or equal to zero up to *less than 90*.

Testing it

If you try the app on your phone with the screen face up, you should quickly get the hang of switching the orientation sensor on/off, and you'll be able to see how the card changes as you rotate the phone. Practice the spin, click, and flip move—then go astonish your friends!

Learning Point: Defying gravity

You've come to grips with the magnetometer part of the orientation sensor (azimuth). The sensor also senses the phone's position in space. It can do this because there's a force (gravity) acting on the phone that you can use to work out which way is up, down, or somewhere in between. The phone uses three accelerometers to detect gravity in three dimensions. These three readings are combined to give you two basic measures of movement: *pitch* and *roll* (see the following diagram). The orientation sensor can also combine pitch and roll into *angle* and *magnitude*, which provides the direction and speed of an imaginary ball balanced on the phone's screen. Here's a summary of all five readings that the orientation sensor can provide:

Azimuth—Turning the phone to face a different direction (for example, holding the phone steady while spinning around in a chair) changes the compass direction, which is called the azimuth.

Imagine you're balancing a marble on your phone screen.

Angle is the direction in which the ball rolls.

Magnitude is the speed at which the ball travels (or the force it feels). A magnitude of 1 is the maximum: it happens when the phone is tilted perpendicular to the ground.

Pitch—Tipping the phone toward its top or bottom edge changes the pitch angle.

Roll—Tilting the phone toward its left or right edge changes the roll angle.

Hungry Spider app

PURPOSE OF THIS APP
This app uses the Creepy Spider app from chapter 8 and turns it into a simple fly-catching game. You control the spider by tilting the phone and try to gobble up all the flies as quickly as possible.

APP RATING
3

ASSETS YOU'LL NEED
Images: Fly.gif and Spider_web.png. A working version of the Creepy Spider app.

Open your Creepy Spider app, and save it as Hungry Spider. Make the following changes and additions to your project.

Hungry Spider			
Screen1 properties	**Title**: Hungry Spider **ScreenOrientation**: Portrait **Scrollable**: No (unselected)		
Components	**What do I rename it?**	**What does it do?**	**What properties do I set?**
`Button`	`RestartButton`	Causes any eaten flies to reappear so the game can begin again.	**Text**: "Restart Game" **BackgroundColor**: Magenta **FontBold**: Yes (selected) **Shape**: Rounded
`Orientation-Sensor` Palette group: Sensors	`Orientation-Sensor1`	Detects how the phone is tilted—the spider always heads toward the ground. The bigger the angle of tilt, the faster the spider crawls.	**Enabled**: Yes (selected)
`Canvas`	`Canvas`	The play area that displays a spiderweb background.	**Width** and **Height**: Fill Parent **BackgroundImage**: Spider-Web.png
`8 ImageSprite`s	`Fly1`, `Fly2` ... up to `Fly8`	Display eight juicy flies, which move around the web.	For all eight sprites: **Picture**: fly.gif **Rotates**: Yes (selected) **Width** and **Height**: Automatic

1. Setting up the screen

We've made some changes to the original Creepy Spider screen. The leaves that provided camouflage for the spider have been replaced by a more neutral background and a spiderweb. This helps the player see the spider and makes it look like the flies are trapped in a web.

All the sprites will move—the flies will move randomly, bouncing off the screen edges, and the spider will always head toward the point of the screen that is closest to the ground (using the orientation sensor to detect gravity). The game will look much better if all the sprites face the same direction they're moving, so for all sprites you'll set the **Rotates** property to **true** by selecting the **Rotates** box. Here's the layout:

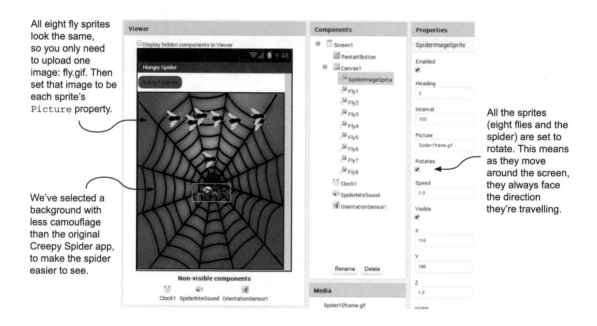

All eight fly sprites look the same, so you only need to upload one image: fly.gif. Then set that image to be each sprite's Picture property.

We've selected a background with less camouflage than the original Creepy Spider app, to make the spider easier to see.

All the sprites (eight flies and the spider) are set to rotate. This means as they move around the screen, they always face the direction they're travelling.

2. Coding the blocks: moving the spider

First you'll get the spider moving around the web in the direction that you tip the phone—later you'll introduce the flies. The orientation sensor provides two useful readings to help you here:

- *Angle*—Tells you which direction a ball would roll if you balanced it on the phone's screen.
- *Magnitude*—Tells you how far the phone has been tipped. A value of 0 means the phone is lying flat (parallel to the ground), and a value of 1 means the phone is tipped onto one of its edges.

You know from previous apps that **Sprite**s have **Heading** and **Speed** properties. If you link a sprite's **Heading** to the orientation **Angle**, the sprite will move toward the ground (just like a ball balanced on the screen). If you link the sprite's **Speed** to the orientation **Magnitude**, the sprite will move more quickly as the phone is tipped further toward one of its edges. Here are the blocks to do just that with your hungry spider:

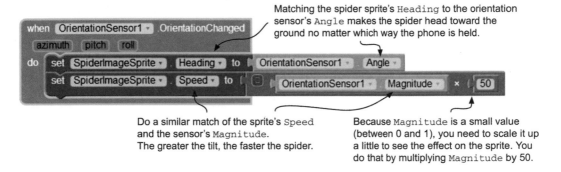

Matching the spider sprite's Heading to the orientation sensor's Angle makes the spider head toward the ground no matter which way the phone is held.

Do a similar match of the sprite's Speed and the sensor's Magnitude. The greater the tilt, the faster the spider.

Because Magnitude is a small value (between 0 and 1), you need to scale it up a little to see the effect on the sprite. You do that by multiplying Magnitude by 50.

Just like in the Compass app, you're using the **OrientationChanged** event to trigger the spider's movement so that whenever the phone moves, the spider reacts right away.

Try the app right now. You should see an animated spider whose movement changes as you tilt the phone. Try getting it to walk slowly in a circle and then dash around the edges of the screen—you'll soon get the hang of it. Although you'll see the flies on the screen, the spider can't interact with them yet. It's time to add that part …

3. Freeing the flies

After all that running around, the spider must be hungry—let's animate some juicy flies for it to chomp. This is a two-step process:

1   Animate the flies so they move randomly around the web.
2   Detect when the spider collides with a fly. When this happens, play a spider-bite sound and make the fly disappear.

To animate the flies, you first need to set a random heading and speed for each of them. Doing this eight times (once for each fly) means a lot of blocks, but there is a handy shortcut you can take to reduce the blocks using a list. You know that lists can contain all kinds of useful items like text, numbers, and colors. Lists can also contain components from the Palette—and once you've filled a list with components, you can set the properties for all those components at once using a loop. Let's break that idea into simple steps.

Start by defining a variable containing an empty list. Call it **FlyList**, because it's going to contain all eight fly sprites.

initialize global FlyList to create empty list

When the app starts, you'll fill the list with your eight fly sprites using the `Screen1.Initialize` event. You'll find the `Fly1` to `Fly8` blocks at the bottom of each `Fly` sprite's list of blocks.

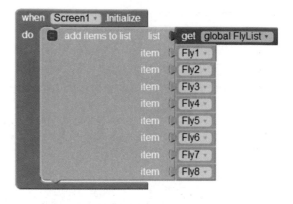

Normally when you make a list you fill it when you first define it, but a quirk of App Inventor means you have to do this two-step process for any list that contains components.

You have a list of sprite components—now what? Well, if you wrote down what you wanted to do in English, you would probably say something like, "For each sprite in the list, set its heading to a random number between 1 and 360 and set its speed to a random number between 2 and 5." That seems straightforward. You know there is a `for each` loop that works through a list, so you could do something like this:

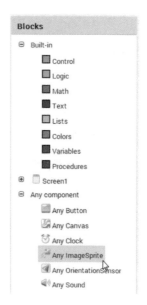

But there's a big problem with this block. Can you see what it is? Which flies get changed by this loop?

The answer is, only `Fly1` is changed. What you really want is to use the `item` variable of the loop to change which fly you're dealing with each time you go around the loop. That way, you set `Fly1`'s `Heading` and `Speed`, then `Fly2`'s, `Fly3`'s and so on.

Fortunately, App Inventor has a built-in set of Any Component blocks you can use to program all the components in a list. It's at the bottom of the Blocks list. App Inventor automatically creates an Any Component for each of the types of objects you've added on the Design screen, so adding your first button to an app adds an Any Button category at the bottom of your blocks.

Open the Any Button blocks now, and look at the sort of blocks you have access to—how are they different from when you click a specific button's blocks, such as **RestartButton**?

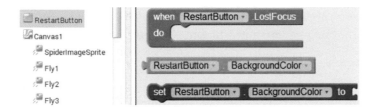

Specific component blocks like **RestartButton** include event blocks like **Button.Click** and blocks that let you find out and set specific properties of the component, such as its background color.

Looking at the Any Component blocks, you'll notice that there are no event blocks. That means it isn't possible to write an app that detects, for example, when any button is clicked. But you'll see that there are blocks for finding out and setting component properties. So you *can*, for example, set all your app

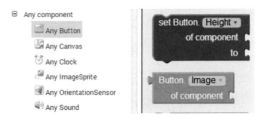

buttons to be yellow or have a bold font. You'll also notice that all the blocks in Any Component have an extra component socket, and this is what you'll use in your **for each** loop.

Here's the new and improved **for each** block:

The for each loop repeats the actions inside the loop for every item in FlyList. So, it does the same thing to all eight fly sprites. It keeps track of which fly it's working on at any time using the item variable.

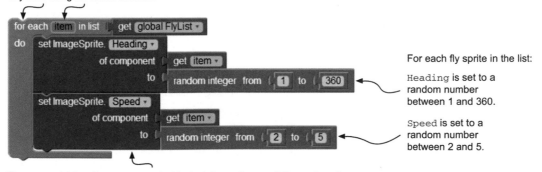

For each fly sprite in the list:

Heading is set to a random number between 1 and 360.

Speed is set to a random number between 2 and 5.

These special Any Component sprite blocks let you change all the sprites at once using the item variable as a reference or index to each component in FlyList.

This might seem a bit complicated—why not forget the `for each` loop and write a separate couple of blocks for each fly? That would certainly work, but 2 blocks per fly equals 16 blocks, and you've just done the same thing with 3. Also, now you have the power to manipulate all the flies at once—you can have them flying in formation at the click of a button, or change their image so they all become butterflies at the end of the game. Any Component blocks are powerful!

You want all the flies' `Heading` and `Speed` properties to be set at the beginning of the app, so insert the `for each` loop into the `Screen1.Initialize` event block that you created earlier:

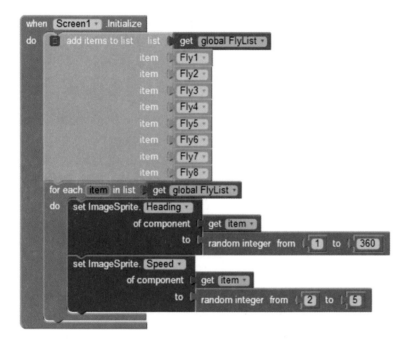

Now if you run the app you'll see that all the flies set off moving in different directions and at different speeds.

When flies reach the screen edge, though, they slide along it until they all end up stuck in a corner. To solve this, you can bounce a fly that reaches an edge so it heads back toward the center of the screen (just like you did with the rat in chapter 7). Unfortunately, detecting when a sprite reaches the edge of the screen is an event—and you can't use Any Components for events—so in this case you need eight sets of blocks:

You can speed up the process of making these blocks by creating the first set of blocks, copying and pasting it seven times, and then changing the fly sprite referred to in the `EdgeReached` event and `Bounce` procedure of each block.

4. Feeding the spider

You have a controllable spider and moving flies. Now you need to say what should happen when they run into each other. When flies collide with other flies, they'll pass over each other. But if the spider collides with a fly, you want to play a spider-bite sound and make the fly disappear. You can do this using the `SpiderImageSprite`'s `CollidedWith` event, just like you used in Cheeky Hamster in chapter 8. The difference here is that you're going to change the fly sprite that the spider collides with by setting its `Visible` property to `false`. Here are the blocks and explanation:

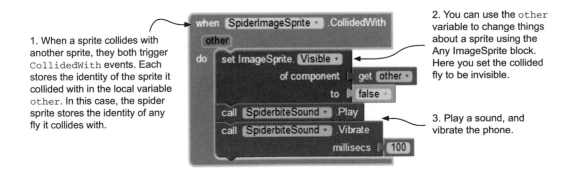

1. When a sprite collides with another sprite, they both trigger `CollidedWith` events. Each stores the identity of the sprite it collided with in the local variable `other`. In this case, the spider sprite stores the identity of any fly it collides with.

2. You can use the `other` variable to change things about a sprite using the Any ImageSprite block. Here you set the collided fly to be invisible.

3. Play a sound, and vibrate the phone.

5. Restarting the game

Once the flies are eaten, the game is considerably less interesting. You need more flies, or you can make the invisible flies visible again. When the button at the top of the screen is clicked, you'll set each fly's **Visible** property back to **true** using a **for else** loop similar to the one you used to set the flies moving.

Taking it further

There are lots of ways you could improve this basic game or adapt the principles to make an entirely new game. Adapt the Hungry Spider app using one or more of these ideas:

1   Add a score counter that increases when a fly is eaten.
2   Add a countdown timer so the spider has to eat the flies before the time runs out.
3   Reverse the spider's direction so it always heads up the screen, away from the ground.
4   Make the game harder by making the spider slower, or make the spider and flies smaller. You could add levels so the game starts easy and gets harder whenever the game restarts.
5   *Extra challenge*—Can you make the spider turn left and right rather than running in a circle so that it ends up upside down? You'll need to create a new set of spider sprites by flipping the current sprites in a program like Paint. Then you'll need to detect the roll of the phone—if it's to the left, use the left sprites, and if it's to the right, use the original (right-facing) sprites.

What did you learn?

In this chapter, you learned the following:

- That smartphones contain sensors that tell you about their physical position in the world
- That the orientation sensor can tell you
  - The compass direction the phone is pointing (using the azimuth)
  - The position of the phone in relation to the ground (using angle, magnitude, roll, and pitch)
- That when the phone moves, the orientation sensor triggers an event called **OrientationChanged**

- That buttons can tell the difference between a short click and a long click
- How to resize objects like sprites so they fill the phone's screen
- How to rotate sprites so they turn to face the direction they're travelling in
- How to set the properties of lots of objects at the same time using a `for each` loop and Any Component blocks

Test your knowledge

1 Which orientation sensor (azimuth, angle, magnitude, roll, or pitch) would be best to use for each of these apps?

   a A driving game, where tilting the phone left and right steers the car

   b A game where you steer a ball through a maze of obstacles

   c A "spin the phone" app that counts how many times the phone can be spun around on a table top

   d Is each of the following statements True or False? You can use Any Component blocks to

     - Set the size of all buttons on the screen
     - Play a sound whenever any text box contains the word *beep*
     - Change the color of all labels to green
     - Display an alert notification whenever a button is clicked for a long time

Try it out

1 In addition to the orientation sensor, phones also have a (related) accelerometer sensor. Create a Sensor Test app that outputs all the phone's sensor readings so you can see how they change as the phone is moved around, like so:

This is a table arrangement containing two columns of text labels.

These blocks output all of the phone's accelerometer and orientation sensor readings into the text labels on the right side of the table arrangement.

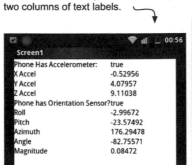

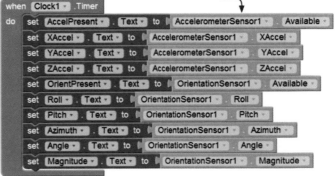

2 Use the phone sensors to create a Smartphone Burglar Alarm app that works like this:

a The user types a password and clicks an Activate button to activate the alarm, after which they put down the phone.

b After 10 seconds, the phone activates the orientation sensor.

c If an **OrientationChanged** event happens, the phone gives the user 10 seconds to type their password and click a Deactivate button.

d If the password isn't entered correctly, the phone sounds an alarm until the password is correctly entered.

e *Extra challenge*—Have the phone send a text message like, "Help! I am being stolen!" to another smartphone.

f *Extra-extra challenge*—Have the text message include some location information about where the phone is at the moment.

3 Create a Maze Game like the one shown. The player steers a ball from a START position through a maze of walls and holes to an END star. The ball, walls, and holes are all separate sprites. The rules of the game are as follows:

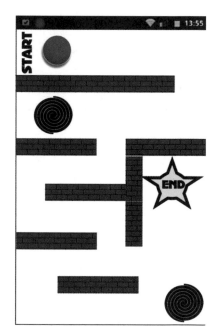

a The ball starts at a specific x, y position (hold this in a variable).

b The ball rolls toward the ground (just like the spider in Hungry Spider).

c If the ball collides with a wall, it bounces off (or, to make the game really hard, you could have it return to the START position).

d If the ball collides with a hole, it returns to the START position.

e If the ball collides with the END star, the game displays a "Congratulations!" message.

You could extend the game by adding scores and levels.

CHAPTER 10

Barcodes and scanners

Barcodes have been around since the 1970s, and there aren't many products now that don't use them. No doubt you've used barcodes in the supermarket at the self-checkout registers.

Barcodes are groups of black and white lines that represent numbers according to the widths and spacing of parallel lines. They can be read by either special optical scanners or smartphone cameras that provide product information that can be read by a computer. The barcode is considered to be one-dimensional (the lines travel in one direction). A *QR code* is a two-dimensional barcode (a *matrix code*). To read such codes, make sure you have a free QR code scanner such as QR Droid.

barcode-tree by Lisa Yarost

The barcode scanner in App Inventor is an easy-to-use, non-visible component that uses the phone's camera to read a QR code or a barcode. The decision you have to make is what to do with the barcode once you've read it. In this chapter, you'll make three apps: one showing how the numbers in a barcode can be used for a petfinder game, the next a practical app for getting information about a product by scanning its barcode, and the third a QR code treasure-hunt app that can be used to communicate clues to treasure hunters.

To have fun with a barcode is pretty simple; to use the actual information embedded in the barcode means you have to learn how to use the activity starter that launches other apps. You may want to launch the browser in response to scanning a barcode, or you might want to develop a clever game that launches another game as a reward for finding a particular barcode!

Learning Point: Using a barcode scanner

Before you take a step further, make sure you have a scanner installed on your phone. QR scanners will read one-dimensional barcodes, too. Scoot on over to the Google Play Store and install a free scanner such as QR Droid or ZXing. App Inventor's barcode scanner talks to the actual barcode scanner installed on your phone and says, "Take a scan. OK: what have you got for me?"

A number of Android apps are commercially available that utilize the mystery and fun of the barcode scanner. One of our favorites is Codemon, which is described as combining the concepts of Pet Collection, Pokemon, and Barcode Battler (these are also fun collection apps that use barcodes). We've put together a much simpler app that retains some of the mystery but is still simple enough to write and customize yourself.

Barcode Petfinder app

PURPOSE OF THIS APP

This game uses the **BarcodeScanner** component and some **if** statements to enable the user to scan existing barcodes on books or drinks or anything and reveal a collection of pets. The challenge in the barcode pet shop is to collect all 10 pets for Sam, who has lost his pets in the long grass!

APP RATING

 2

ASSETS YOU'LL NEED

Grass background, 10 pet images, and a picture of pet owner Sam.

As you may know already, a typical barcode is made up of 14 digits. In order to put some challenge into this game, the user doesn't know the key to each of the pets. The keys are 000, 11, 12, 13, 14, 15, 16, 17, 18, and 19. For example, the barcode number 0004011234598 unlocks the hamster, the chameleon, and the donkey because it contains 000, 11, and 12 but none of the other keys. When you're designing the game, you'll program in a different number to correspond to each of the animals.

Barcode Petfinder			
Screen1 properties	**AlignHorizontal**: Center **AlignVertical**: Center **ScreenOrientation**: Portrait **Scrollable**: No **Title**: Barcode petfinder		
Components	**What do I rename it?**	**What does it do?**	**What properties do I set?**
Horizontal-Arrangement	Horizontal-arrangement1	Allows you to position the button centrally.	
Button	Scan_barcode_button	Invokes the barcode scanner.	**BackgroundColor**: Dark grey **Font**: Bold **FontSize**: 16 **Text**: "Scan some barcodes to track down Sam's missing pets"
Canvas	Canvas1	Allows you to position Sam and the pets.	**BackgroundImage**: grasses.jpg **Width**: Fill Parent **Height**: 400
10 **ImageSprites**	Snake, Donkey, Bird, Tortoise, Panda, Dog, Guineapig, Hamster, Chameleon, Cat	Each pet starts out not visible. When its number is part of a barcode that has been scanned, it appears to be added to the collection.	**Image**: Hamster.gif and so on **Width**: 50 pixels **Height**: 50 pixels **Visible**: (Unselect) Once you've assigned the images to the names, drag them around the canvas to spread them out. Leave the middle free for Sam.
ImageSprite	Sam_Sprite	Appears as a still image. Sam is the owner of the pets.	**Image**: Sam.png **Width**: 100 pixels **Height**: 100 pixels. Drag to position in the center. **Visible**: Leave this box selected so that Sam is visible all the time.
BarcodeScanner Palette group: Sensors	BarcodeScanner1	Connects with the code scanner already installed on the phone, and reads the barcode number.	No properties to set
Media files			

12 files downloaded from our website:
    Snake.png and 9 other animal .png files
    Sam.png
    Grasses.jpg

To code the petfinder, you need to begin by scanning the barcode when the user clicks the Scan button. Next the result of the barcode scanner needs to be looked at using an `if` statement; and if the numbers contain any of the strings that "unlock" a pet, the pet is made visible.

1. Opening the scanner and scanning a barcode

This small set of blocks does quite a lot. It enables the user to click the Scan button, and then it opens the scanner so the built-in scanner can scan the barcode.

1. Choose the event handler
`Scan_barcode_button.Click`.

2. Slot in the `call`
`BarcodeScanner1.DoScan` method.

2. Collecting the barcode scanner result

Pull out the event handler for the **BarcodeScanner**. This takes the information from the scanner and holds it as **result**.

The result is the data
provided by the scanner.

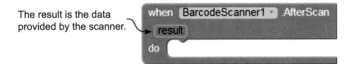

3. Looking for secret codes in the barcode scanner result

Earlier, we explained that each of the animals matches a string of numbers. The hamster, for example, matches 000. This is something we made up; in testing, we've found that using mostly two-digit strings means the user doesn't easily find all 10 pets but can find them by scanning a number of products.

This block looks at the result returned by the barcode scanner and says, "Is 000 in there? If it is, I'm going to do something." The next block will tell it what to do.

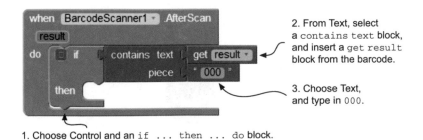

2. From Text, select
a `contains text` block,
and insert a `get result`
block from the barcode.

3. Choose Text,
and type in 000.

1. Choose Control and an `if ... then ... do` block.

4. Revealing the hamster

The hamster sprite is of course always on the screen—it's just invisible (as are all the other sprites). These blocks change the hamster to visible so the user feels that they have "found" it.

1. Pull out the Hamster drawer, and select `Hamster.Visible`.

2. Go to Logic, and choose `true` to slot in.

5. Revealing all the pets

You have to repeat the previous step nine more times for the rest of the pets to be included. All the blocks tuck into the one event handler. And, of course, each time you have to use the blocks from the animals drawer and change the secret numbers needed to find them: Hamster 000, Chameleon 11, Donkey 12, Panda 13, Snake 14, Tortoise 15, Dog 16, Cat 17, Bird 18, and Guineapig 19.

As you can see, the only thing that changes about each **if** statement in the event handler is the number in the text block and the name of the animal. So, the first **if** block has the text block with "000" and the **set** block with **Hamster.Visible**. The second **if** block has the text block with "11", and the **set** block is for the **Chameleon.Visible**. As the user scans a barcode, if it contains 000, the hamster become visible; if the barcode contains 11, the chameleon becomes visible; and so on.

Taking it further

1   Use the same logic for the program, but have the user collect cars.

2   If you want to make Barcode Petfinder challenging, you can include a timer and a score count and have users find the greatest number of pets in the least time.

3   You can make the app a lot more complicated by making pets disappear if certain barcodes are scanned or by earning food for pets with certain barcodes.

Book Finder app

PURPOSE OF THIS APP
This app lets you scan the barcode of a book and then search for that book on the web.

APP RATING

3

ASSETS YOU'LL NEED
Basket image, Scan Barcode image.

As we mentioned earlier, the barcode contains some information that could be genuinely useful to you. For example, if you have the barcode of a book and want to find out how much it costs or where you can buy it, the key is, of course, the internet! The barcode on a book relates directly to the ISBN number, which uniquely identifies that book. By scanning the barcode and launching a search engine (like Google or Yahoo!), you can go straight to a website that contains information about the book. It works for other products too: pizza, salad, lemonade, ice cream … (it must be lunchtime!). In order to launch the internet browser from App Inventor, you need to use a component that's new to you: the **ActivityStarter** component.

Learning Point: What is the ActivityStarter component?

We have a phrase in Britain (which comes from an advertising campaign for paint): "It does what it says on the tin." This is just such an example. The `ActivityStarter` component … starts activities. If you want to start another app from within your app, you have to find out the package and class name (a way of organizing code in Java) and set the properties of the component to match. This could include searching the web for something, going to a particular web page, opening a map on Google Earth, starting someone else's app from in your app … almost anything a smartphone can do.

Again the wonderful people at MIT have a useful list of package and class names for activities you may want to start: it's at http://mng.bz/0x89. Our example should help too!

Book Finder			
Screen1 properties	`AlignHorizontal`: Center `AlignVertical`: Center `ScreenOrientation`: Portrait `Scrollable`: No `Title`: Book Finder		
Components	**What do I rename it?**	**What does it do?**	**What properties do I set?**
`Screen`	`Screen1`		`Image`: Basket.png
`Label`	`Title_label`	Displays the title for the user	`FontSize`: 25 `Text`: "Barcode Bookfinder" `Width`: Fill Parent
`Horizontal-Arrangement`	`Horizontal-arrangement1`	Allows you to position the button and label next to each other	
`Button`	`Scan_barcode_button`	Invokes the barcode scanner	`BackgroundColor`: None `Font`: Bold `FontSize`: 18 `Image`: barcodeimage.png `Text`: "Scan Barcode" `TextAlignment`: Center `TextColor`: Red `Width`: 100 pixels `Height`: 100 pixels
`Label`	`Barcode_label`	Reveals the ISBN number read by the barcode scanner	`BackgroundColor`: Yellow `FontSize`: 20 `Text`: "ISBN number here" `TextColor`: Black
`Horizontal-Arrangement`	`Horizontal-Arrangement2`		

Components	What do I rename it?	What does it do?	What properties do I set?
Button	`Search_for_book _button`	Launches the activity starter to automatically search for the book through Google	**BackgroundColor**: None **FontSize**: 18 **Image**: Basket **Text**: "Search for Book" **TextAlignment**: Center **TextColor**: Red **Width**: 300 pixels **Height**: 300 pixels
ActivityStarter Palette group: Connectivity	`ActivityStarter1`		
BarcodeScanner Palette group: Sensors	`BarcodeScanner1`		

Media files

2 files downloaded from our website:
   Basket.png
   Barcodeimage.png

To get started, you have to first code the Scan Barcode button to enable the user to click it to open the barcode scanner. This involves adding a `Scan_barcode_button.Click` event and calling `BarcodeScanner1.DoScan`. Second, you need to create a set of blocks that prints the result from the barcode scanner on screen, joined with the text "ISBN" to show the user the book's unique code. You do this by using the clever `join` block, which lets you take some of your own text ("ISBN") and join it to the number the scanner has picked up from the barcode. Finally, you code the button that starts the activity starter. The activity starter opens Google and quickly searches for the barcode that your scanner has read.

1. Creating the event handler to scan the barcode

This first block uses the button click to call the barcode scanner.

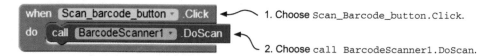

1. Choose `Scan_Barcode_button.Click`.

2. Choose `call BarcodeScanner1.DoScan`.

2. Using the scanner result to print the ISBN number

Now you'll set the barcode label text so it reads "ISBN" with the ISBN number (which was read by the barcode scanner) right next to it. This reassures the user that the correct book has been scanned: they can check the barcode, because the ISBN number is usually printed on the book as well as the code.

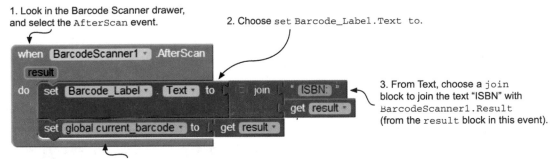

1. Look in the Barcode Scanner drawer, and select the `AfterScan` event.

2. Choose `set Barcode_Label.Text to`.

3. From Text, choose a `join` block to join the text "ISBN" with `BarcodeScanner1.Result` (from the `result` block in this event).

4. Later, you'll use the result from the scanner in another event handler. So create a new variable called `global current_barcode`, and insert the `get result` block from this event handler.

Next you need to create a new variable called **current_barcode**. It holds the result

of the barcode scanner so it can be used in other event handlers later. Initialize it to be an empty text box.

3. Searching the web

To open a specific web page from the app you've created in App Inventor, you need to set the properties of two blocks from the Activity Starter component. We'll explain each separately and then let you see how the blocks fit together.

You need to first tell App Inventor that you want the activity starter to go to the internet by setting **ActivityStarter1.Action** to **android.intent.action.VIEW** (use a text block—type it exactly as printed here).

Next you tell it which website to view by setting its **Data.Uri** (Uniform Resource Identifier). This automatically goes to the page you're looking for, much like a link in a website. If you wanted your app to automatically call Facebook, for example, you could you set this to https://www.facebook.com/. But you want the app to visit the page that would come up had you gone into Google and typed in the barcode of the book you're scanning. So the URI you want to visit is http://www.google.com/m?q=. Then you add **BarcodeScanner1.Result** so you find the book that you've scanned through Google. The m?q= means, "Exactly which URI are you looking for?"

Learning Point: What is a URI?

A Uniform Resource Identifier (URI) is a string of characters (number, symbols, letters, or all three) used to identify a name or a web resource. You may have heard of Uniform Resource Locators (URLs) and Uniform Resource Names (URNs), both of which count as URIs. If you think of URLs as addresses and URNs as names, it may help. Strictly speaking, a URI is either the address or the name or both together.

Now that you've set the activity starter, you need to call it using the block shown at right.

Put it all together, and you get this:

Now your user can scan the barcode of a book and launch Google to search for the book automatically, all from their phone. Good, eh?

Taking it further

1 Combine ideas from chapter 6 (lists) and chapter 11 (TinyDB) to write an app that stores a list of book barcodes along with a user's comment and star rating for each book. Scanning a book barcode retrieves the comment and star rating.

2 If you want to know how to open other apps using **ActivityStarter**, explore the link offered earlier (http://mng.bz/0x89). This page has lots of technical information—but that's what Inventors like!

QR Treasure Hunt app

PURPOSE OF THIS APP
This game uses the **BarcodeScanner** component to read clues and assign points to the players.

APP RATING

3

ASSETS YOU'LL NEED FOR THE APP
Clue text file, amethyst.png, goldcoin.png, pearl.png, ruby.png, sapphire.png, scroll.png, and TreasureChest.png

ASSETS YOU'LL NEED TO PLAY THE GAME
Printed-out QR codes.

How does the game work?

This is a party game mixed with an app, which your friends will love. Here's what you need to do:

1   Come up with a set of questions that relate to places and that could be answered by your friends. The example we have provided is one that our own children could play in the house and garden during the summer.

2   Using a QR generator like goQR.me, type in the questions and print each of the QR codes. You can create your own QR codes for websites you've developed or for favorites that aren't your own. Just go to a QR site such as http://goqr.me/ and follow the instructions there, keeping the questions short. Each of the QR clues leads the players to the next location. We recommend numbering the clues on the back so you can make sure you put them in the right locations.

3   Hide all the clues in the appropriate places. Test the hunt before you try it with your friends, to make sure it goes well.

4   Email the APK (Android package file) for your app to your friends so they can join in the treasure hunt.

5   Do it all again. The QR Treasure Hunt app is designed so that all you need to change are the QR codes on the clue printouts each time. The app refreshes each time it's closed.

Learning Point:
How can I shorten my QR codes?

One thing to remember is to keep your URL reasonably short (below 300 characters). Services like http://tinyurl.com enable you to shorten website addresses in order to do this.

QR Treasure Hunt			
Screen1 properties	`AlignHorizontal`: Left `AlignVertical`: Top `BackgroundColor`: Cyan `BackgroundImage`: None `Icon`: TreasureChest.png `Scrollable`: Yes (selected) `Title`: QR Treasure Hunt		
Components	**What do I rename it?**	**What does it do?**	**What properties do I set?**
`Horizontal-Arrangement`	`Horizontal-Arrangement1`	Allows you to position the button and text box next to each other	
`Image`	`TreasureChestImage`	Looks good	`Picture`: TreasureChest.png `Height`: 100 `Width`: 100
`Label`	`TitleLabel`	Gives instructions to users	`Font`: Bold `Font`: Italic `FontSize`: 12 `FontTypeface`: Serif `Text`: "Scan QR Codes for Treasure"
`TableArrangement`	`TableArrangement1`	Arranges buttons, jewels, and text boxes	`Columns`: 3 `Rows`: 5

5 `Buttons`	`Clue1_Button`
	`Clue2_Button`
	`Clue3_Button`
	`Clue4_Button`
	`End_hunt_Button`
		Invoke the QR scanner to read the QR code	`Font`: Bold
			`Font`: Italic
			`FontSize`: 12
			`FontTypeface`: Serif
			`Image`: Scroll.png
			`Text`: "Scan for Clue 1", "Scan for Clue 2", "Scan for Clue 3", "Scan for Clue 4", "Scan to finish"
			`TextAlignment`: Center
			`Width`: 60
			`Height`: 60
			`Visible`: Showing

Components	What do I rename it?	What does it do?	What properties do I set?

5 `Images`	`Amethyst`
	`Pearl`
	`Ruby`
	`Sapphire`
	`Gold`
		Revealed as the clues are scanned	Picture: Amethyst.png (change treasure each time)
			`Visible`: No (unselected)
			`Width`: 25 pixels
			`Height`: 25 pixels

5 `TextBoxes`	`Result_Clue1`
	`Result_Clue2`
	`Result_Clue3`
	`Result_Clue4`
	`Result_End_Game`
		Reveal the clues	`FontSize`: 12
			`Hint`: (delete the text)
			`MultiLine`: No (unselected)
			`Text`: (delete the text)
			`Width`: 200 pixels
			`Height`: Automatic (enables the text to wrap around and appear in rows instead of disappearing)

5 `BarcodeScanners`
Palette group: Sensors
	`BarcodeScanner1`
	`BarcodeScanner2`
	`BarcodeScanner3`
	`BarcodeScanner4`
	`End_Hunt_Scanner`
		Scan QR codes for clues	

Media files

7 files downloaded from our website:

Treasure.png
Scroll.png
Amethyst.png
Pearl.png
Ruby.png
Sapphire.png
Gold.png

The coding of this app is reasonably simple but effective. You first need to code the buttons so they open the barcode scanner. Next you use the result of the scan to reveal the treasure (like gold or perhaps a sapphire) as a reward for the user and the clue to find the next treasure.

1. Scanning the QR codes

Pull out an event handler, and call a method that lets the user click the clue button and scan the QR code. Do this for each of the clues so you have five blocks, each one like this.

1. Choose `Clue_1_Button.Click.`

```
when  Clue1_Button ▾ .Click
do   call  BarcodeScanner1 ▾ .DoScan
```

2. Choose the `BarcodeScanner1.DoScan` **event.**

2. Revealing the treasure and the clues

As the user scans the QR code, the treasure becomes visible and the clue for the next treasure appears in the text box. For example, scanning a particular code might earn the user a ruby.

Do this for each of the results so you have five blocks like this.

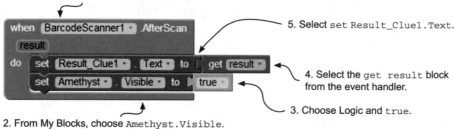

1. Choose the `BarcodeScanner1.AfterScan` event handler.

5. Select `set Result_Clue1.Text`.

4. Select the `get result` block from the event handler.

3. Choose Logic and `true`.

2. From My Blocks, choose `Amethyst.Visible`.

Following is the QR table we used to make our own treasure hunt. Our kids are young, so you may want to make the clues a bit harder to keep your users guessing! We created the quiz by going around the house and garden and finding four well-spaced-out places by the sunflowers, the piano, the kitchen table, and the trampoline. Then we tried to think up clues to lead the kids to these places:

Clue 1	Which flower produces seeds that the hamster would enjoy eating?	
Clue 2	Where could you play chopsticks?	
Clue 3	Rearrange the words "tikhnec btlea" to find the next clue.	
Clue 4	On which piece of equipment would you do a seat drop?	
End of hunt	Congratulations! You've found the treasure.	

Taking it further

Later in the book, you'll learn how to save into a database on the phone. You may want to use this knowledge to let the users save their treasure and clues as they go along.

What did you learn?

In this chapter, you learned the following:

- What barcodes and QR codes are
- How to use the **BarcodeScanner** component
- How to use the **.AfterScan** block
- How to use logic to make an image visible
- How to use the **ActivityStarter** component to search on the web
- How to produce your own QR code

Test your knowledge

1. What is the difference between a QR code and a barcode?
2. Name three things you can do with an activity starter.
3. What is a URI?

CHAPTER 11

Using speech and storing data on your phone

In this chapter, we'll look at the different ways you can change words (text) into the Android voice and how you can record your own voice and change that into text. We'll also examine how you can store items such as text and pictures on your phone.

What is the difference between *text to speech* and *speech to text*?

	User/programmer	App Inventor	Need to be online?
Text to speech	Inputs text	Speaks aloud	Nope
Speech to text	Speaks aloud	Uses Google Voice to convert to text	Yessir

In recent years speech recognition has improved a great deal, but it still isn't perfect. Text to speech is more reliable and effective but still has some funny quirks, such as mispronouncing words. Technical words are often mispronounced—for example, megapixel is pronounced "maygaypixel." You'll also have problems with Roman numerals: King George V is pronounced "King George Vee" by text to speech. But speech to text and text to speech both have the potential to allow you to produce some fun apps, so let's give them a go.

The possibilities presented by text to speech are massive, from creating apps for visually impaired people to including spoken words in a game. The most basic example would be text added to a button so that when the user clicks the button, the text is read aloud. But text can be input by the user, too, or received via an SMS text from someone contacting the user, and automatically read aloud.

Learning Point: What is SMS?

SMS means *Short Messaging Service.* It's the system that lets mobile phone users send and receive texts. The messages are limited to 160 characters (letters, numbers, or symbols). Longer text messages are sent as multiple messages and put back together by the receiving phone service.

Once you've seen the basic functionality of speech recognition and text to speech, you can use this knowledge to create other apps. We have included in this chapter the functionality to save and reuse data in App Inventor's very useful local (stored on the phone) database called TinyDB.

Have you ever woken up in the morning after a crazy dream and discovered that by the time you see your friends you've forgotten the details, so you can't have them analyze it for you? Perhaps it's just me (Paula), but when I wake up I can hardly hit the button on my huge, cartoon-like alarm clock, never mind type onto a phone keyboard to write down dream details, but I can just about speak. The following app enables you to use Google speech to text to record your dream.

The first app you'll put together is a simple dream-recorder page using speech to text. To ensure that your dream recorder is kept safe, you'll include a password so that only you can access your speech-to-text notes. As we mentioned earlier, Google Voice is a bit dicey (or maybe it's my accent that it can't understand), so what you say won't always be what appears onscreen. But hey, that could make the dream more interesting!

My Dream Recorder app

PURPOSE OF THIS APP
This app uses the speech-to-text facility to record your dreams. It can only be accessed through a password-protected screen, leading to a dream-recorder screen. To create this app, make sure you have a device to test it (emulator doesn't support two screens). And note that you need to be online to use speech recognition.

APP RATING
3

ASSETS YOU'LL NEED
Cloud image background.

My Dream Recorder			
Screen1 properties	**BackgroundImage**: Cloud.png **Icon**: Cloud.png **Title**: My Dream Recorder		
Components	**What do I rename it?**	**What does it do?**	**What properties do I set?**
TextBox	**Passwordtextbox1**	Enables the user to input a password secretly	**BackgroundColor**: Cyan **FontSize**: 20 **TextColor**: Blue **Width**: 100 pixels **Hint**: "Input your password"
Button	**SubmitButton**	Enables the user to submit their typed-in password	**BackgroundColor**: Blue **FontSize**: 14 **Shape**: Rounded **Text**: "Submit Password" **TextColor**: Yellow **Width**: 100 pixels **Height**: 50 pixels
Notifier	**Wrongpassword-notifier**		

My Dream Recorder			
Screen2 properties	`Backgroundcolor:` Cyan `Title:` Dreamscreen		
Components	**What do I rename it?**	**What does it do?**	**What properties do I set?**
`Button`	`DreamButton`	Opens `SpeechRecognizer`	`BackgroundColor:` Blue `FontSize:` 20 `Text:` "Tell me your dream" `Text` color: Cyan
`Label`	`Dreamdescription`		`FontSize:` 14 `Text:` "When you speak your dream description will be here"
`Speech-Recognizer` Palette group: Media	`SpeechRecognizer1`	Accesses Google Voice to record your words and convert them to text	
`TinyDB` Palette group: Storage	`TinyDB1`	Stores the dream notes	
Media files			
1 file downloaded from our website: Cloud.png			

NOTE

This is the first time you've used two screens in an app, and it does make a difference in how you put the app together. It makes sense to first create the password-protected screen, next complete the blocks for that screen, then add the **Dreamscreen** and complete its blocks, and finally test the whole thing on a phone. You can toggle between the two screens from the Designer, which then changes the blocks in the editor.

Once you've set up the user interface, you can get down to the nuts and bolts of how the app works. You start by putting together the blocks for **Screen1** (which is effectively a password interface to access **Dreamscreen**). So, first you need to define the password: you'll check the password and either open the **Dreamscreen** or give an error message. Then you need to create **Dreamscreen**.

1. Defining the password

Before you use the password in the programming of this app, you have to define it as a variable as shown here.

1. From Variables, choose an `initialize global name` block, and change the name to `mypassword`.

2. Use a Text block, and type in the password `appinventor`, which becomes the password for the dream recorder.

2. Checking the password and opening the second screen

When the user clicks **SubmitButton**, you want them to access a control event that you can imagine says, "If the password the user has input matches the one you've stored, open **Dreamscreen**. If the password doesn't match the stored password, show an error message that tells the user they have input the wrong password and should try again."

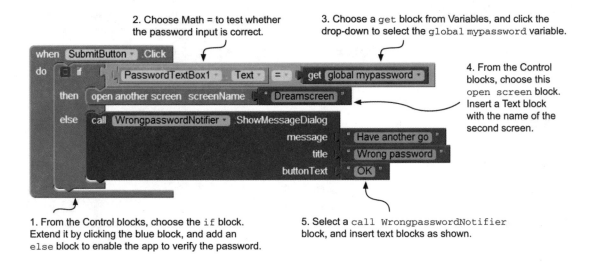

2. Choose Math = to test whether the password input is correct.

3. Choose a `get` block from Variables, and click the drop-down to select the `global mypassword` variable.

4. From the Control blocks, choose this `open screen` block. Insert a Text block with the name of the second screen.

1. From the Control blocks, choose the `if` block. Extend it by clicking the blue block, and add an `else` block to enable the app to verify the password.

5. Select a `call WrongpasswordNotifier` block, and insert text blocks as shown.

In the **open another screen screenName** block, you insert a Text **Dreamscreen** block even before the second screen exists. It's possible to do this because you have to type the name you're going to call the second screen in the text box; then, once the screen exists and the user clicks **SubmitButton**, the app will open the other screen.

3. Adding the second screen

In the App Inventor Designer, when you click the Add Screen button, you're asked to give your new screen a name. Once submitted, it can't be changed, so be careful! Call the added screen **Dreamscreen**. When you've added it, two buttons appear at upper left on your screen in the Designer, with the names of the two screens.

The second screen can be simple: it has a button with the text "Tell me your dream". The text produced by the speech recognizer will appear below the button in a label. Putting this part of the app together means you need to know how to store data in the **TinyDB** database; take a look at the Learning Point "Storing data in TinyDB."

Learning Point: What exactly is a database?

A *database* is a collection of related data that is organized so as to allow quick retrieval of the data. Most apps and programs have a database. Can you think of all the databases you come into contact with every day? Your MP3 playlist, Facebook, your television channels, your running apps, Google, and your phone contacts list are just a few, before you've even gotten to work or school!

Learning Point: Storing data in TinyDB

The introduction of the **TinyDB** component takes things to another level and allows you to store information when the app is closed. Nearly every app or program has a database of some kind that needs to be added to. For example, it could be used to keep track of the highest score for a game.

App Inventor has a great component called **TinyDB** that allows you to use some of the advanced functions of a database without having advanced knowledge. In the My Dream Recorder app, for example, the **TinyDB** component allows you to store some text (your dream description). Then, when you next open the app, the text is still there. This is called *persistent data*—it's obstinate and stays there despite you switching off the app! This is in contrast to non-persistent data, which gives up easily. For example, in the Cheeky Hamster app that you created in chapter 6, as each seed lands in the bowl, you score a point. But even if you run up a huge score, when you reopen the app, the score returns to 0. This is because although you dutifully use a variable to store and add to the score while the app is open, there is nowhere to store it once the app is closed; so the score resets to its default of 0.

USING TINYDB

You don't have to set up a database to use TinyDB, but you do need to add a **TinyDB** component to your interface. It will laze around with the other nonvisible components until you give it a job to do.

TAG-VALUE

In order to use a **TinyDB** component, once you're into the Blocks Editor you have to assign it a tag-value. A *tag-value* is like a variable name, but each piece of data that lives in TinyDB has its own tag-value and stays in your Android device's memory—a variable doesn't. As mentioned earlier, when you quit an app, anything temporarily stored in a variable disappears, but anything stored in TinyDB sticks around. For example, in My Dream Recorder, you need to store the result of the speech recognizer so it's there the next time you open the app.

You could think of the TinyDB database as a table of tag value pairs. The tag is the title of the item to be stored, and the value is the item to be stored.

Tag	Value
Dreamdescription	Result (of the Google Voice recognizer, such as, "Last night I dreamed that my pillow was an enormous marshmallow, and I ate it")

In this case, when you ask TinyDB to retrieve the value associated with the tag **Dreamdescription** it will retrieve the result of the Google Voice recognizer. The tag is always, always, always text, because it's the name of the tag; but the value can be either a single piece of data (image, number, or text) or a list. Once you write over it, it's gone.

This may seem a bit difficult. But after you've seen TinyDB in action in the My Dream Recorder app, you'll practice using it again right away in the Inspiration Scrapbook app, part 2.

Now that you've created the password screen and the second screen, you can get down to the business of using speech recognition. You'll first choose a **DreamButton.click** event handler that calls the **SpeechRecognizer** component, and then you'll set the text box to display the result of the speech recognizer—that is, the text the user has spoken aloud. Almost at the same time, you'll store the text in TinyDB and make sure the next time you open the app, the text (the description of your dream) appears in the text box.

4. Opening the SpeechRecognizer component

Opening the **SpeechRecognizer** component is as simple as activating the **DreamButton.Click** event handler and slotting in the **SpeechRecognizer1.GetText** block.

5. Using the SpeechRecognizer text

After the speech has been recorded by Google Voice, you want the result of that recognition to appear onscreen. The next event handler enables you to take the result of the speech recognizer and do two things: show the text onscreen in **Dreamscreen**, and save it to TinyDB so it's there when you next open the app.

1. Choose SpeechRecognizer1.AfterGettingText.

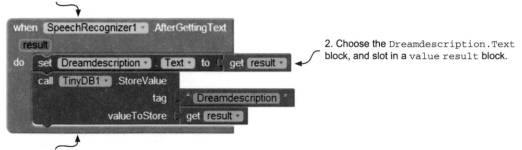

2. Choose the Dreamdescription.Text block, and slot in a value result block.

3. The TinyDB1.StoreValue block lets you store the results of the SpeechRecognizer.

6. Initializing Dreamscreen (or, setting the rules for Dreamscreen)

When you first open the app, it has an empty label in which the text from the `Speech-Recognizer` component appears. In order to make this text available when you reopen the app, you need to set `Dreamdescription.Text` to the contents of the `TinyDB` component, as in the following blocks:

1. Choose the `Dreamscreen.Initialize` block.

2. Choose the `TinyDB1.GetValue` block, and slot in the Text block for `tag Dreamdescription`.

```
when Dreamscreen .Initialize
do  set Dreamdescription . Text to  call TinyDB1 .GetValue
                                              tag  " Dreamdescription "
                                    valueIfTagNotThere  " "
```

Happy dreaming!

Taking it further

1 Extend the My Dream Recorder app so the password is also kept in a TinyDB and can be changed by the user.

2 Add to the My Dream Recorder app so you can record more than one dream per day and browse through them.

Inspiration Scrapbook app, part 1

PURPOSE OF THIS APP
This app is designed to help spur you on when you need some inspiration. The user clicks the photograph of someone who inspires them, and the Android voice reads a quotation from that person.

APP RATING

 3

ASSETS YOU'LL NEED
Images of inspiring people (we chose J.K. Rowling, Nelson Mandela, Michael Jordan, and Oprah Winfrey) and a list of quotations from these people.

Most of you will know who our inspirational people are, but for any of you who don't or who want a refresher, here is a little about each:

- *Nelson Mandela* was South Africa's first black president. He is a peacemaker who strove to abolish apartheid in South Africa after being imprisoned for 27 years for planning to sabotage the then government. He won the Nobel Peace Prize in 1993 and has become a symbol of determination and forgiveness.
- *Oprah Winfrey* is an American talk-show host, an actress, a business woman, and the founder and supporter of many charities. She has overcome many difficulties to become one of the most successful and influential women of the 21st century.
- *Michael Jordan* is an American former professional basketball player, a hugely successful entrepreneur, and a contributor to many charities.
- *J.K. Rowling* is the British author of the hugely popular Harry Potter series of books. They're the best-selling books in history, and the resulting movies are the highest-grossing film series in history. She overcame poverty as a single parent and within five years became a millionaire.

Inspiration Scrapbook			
Screen1 properties	**BackgroundColor**: Black **Scrollable**: Yes (selected) **Title**: Inspiration Scrapbook **Icon**: Mandela.png		
Components	**What do I rename it?**	**What does it do?**	**What properties do I set?**
Horizontal-Arrangement	**Horizontal-Arrangement1**	Houses the title button so you can position the button in the center	**AlignHorizontal**: Center **Width**: Fill Parent
Button	**Inspiration-TitleButton**	Displays the title, and reads out a message when clicked	**Picture**: Inspiration.png
TableScreen-Arrangement	**TableScreen-Arrangement1**	Allows you to position the buttons in a table form	**Columns**: 2 **Rows**: 2
4 **Buttons**	**Mandelabutton** **Oprahbutton** **MJordanbutton** **JKRowlingbutton**	When clicked, each button accesses a list of quotes from the corresponding inspirational person	**Image**: Nelsonmandela.png, Oprahwinfrey.png, MichaelJordan.png, and JKRowling.png
TextToSpeech Palette group: Media	**TextToSpeech1**	Transforms the text from the quotes into speech that you can hear	

Media files
6 files downloaded from our website:

NelsonMandela.png
OprahWinfrey.png
MichaelJordan.png
JKRowling.png
Inspiration.png
Quotes.doc

The text file contains a table with all the quotes so you can cut and paste to save time! Inspiration.png is a graffiti-style image to use in the title button.

On the companion website, we have placed three quotes per person. Here are a few examples:

Person	Quotation
Nelson Mandela	"It always seems impossible until it's done."
Oprah Winfrey	"Real integrity is doing the right thing, knowing that nobody is going to know whether you did it or not."
Michael Jordan	"I've failed over and over and over again in my life and that is why I succeed."
J.K. Rowling	"If you want to see the true measure of a man, watch how he treats his inferiors, not his equals."

This app is relatively simple but effective. If you follow the guidelines in the properties table and the images of the interface, you'll produce a very personalized and enjoyable app. We imagine it being used this way: when you need a bit of inspiration, you can click a photograph once and enjoy the random quote that is read out. Having the quote be randomly accessed leaves an element of chance and will give the user a feeling of serendipity if the quote suits their particular situation.

Learning Point: Choosing how your app will sound

If the default Android voice sounds too much like your bossy gym coach, you can adjust it on your phone. To access the optional defaults, go to Settings > Language & Input > Text-To-Speech Output, click the gear icon next to Google Text To Speech, and then click Language on the settings screen. If you want to see illustrated instructions, go to www.wikihow.com/Change-the-Android-Voice.

When digging around trying to figure out how to do this, we found a very funny American thread in which the contributors agreed that mobile devices should have UK voices because they sound more natural and make the users feel like secret agents receiving instructions. We prefer a friendly female American voice, making the text sound more like a suggestion than a command.

Learning Point: Who inspires you?

Don't forget, these are people *we* find inspirational. You may be inspired by other people. Customize this app for yourself. A good site for quotes is www.brainyquote.com. You can search by name or topic area, such as motivational quotes, quotes about love, and quotes about education.

For this app, you're using the **TextToSpeech** component. First you need to create an event handler that responds to the user clicking a button to read out a message. Then you'll define a variable that becomes the list of quotes. Next you'll insert the quotes into the list and add a quote button so that when the user clicks it, a random quote is selected from the list.

1. Inserting the title button

When users open the app, they might be puzzled about what it does. So, the title is created to look like a button. The following blocks activate a text button that reads out an inviting message:

1. From `InspirationtitleButton`, select the `Click` event handler and insert the `TextToSpeech1.Speak message` block.

2. Select Text, and type in a welcoming message to help the user.

2. Defining the list variable

Depending on how many inspirational people you put in your app, you'll need to repeat this process a number of times. The following example is for the Nelson Mandela list.

Before you establish your list, you have to define a variable. Go to the **variable** block, click the word *variable*, and change it to **Nelsonquotes**.

Now set up your quote list. The **call make a list** block is in the Built-in > Lists drawer. Insert Text blocks, and type in the quotes.

1. Create a variable called `Nelsonquotes`.

2. From the Lists blocks, choose `make a list`, and insert three text boxes.

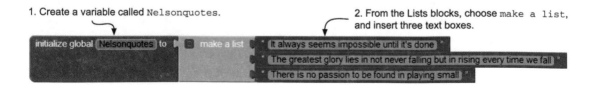

3. Adding the quote button

You want the Nelson Mandela quotes to be read out when the Nelson Mandela photograph button is clicked.

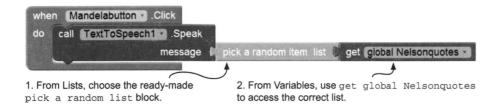

1. From Lists, choose the ready-made `pick a random list` block.

2. From Variables, use `get global Nelsonquotes` to access the correct list.

Inspiration Scrapbook app, part 2

PURPOSE OF THIS APP

This app takes Inspiration Scrapbook, part 1 to another, more inter-active level. You keep your two favorite inspirational photographs and lists of quotations but replace the other two with the ability to take a photograph of someone who inspires you and insert quotes from them.

APP RATING

4

ASSETS YOU'LL NEED

Images of inspiring people (for this part of the app, we're going to introduce you to a couple of giants of the computing world).

Learning Point:
Tim Berners-Lee

Tim Berners-Lee is a British computer scientist who is said to be the inventor of the World Wide Web. Marissa Mayer is an American computer scientist who was a computer engineer for Google and is now the Chief Executive Officer (CEO) of Yahoo.

Person	Quotation
Marissa Mayer	"I always did something I was a little not ready to do. I think that's how you grow. When there's that moment of 'Wow, I'm not really sure I can do this,' and you push through those moments, that's when you have a breakthrough."
Tim Berners-Lee	"Anyone who has lost track of time when using a computer knows the propensity to dream, the urge to make dreams come true and the tendency to miss lunch."

NOTE

Don't forget, this app only works with an Android device that has a camera. You can put it together on your PC, but testing will need to be done on the phone.

In case you're coming straight to part 2, we have included the entire design table for you to follow. Brace yourself: there are a few new concepts to learn as you put together part 2.

Inspiration Scrapbook, part 2			
Screen1 properties	`BackgroundColor`: Black `Scrollable`: Yes (selected) `Title`: Inspiration Scrapbook Part 2 `Icon`: Inspiration.png		
Components	**What do I rename it?**	**What does it do?**	**What properties do I set?**
`Horizontal-Arrangement`	`Horizontal-Arrangement1`	Houses the title button so you can position the button in the center	`AlignHorizontal`: Center `Width`: Fill Parent
`TableScreen-Arrangement`	`TableScreen-Arrangement1`	Allows you to position the buttons in a table form	`Columns`: 2 `Rows`: 3
`Image`	`Title`	Displays the title	`Picture`: Inspiration.png
2 `Buttons`	`Mayerbutton` `BernersLeebutton`	When clicked, each button accesses a list of quotes from the corresponding inspirational person	`Image`: Mayer.png, Berners-Lee.png
`TextToSpeech` Palette group: Media	`TextToSpeech1`	Transforms the text from the quotes into speech that you can hear	
`TextBox`	`Submitquotetext-box`	Enables the user to type in quotation text of their choosing	`FontSize`: 14 `Hint`: "Insert quote text for your personalized quotations and click Submit quote ==>"

Components	What do I rename it?	What does it do?	What properties do I set?
Button	Submitquotebutton	Sends the text from the text box to TinyDB (database)	**BackgroundColor**: Orange **Font**: 14 **Text**: "Submit quote"
Button	Takepicturebutton	Opens the phone's camera to enable the user to take a picture	**BackgroundColor**: Orange **Font**: 14 **Text**: "Take picture"
Button	Ownpicturebutton	When clicked, reads out a message	**Image**: Yourpicturehere.png
Camera Palette group: Media	Camera1	Permits the user to take a picture	
TinyDB Palette group: Storage	QuotesTinyDB	Stores the user's quote	
TinyDB Palette group: Storage	PhotoTinyDB	Stores the user's database	

Media files

5 files downloaded from our website:

> Mayer.png
> BernersLee.png
> Inspiration.png
> Yourpicturehere.png
> Quotes.doc

The first two are photographs of the inspirational people. The text file contains a table with all the quotes so you can cut and paste to save time! Inspiration.png is a graffiti-style image to use in the title, and Yourpicturehere.png is a graffiti-style image to use as a placeholder for the photograph the user takes.

Do steps 1–3 from the Inspiration Scrapbook, part 1 section. Then start here with step 4 to adapt the app.

You need to add a button to enable the user to store the submitted quote and then take a picture of their own inspirational person using the **Camera** component. Next, you'll send the picture produced by the camera to TinyDB. The last bit checks whether the user has already added a quote and a photo before reading out or displaying the result.

4. Storing the text from the text box in TinyDB

To store the text from the text box, you have to create a tag for **QuotesTinyDB**. You want this event to be triggered by the user clicking **Submitquotebutton**. Then it's just a case of choosing the **StoreValue** block, giving the tag a name, and saying what will be stored in the tag—in this case, the text the user inputs into **Submitquotetextbox**.

1. Use the call `QuotesTinyDB.StoreValue` block to store the quote the user submits.

2. This is where you assign a name to the tag. Call it `Ownquote` by inserting a text box with `Ownquote` typed in it. Then choose the `Text` block from `Submitquotetextbox` drawer to store the text the user enters in the text box.

5. Taking the photograph

This is the first time you've used the camera as part of an app, so it's worth explaining a little about using the **Camera** component. You use **Takepicturebutton** to take the picture with the app. You then slot in the

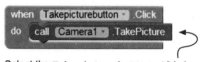

Select the `Takepicturebutton.Click` event handler, and insert the call `Camera1.TakePicture` event.

Camera1.TakePicture block, which instructs the app to take a picture. In this app, this gets you as far as opening the camera—the user has to click the "shutter" and save the picture.

6. Submitting the photo taken with the camera to TinyDB

But where does the picture go? Well, once you use the **Camera1.AfterPicture** event handler, you'll see that **image** is available as a variable. Click it, and choose to **get** the image.

Now you want to move it to **PhotoTinyDB**. You also want to resize it, because the user's camera may well take a photo in the range of 2048 x 1536 pixels, which is massive. The space you allocate on the screen for the photo is 100 x 100 pixels.

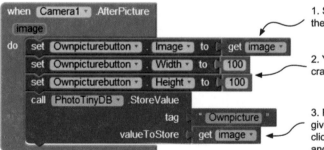

1. Set the `Ownpicturebutton` image to become the value `image` (which will be sent to TinyDB).

2. You need to resize the photo, or it will look crazy. Set both `Width` and `Height` to 100.

3. Follow the same procedure as before: give `PhotoTinyDB` a tag of `Ownpicture`, click `image` in the event handler, and then click `get image`.

Learning Point: Megapixels

Previously we've looked at pixels—but cameras are often described as having *megapixels* (for example, 3.2 megapixels). A megapixel is roughly 1 million pixels (1,048,576, to be precise). Don't forget that this is the total number of pixels in the image, so an image taken with a 3.2 megapixel camera produces an image with the dimensions 2048 x 1536: 3,145,728. You multiply the width by the height of the image to get the total number of pixels; round down and divide by a million to get the answer in more manageable megapixels.

---

7. Activating Ownpicturebutton

One lovely feature of this app is that it's very personalizable. The next feature allows the user to hear their own quote read aloud when the photo button is clicked. It first checks whether there is anything in the **QuotesTinyDB** and, if there isn't, reads aloud a standard message to encourage the user to take a photo and add a quote.

1. Choose the Ownpicturebutton.Click event handler, and insert an if ... then block from the Control blocks.

2. Using a Math > 0 block, check the length of the value in QuotesTinyDB to find out if there is data in QuotesTinyDB.

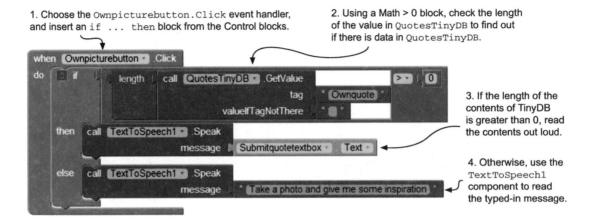

3. If the length of the contents of TinyDB is greater than 0, read the contents out loud.

4. Otherwise, use the TextToSpeech1 component to read the typed-in message.

8. Understanding how to check TinyDB

Often when you're dealing with variables and databases in a program you want to check whether there is anything in the database or variable. In this case, when the user first opens the app, the button that becomes the photograph needs to do something to prompt the user to use the app, and the text box needs to contain a hint to encourage the user to submit a quote. Following is a table that describes the functions of these features, depending on whether the user has just opened the app or is already using it.

Feature	What is the user doing?	What do you want it to look like?	What do you want it to do?
Text box	Just opened the app for the first time	An inviting greyed-out text box	Contain the hint "Insert quote text"
Text box	Has input a quote	The text of the user's quote	Hold the text until it's submitted to TinyDB, and then display it
Your Picture Here button	Just opened the app for the first time	An inviting button	Read out the message "Take a photo and give me some inspiration"
Your Picture Here button	Has taken a photo	A 100 x 100 image taken by the user	Read out the quote that the user has input

You can see that the function of the text box and the Your Picture Here button changes once the user has submitted the quote and the photo to the respective TinyDBs. This is important, because you need the app to check whether anything is in the TinyDBs before deciding what to display or do.

When the app starts, you want to set the rules for it (this is called *initializing* it) to make sure everything is working correctly. You need to check whether the tag-values in the TinyDBs are 0 (whether there is nothing in them).

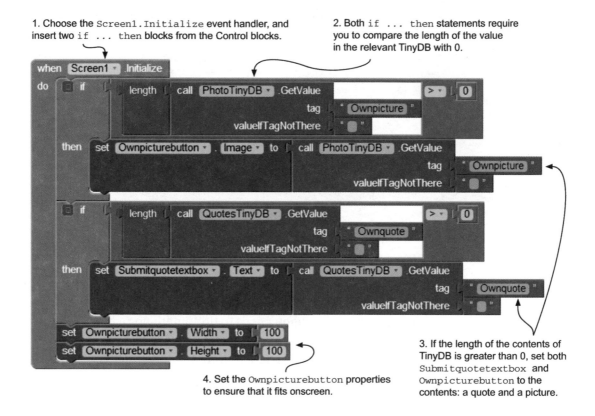

1. Choose the `Screen1.Initialize` event handler, and insert two `if ... then` blocks from the Control blocks.

2. Both `if ... then` statements require you to compare the length of the value in the relevant TinyDB with 0.

3. If the length of the contents of TinyDB is greater than 0, set both `Submitquotetextbox` and `Ownpicturebutton` to the contents: a quote and a picture.

4. Set the `Ownpicturebutton` properties to ensure that it fits onscreen.

Your users will enjoy being able to personalize the app using inspirational people from their own lives. By learning how to take words and pictures that are input by the user and add them to a database (TinyDB), you're able to create something individual for each user.

Taking it further

1 Completely redesign the interface of the Inspiration Scrapbook app. Change the buttons, change the inspirational people, and tailor it to make it your own.

2 Create an Inspiration Scrapbook app for a friend or relative, choosing people who inspire them and including a photo of yourself saying something encouraging. Then email it to them to install on their Android device!

3   Try combining what you've learned in My Dream Recorder and Inspiration Scrapbook, part 2, to develop an app that requires the user to input their inspirational quotes orally rather than typing them in.

4   See if you can figure out how to extend Inspiration Scrapbook, part 2 to create a list of new quotes from the user to be randomly read out rather than just one quote.

5   Use your knowledge (gained from previous chapters) to add an index to Inspiration Scrapbook to enable the user to listen to each quote in turn rather than being given a random one.

6   Create a Don't Bug Me, I'm Studying app that sends a message telling the texter when you'll be free to respond. It should also read out texts to save you from trying to multitask while ensuring that you don't miss any essential gossip that might need an instant follow-up.

What did you learn?

In this chapter, you learned the following:

- How to use a second screen in your app
- How to password-protect apps
- How to use the **TextToSpeech** component
- How to use the **SpeechRecognizer** component
- What TinyDB does
- About tag pairs used in TinyDB
- How to use the **Camera** component

Test your knowledge

1   If you don't want someone to see what you're typing, what type of text box do you use?

2   What can't you do to the name of a screen once you've created it?

3   How do you reference one screen in the blocks of another?

4   Why don't you need an index with the lists for the Inspiration Scrapbook app?

5   What type of data can be stored in TinyDB?

6   What type of data does the tag name always have to be?

7   What did you dream last night? I dreamed that this book was the wallpaper of my bedroom and that I was sleeping inside a sleeping bag made out of the pages of the book. Analyze that!

CHAPTER 12

Web-enabled apps

You've already seen that App Inventor lets you connect with other people using text messages (see chapter 6). In this chapter, we'll look at other tools that let you send and receive information, this time using the internet. You'll see how you can show pages from websites, read information from online sources, and store data in the cloud using the **WebDB** component.

You'll need a data connection to use these features on your phone—so that means either a Wi-Fi connection or a phone network data connection. Most people pay (or have a monthly data allowance) for their phone's data connection, so we suggest using Wi-Fi while you're playing with these features—and if you're using a data connection, please check with whoever pays the phone bill first. We've tried to use examples of websites and services that will be around for a while, but it's always possible that a service will change or disappear. If that happens, let us know on the Manning online forum for this book.

You'll start by looking at how each of the components works with some simple examples. We'll also make suggestions about how you could use these features in the apps you've already created.

Browsing the web

App Inventor offers two options for viewing the World Wide Web:

1 **WebViewer** *component*—This option displays web pages in your app. The **WebViewer** uses a mini browser that is part of App Inventor. It doesn't have lots of functions like you might be used to in Chrome, Firefox, Safari, or any of the many other browsers

you can use. But it's fine if all you want to do is browse and navigate some web pages.

2 **ActivityStarter** *component*—This option jumps out of your app and displays web pages in a web browser installed on your phone. Using **ActivityStarter** allows the user to view the web page in whichever app they choose, so they get all the functions they're used to. It's also possible for you to provide no choice of app and to specify exactly which app should be used—but if the user doesn't have the app on their phone, it may cause an error (so we don't recommend doing that). The user returns to your app by quitting the web browser app.

The advantage of the **WebViewer** component is that it's simple and your app stays in control of the screen—the user isn't going to get lost in other apps that are open. The advantage of the **ActivityStarter** component is that the user can choose the web browser app that they're most used to—and it will have more features than the **WebViewer**, such as the ability to bookmark a web page.

Let's take a look at the two options in practice.

Using WebViewer

To set up the components for a **WebViewer** test, follow these steps:

1 Set up a new app, and call it **TestWebViewer**.

2 Set **Screen1.Title** to "WebViewer Example" and **Screen1.ScreenOrientation** to Landscape.

3 Add a **HorizontalArrangement** with five buttons, as shown :

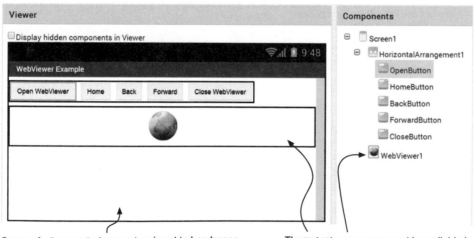

Screen1 ScreenOrientation is set to Landscape to make it easier to read web pages.

The **WebViewer** component is available in the User Interface section of the Palette.

4   Add a `WebViewer` component from the Palette's User Interface section.

5   Set `WebViewer1`'s properties as shown. In addition, set `WebViewer1`'s `Width` and `Height` properties to Automatic.

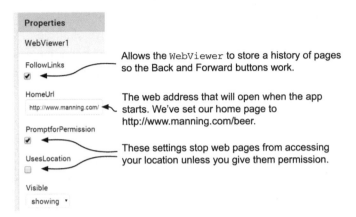

You've finished the basic user interface for a web browser. You could improve it by, for example, including a text box where the user could type their own web address (URL). But it's unlikely that a user would choose to use the App Inventor `WebViewer` for casual browsing; it's better suited to providing a specific link to a web page you direct the user to. For example, you could

- Provide additional information for a game you've made, such as help, hints, and tips
- Link to the Google Play Store, where you might have other games for sale
- Set up an online survey to find out what users think of an app (for example, using Google Docs or SurveyMonkey)

Learning Point: Uniform Resource Locator (URL)

The correct computer science name for a web address is a *uniform resource locator* or *URL*. A URL like http://www.manning.com/beer contains three elements:

- http:// stands for *HyperText Transfer Protocol* and means you'll be viewing web pages with hypertext—or web pages with links.
- www.manning.com is the *domain name*—a unique address of a computer that you want to access (the .com tells you it's a company).
- /beer/ is the *pathname* of the file you want to view, just like the directories on your computer at home.

When a URL ends in a filename like /instructions.html, that file is retrieved. If the address ends in a forward slash (/), the app looks for a file called index.html in that pathname.

If you preview the app, you'll see the web page for this book appear on your screen—and you can navigate between pages by clicking hyperlinks. But the buttons you made don't do anything yet. Add the code blocks for the buttons as shown next. As you can see, the **Web-Viewer** includes ready-made functions for browsing, which makes it easy to code the navigation buttons:

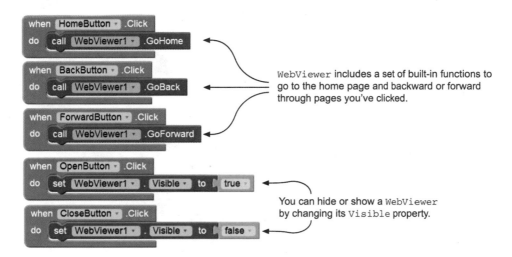

WebViewer includes a set of built-in functions to go to the home page and backward or forward through pages you've clicked.

You can hide or show a WebViewer by changing its Visible property.

Here's how the app looks on a phone. You can pinch with two fingers to zoom in and out of the web page:

There are a couple of limitations to the browsing experience:

- The buttons scroll with the web page—so if you want to use them, you have to scroll back to the top of the screen.
- If the user presses the phone's Back button (rather than the Back button you've created), the app quits. There is a workaround for this in chapter 14—see the Zombie Alarm app.

It's also possible to change the current web page in the blocks using the **GoToUrl** block. In the example, we've

set the web page to the App Inventor home page by hard-coding the web address into a text block. You could just as easily include a text box in the app as an address bar and use whatever the user types into it as the input for **WebViewer1.GoToUrl**. Now let's look at the more flexible **ActivityStarter** component.

Using ActivityStarter

To set up the components for an **ActivityStarter** test, follow these steps:

1. Set up a new app, and call it **TestActivityStarter**.
2. Set **Screen1.Title** to "ActivityStarter Web Browser Example".
3. Add a **Button**, an **ActivityStarter** (from the Connectivity Palette group), and a **Notifier** (from the User Interface Palette group).
4. Set the **ActivityStarter** properties as shown next.

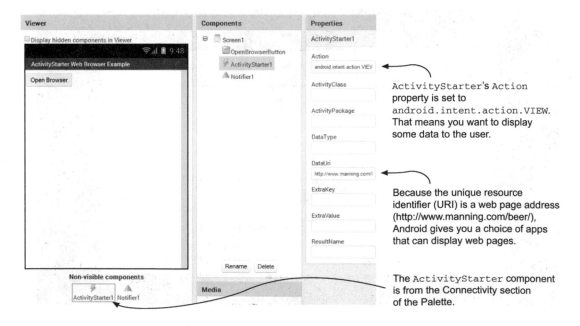

To activate the **ActivityStarter**, you use the block **call ActivityStarter1.StartActivity**. You could do that from the **OpenBrowserButton.Click** event, like this.

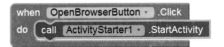

But you're about to take the user out of your app and into their browser, so you add the **Notifier** to provide a warning and tell them how to return to your app once they're finished. Here's how the sequence will work:

1. The user clicks Open Browser, triggering …

2. … the Notifier, which checks that the user wants to open the browser and tells them how to get back to this app.

3. Clicking OK presents a list of apps that can open web pages if you have more than one browser installed.

4. The browser opens. Clicking the phone's Back button returns the user to the app (step 1).

From this sequence, you can work out that the **Button.Click** event opens the **Notifier**, and then the **Notifier.AfterChoosing** event triggers the **ActivityStarter**. Here are the blocks:

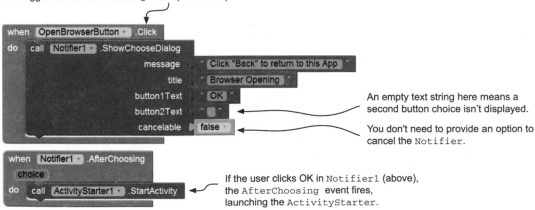

The button Click event triggers the Notifier. You need to use a ShowChooseDialog notifier so you can trigger the AfterChoosing event (see below).

An empty text string here means a second button choice isn't displayed.

You don't need to provide an option to cancel the Notifier.

If the user clicks OK in Notifier1 (above), the AfterChoosing event fires, launching the ActivityStarter.

Your app should now launch a web browser successfully—give it a try. `ActivityStarter` is versatile and can launch other apps such as the camera, Google Maps, and even other apps you've written. Also, if you enter a URL to a specific resource related to an app, Android will present more options in the app list. For example, if you have the YouTube app installed and you use a YouTube URL, then you'll have the option to view the video in your browser or YouTube app. There's full documentation about how to do this on MIT's App Inventor website here: http://mng.bz/0x89.

Using data from the web

`WebViewer` and `ActivityStarter` can help you access whole web pages, but what if you just want to extract some data from the web to use in your app? Maybe you want to know the temperature forecast at a location for a fashion app that gives you options for what to wear that day. Lots of web services out there provide this kind of data in machine-readable form that an app can use, as well as in human-readable web pages. For example, lots of weather sites provide web pages of weather forecasts and maps—but if you know how, you can access the data directly and use it in your own apps.

You can access this data using an *application programming interface* (API). You can think about it this way: when you request a web-page weather forecast, you're asking for text, graphics, links, maps, and so on, all neatly packaged in a nice, easy-to-read format (you hope). When you request weather data via an API, you're saying, "Just give me the data—I don't want all that other fancy stuff! I want temperatures, wind speed, atmospheric pressure, cloud cover, and those kinds of things." When you request data like this, we say that you're making an *API call*. There are lists of publicly available APIs, such as that at www.programmableweb.com.

API keys

Most public APIs ask you to apply for a key to use the API—you provide an email and some other details, and you get a *key* (which is actually a code) sent back. You don't have to do this for web-page browsing—so what's the difference? When you request a web page, it's sent to your machine, and then you spend some time reading it before you ask for the next page. This doesn't put much strain on the web servers (the computers that hold the web pages). With APIs, you're using a computer (smartphone) to request data—and computers can make lots of requests quickly. If your computer got stuck in a loop and made too many requests too quickly, the web server might crash. An API key limits the number of requests any one computer can make in a certain time, so you can't crash the servers.

Weather Watch app

PURPOSE OF THIS APP

World Weather Online is a business that provides weather forecast information. You're going to use their free local weather API to tell the user today's weather forecast for any town or city.

APP RATING

4

ASSETS YOU'LL NEED

You'll need to create a World Weather Account and request a key. We'll tell you how.

WeatherWatch			
Screen1 properties	`Title`: Weather Watch		
Components	**What do I rename it?**	**What does it do?**	**What properties do I set?**
TextBox Palette group: User Interface	`LocationTextBox`	Where the user enters the location for the weather forecast	`Hint`: "Enter a location."
Button	`GetWeatherButton`	Starts the API call	`Text`: "Click for weather"
Label	`WeatherLabel`	Displays the weather forecast description	`Text`: "Today the weather will be…"
Label	`RainfallLabel`	Displays the rainfall in mm	`Text`: "Rainfall –"
Label	`FarenheitLabel`	Displays the maximum and minimum temperatures in farenheit	`Text`: "Farenheit –"
Label	`CelsiusLabel`	Displays the maximum and minimum temperatures in celsius	`Text`: "Celsius –"
ListPicker	`WeatherList-Picker`	Helps you test the app by showing all the weather data in a single list	`Text`: "List of all weather data"
Label	`WWOLabel`	States an attribution to the World Weather Online service. This is a legal requirement	`Text`: "Powered by World Weather Online"
Web Palette group: Connectivity	`Web1`	A non-visible component that provides functions for accessing web pages and services	Default

1. Request an API key

First head to www.worldweatheronline.com and register for an account. Sign in, and request an API key for the Free Local Weather API. At the time of writing, you can do all this directly from www.worldweatheronline.com/free-weather-feed.aspx. The key will be a string of 24 characters. In the examples that follow, always make sure you're using your key.

2. Work out the API call

World Weather Online lets you try out API calls from your browser using your key. This is really helpful for a beginner. Head to this page: https://developer.worldweatheronline.com/page/explorer-free.

Enter your 24-character API key in this text box.

Click the Get Local Weather link, which lets you access weather forecast data for a specific location.

A window opens where you can change lots of API options. There's an explanation of each option on the right side of the page. Under the options, you can see the API call (which looks like a web address) and an example of the data that would be returned.

In the app, the user will set the location using a text box, but for now you'll pick a city name to see how it works. We chose Orlando because it's a unique city name (and it makes us think of summer holidays). After some experimentation, we figured out the best way to format the output so that App Inventor can handle the data easily (there are lots of other ways to do it). The table on the next page lists the parameters you need to set.

Setting the API values tells World Weather Online what data you want and how you would like it formatted. In this API, only the top two values are mandatory (location and output format); everything else is optional.

Clicking the Try It button makes an API call and runs it. You can see the results below. You can also copy and paste this API call into a regular browser window to test it.

You can ignore the Response Code and Response Headers at this stage.

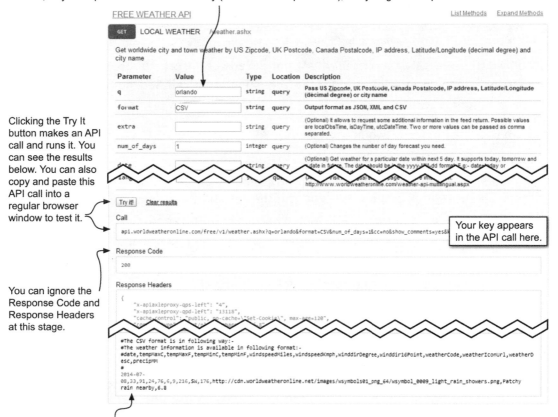

The Response Body shows you the data that the API call will produce.
The comments at the top that start with a # explain the order of the data below.

Parameter	Value	Explanation
Q	Orlando	The weather forecast location.
format	CSV	Comma-separated values. The data will be output as a long string of text with a comma between the data items. App Inventor has some handy blocks that can automatically turn this into a list.
num_of_days	1	Gives you a forecast just for today. Increasing the value gives you multiple forecasts (one for each day).
cc	No	When set to Yes, gives you the weather right now as well as the forecast. To keep things simple, set it to No.
show_comments	Yes for testing No for the app	Comments help explain the data, which is handy when you're figuring out the API call. Later, when you're ready to use the API call in App Inventor, you'll set this to No to strip out the comments and simplify the data you receive.

If you enter these values and click the Try it! Button, you should see that the API call looks like this:

```
api.worldweatheronline.com/free/v1/weather.ashx?q=orlando&format=
CSV&num_of_days=1&cc=no&show_comments=yes&key= your key goes here
```

The only difference is that you'll see your key at the end of the call. To use the API call, you'll need to include the protocol (http://) at the beginning of the call. See the Learning Point "Uniform Resource Locator (URL)."

You can break the API into two parts:

- *http://api.worldweatheronline.com/free/v1/weather.ashx*—The protocol and domain
- *q=orlando&format=CSV&num_of_days=1&cc=no&show_comments=yes&key= your key goes here*—The API call or query that encodes the options you entered:
  - */?q=orlando*—A query that asks for the weather in Orlando.
  - *&format=CSV*—The format of the results.
  - *&num_of_days=1*—One-day forecast, for today.
  - *&cc=no*—Don't send the current conditions weather data.
  - *&show_comments=yes*—Show additional comments.
  - *&key= your key goes here*—Your API key.

If you run the API in a web browser, here's what you get:

Comments start here.

Data starts here.

You can see that there is lots of weather data. If you can work out how to get the data into App Inventor, you can select the parts you need and display them in an app. You'll give the user a description of the weather (**weatherDesc**), the minimum and maximum temperatures in Celsius (**tempMinC**, **tempMaxC**) and Fahrenheit (**tempMinF**, **tempMaxF**), and the rainfall in mm (**precipMM**).

Now that you know the API call works and understand the data, it's time to switch off the comments in the API call so App Inventor only has to deal with the data. Change **&show_comments=no** so the API call becomes

```
http://api.worldweatheronline.com/free/v1/weather.ashx?q=orlando&format=
CSV&num_of_days=1&cc=no&show_comments=no&key= your key goes here
```

If you put this address into your browser, you'll just see the weather data, like this:

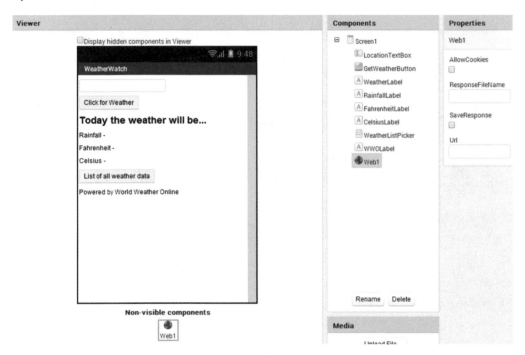

```
2014-07-
08,33,91,24,76,6,9,216,SW,176,http://cdn.worldweatheronline.net/images/wsymbols01_png
_64/wsymbol_0009_light_rain_showers.png,Patchy rain nearby,6.8
```

3. Setting up the screen

Switch to App Inventor, and start a new project called **WeatherWatch**. Here's the screen layout:

You have a new, non-visible **Web** element in the layout. This is what makes the API call to the internet and triggers a **Web.GotText** event when the data arrives back at the phone. You can also see a label that gives credit to World Weather Online for providing the data. This is important, because you can't just claim data as your own; it's only fair and legal to say where it came from. API providers usually tell you in their terms and conditions what you need to do if you use their API. This usually includes the following:

- *Keeping your key private*—It's OK to use it in an app, but don't tell the user what it is.
- *Limiting the number of API calls you make*—World Weather Online asks that you don't exceed 12,000 requests per day.
- *Crediting the API provider*—This generally means a text label, and sometimes a logo and web link.

When the user types a word and clicks **GetWeatherButton**, you make an API call string that follows the Orlando example. You can make the string using a standard Text **join** block. At first we tried this:

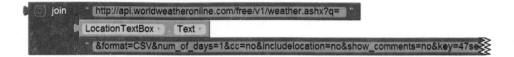

This worked fine for most locations, but if the location was "San Francisco" the app generated an error message. What's the difference between "Orlando" and "San Francisco"? (The answer isn't Mickey Mouse or the Golden Gate Bridge.) San Francisco has a space in the middle, and it turns out that API calls (and web pages) need space characters to be specially encoded. You could do this by hand, but App Inventor has a block that does it for you; just add a **Web1.UriEncode** block like so:

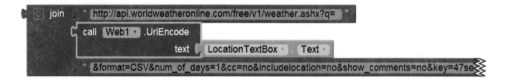

Now you can use the API call string above by setting **Web1**'s **URL** property—that's the address the **Web** component will access. Carrying out the API call is a two-step process:

1 Use a function called **Web.Get** that asks the website at the URL for the data and then waits until something comes back.

2 When **Web1** gets some data, it triggers a **Web.GotText** event. Then you can do something with the data you've received.

It's important to understand that accessing the web has this built-in delay. You ask for something, wait, and then, when it arrives, do something—it's a bit like waiting for a mailman to deliver a parcel before you can do a project. Here are the blocks to make the call:

This Text `join` block makes the API call by adding the location
from `LocationTextBox` into the API query string.

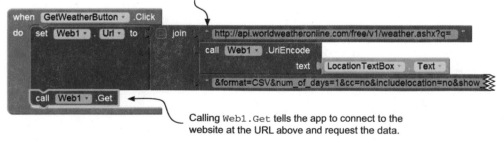

Calling `Web1.Get` tells the app to connect to the
website at the URL above and request the data.

The result of calling **Web1.Get** is a list of the data you saw in your browser. You'll take this list and put it into a list variable called **WeatherList**. Then you can select the items you need. This looks complicated at first, but a little trial and error helps—that's why you added the **ListPicker** at the bottom of the screen, as an easy way to view the data that has been downloaded.

Here are the blocks that take the returned data and store it in an App Inventor list:

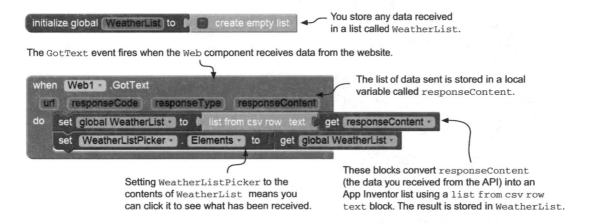

You store any data received in a list called WeatherList.

The GotText event fires when the Web component receives data from the website.

The list of data sent is stored in a local variable called responseContent.

Setting WeatherListPicker to the contents of WeatherList means you can click it to see what has been received.

These blocks convert responseContent (the data you received from the API) into an App Inventor list using a list from csv row text block. The result is stored in WeatherList.

Run the app now:

1 Type a city (we typed *orlando*).
2 Click the Click for Weather button.
3 Click the List of All Weather Data button at the bottom of the screen.

You should see a list like this. Each line in the list is an item of weather data—it looks like it's worked!

Now you just need to select the right elements from the list (description, temperatures, rainfall) and display them in the text labels. Here are the blocks to complete the app:

```
when Web1 .GotText
  url  responseCode  responseType  responseContent
do  set global WeatherList to  list from csv row  text  get responseContent
    set WeatherListPicker . Elements to  get global WeatherList
    set WeatherLabel . Text to  join  " Today the weather is ...\n "
                                      select list item list  get global WeatherList
                                                       index  12
                                      " \n "
    set RainfallLabel . Text to  join  " Rainfall "
                                      select list item list  get global WeatherList
                                                       index  13
                                      " mm\n "
    set FahrenheitLabel . Text to  join  " Fahrenheit - Min: "
                                        select list item list  get global WeatherList
                                                         index  5
                                        " Max: "
                                        select list item list  get global WeatherList
                                                         index  3
    set CelsiusLabel . Text to  join  " Celsius - Min: "
                                     select list item list  get global WeatherList
                                                      index  4
                                     " Max: "
                                     select list item list  get global WeatherList
                                                      index  2
```

These blocks select the data items you want to display from the elements in `WeatherList` (12 = `weatherDesc`, 13 = `precipMM`, 5 = `tempMinF`, 3 = `tempMaxF`, 4 = `tempMinC`, and 2 = `tempMaxC`). The line breaks and explanation text are added to help the user make sense of the data.

Taking it further

1 Display a weather icon: change the image depending on the maximum temperature and rainfall forecast.

2 Use the phone's GPS coordinates (latitude and longitude) as the location for the forecast.

3 Display a different weather icon depending on the weather condition code. See the list here: www.worldweatheronline.com/feed/wwoConditionCodes.txt.

Storing and sharing data in the cloud with TinyWebDB

Your App Inventor apps are stored *in the cloud*, which means they're saved on web servers that are connected to the internet. The advantage of this is that you can access them from any computer without worrying about saving them to flash drives. Of course, you can download them to your own computer, too—and that's always a good idea, just in case those web servers fail. In addition to being able to access your apps and data from any computer or smartphone, cloud access also lets you share things with the world—a Facebook update can be seen by all your friends, for example.

In chapter 11, you saw how you can use the `TinyDB` component to store data on your phone so it's available even after the user has quit the app and restarted it. App Inventor has an almost identical component called `TinyWebDB` that stores data in the same way—but to a web server in the cloud. You'll use it to enhance the My Dream Recorder app so that you can store your most recent dream online—and your friends can read about it using an app called Dream Sharer.

Learning Point:
Staying safe online

The examples you've seen so far involve getting information *from* the internet, but in this app you'll be posting information *to* the internet. Before you do, there are two things you need to know about `TinyWebDB`:

- The information you send and receive over `TinyWebDB` needs a private tag, but don't assume it's secure. Don't post personal details like names, addresses, telephone numbers, or passwords.
- Once you post an item online, you should assume it's there forever as part of your digital footprint. So be nice, and don't post anything you wouldn't want your parents, teachers, or future boss to see!

Limitations of the TinyWebDB test service

For this next app, you're going to use a test service for `TinyWebDB` that is provided by App Inventor. This is the default service for any new app, and it's useful for testing, but it's shared by all App Inventors and only has space for 1,000 entries. Once these are used up, it starts overwriting previous entries. That means if you store data on the service, it might not be there long. But once you're happy that your app works, you can set up your very own `TinyWebDB` service that only you can use. For instructions on how to do this, head over to the App Inventor site and search for "Creating a custom TinyWebDB service"; at the time of writing, the pages were here (but this may change in the future): http://mng.bz/fo9Y.

Dream Sharer app

PURPOSE OF THIS APP
In the My Dream Recorder app, you stored your most recent dream text in your smartphone. The idea in this enhanced version is that your friends can also use My Dream Recorder, and then you can all use a new app called Dream Sharer to see everybody else's dreams, too.

APP RATING

3

ASSETS YOU'LL NEED
None.

In the original version, you stored your dream text in TinyDB with a tag called **Dreamdescription**. That worked fine because you were the only person using it. But if you and all your friends use the same tag online, they will overwrite one another, and you'll only ever be able to retrieve the most recently posted dream. To solve this, you'll first make some modifications to the original My Dream Recorder app by letting each user invent their own username that will then be used to tag their dream:

1   Load the My_Dream_Recorder project (from chapter 11), and save the project as My_Dream_Recorder_Web.

2   Switch to **Dreamscreen**, and add the following objects:

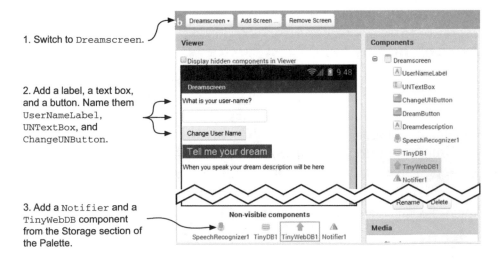

1. Switch to Dreamscreen.

2. Add a label, a text box, and a button. Name them UserNameLabel, UNTextBox, and ChangeUNButton.

3. Add a Notifier and a TinyWebDB component from the Storage section of the Palette.

Retrieving the username and dream

When the user opens the app and enters their password, you want to see if they have already used the My Dream Recorder app on this phone. If they have, you'll retrieve their username so they need not enter it again. Then you'll retrieve the last dream recorded against that username. When **Dreamscreen** is initialized, do this:

1 Read the value of the TinyDB data tagged with **StoredUserName**, and store the result in a variable called **username**.
2 Change the **Text** property of **UNTextBox** to display the username.
3 Dreams are recorded with the **username** tag, so get the value of the TinyDB data tagged with the value of **username**, and display it in **Dreamdescription.Text** (just like you did in the original app—only the tag has changed).

This means if the user has used the app before, their previous username and dream are displayed. If they haven't used the app, they see an empty username text box, and no dream is displayed. Here are the blocks:

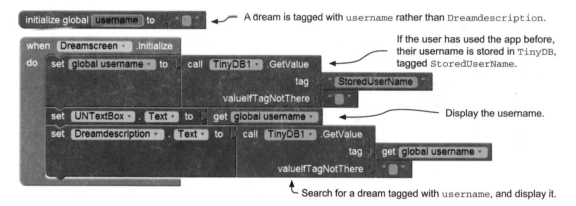

Checking that a username has been entered

In the original app, when the user clicked **DreamButton**, the speech recognizer started up. In this new version, you'll first check that a username has been retrieved or entered (because if there's no username, you have nothing to tag the dream with). To do this, add an additional **if . . . else** block that checks that the username variable isn't empty:

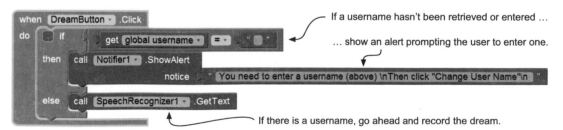

The user can change the username at any time by clicking **ChangeUNButton**. The **username** variable is updated and stored with the TinyDB tag **StoredUserName**. The next time the user accesses the app, this username is automatically retrieved by the **Dreamscreen.Initialize** event.

The final changes to My Dream Recorder are as follows:

1 Change the tag for the stored dream so it can be retrieved using **username**.

2 Add a block to store the dream data to the cloud using **TinyWebDB**.

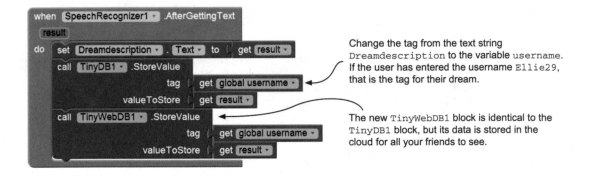

Change the tag from the text string Dreamdescription to the variable username. If the user has entered the username Ellie29, that is the tag for their dream.

The new TinyWebDB1 block is identical to the TinyDB1 block, but its data is stored in the cloud for all your friends to see.

This means if the user records a dream, it's both stored locally on their smartphone *and* uploaded to the **TinyWebDB** server (as long as their phone has an internet connection).

Dream Reader

As the final step, you need to create a simple app to read from the cloud the dream data that your friends have uploaded:

1 Set up a new app, and call it Dream Reader.

2 Set **Screen1.Title** to "Dream Reader".

3 Add the following components:

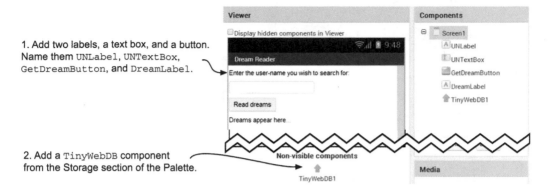

1. Add two labels, a text box, and a button. Name them UNLabel, UNTextBox, GetDreamButton, and DreamLabel.

2. Add a TinyWebDB component from the Storage section of the Palette.

As long as you know your friend's username, you can retrieve the text of their dream from **TinyWebDB**. This is a two-step process, just like with the Weather Watch API:

1 Request the data using a call to **TinyWebDB1.GetValue**. The tag you're searching for is the user-name that the user typed in **UNTextBox**.

2 You wait until some data comes back, and when it does, the **TinyWebDB1.GotValue** event fires. It holds the data retrieved

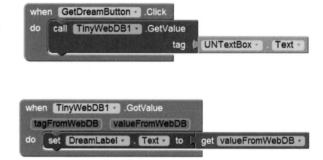

in a local variable called **valueFromWebDB**. You can then do something useful with the data, like display it onscreen in the **Dream-Label** you created.

The two apps should now work together. Use My Dream Recorder to save your dreams to your phone and the web. Use Dream Reader to see your friends' most recent dreams, once you've swapped usernames.

The idea behind this app could also be used to create your own instant-messaging app or even to make simple online games. You could also use **TinyWebDB** to create a shared online high-scores list for a game.

What did you learn?

In this chapter, you learned the following:

- How to display web pages using the **WebViewer** built-in browser or through other apps via the **ActivityStarter**
- The different parts of a uniform resource locator (URL), also called a web address
- That some websites let you access raw or unformatted data using an application program interface (API)
- How to process the results of an API call to extract just the data you need
- That getting data from the web is a two step process—1) request the data, 2) then wait until it's returned—triggering a **GotValue** event
- How to store and retrieve data from the cloud (web servers) using TinyWebDB

Test your knowledge

1. What are the advantages and disadvantages of **WebViewer** versus **ActivityStarter** for accessing web pages?
2. Why do some websites ask you to apply for an API key before you can make an API call?
3. Here's part of an API query from api.worldweatheronline.com. What data do you think it will return?

    ?q=Liverpool&format=json&date=today&key=1234567890

4. For what reasons might a user want to store the same data both locally on their phone *and* in the cloud on a web server?
5. Why is it a good idea to set up your own TinyWebDB service rather than use App Inventor's test service?

Try it out

1. Create a webquest that takes users on a tour of websites about a single topic, such as Atlantis.
2. Create a quiz where the questions have hints that are linked to helpful websites.
3. Try using ActivityStarter to open different sorts of web-based applications like Youtube videos, Facebook, or Twitter.
4. Browse the list of public APIs on www.programmableweb.com. Apply for a key for an API that looks interesting, and then write an app to access the data.
5. Try writing a simple multiplayer text-based, two-player game using TinyWebDB, for example Hangman or Battleship.

CHAPTER 13

Location-aware apps

In this chapter, we'll be looking at the fascinating subject of how your phone knows where it is, what you might want to do with that information, and how you would use this in an app.

Perhaps you already know that a global positioning system (GPS) has something to do with satellites and location. In fact, GPS is a system of 24 satellites that orbit at a speed of 3.9 km per second, sending out a signal of their position. You can "see" at least four of these satellites from anywhere on Earth. Your phone uses their signals alongside a lot of math to work out your precise location. In this chapter, we'll explain how you can use GPS data to show latitude, longitude, and even street addresses.

The GPS system was first used by the US Navy and went on to be used by other members of the international armed forces as well as emergency services and then civil engineers to enable them to measure geographical areas more precisely. Of course, now every new mobile phone has the ability to access GPS, which (among other things) can be used for fun stuff like getting to know a new city using suggested information and images from the internet (such as apps like Layar and Around Me), or using a GPS-enabled exercise app to track your cycle rides or runs and see if you're getting fitter and faster (apps like MapMyRide and Nike+).

Your phone contains a location sensor that can determine your latitude, your longitude, and where you are. The App Inventor component called `LocationSensor` (in the Sensors Palette group) lets you use the information picked up by the phone's location sensor.

In this chapter, you'll design two adventurous apps using GPS technology.

Learning Point: Latitude and longitude

The globe of course is round(ish!), so to pinpoint exactly where we are on Earth, a system was developed that measures how far up you are (latitude) and how far around you are (longitude). The zero line for latitude is an imaginary line called the *equator* that runs around the "center" of the Earth. As you get closer to the North Pole, you have a bigger and bigger positive latitude (up to 180); and as you get closer to the South Pole, you have a bigger and bigger negative latitude (to -180).

The zero line for longitude is in Greenwich (near London, England). As you head east from Greenwich, the longitude goes from 0 to 180; and as you head west, it goes negative as far as -180.

All other coordinates are measured in relation to these two fixed points. A good way to remember which way around these are is that "LA"titude is the vertical one, like "AL"titude.

The following diagram shows a flattened-out globe that gives a rough approximation of the latitude and longitude of all places. What is the location with 0 latitude and 0 longitude? Can you estimate the latitude and longitude of where you live? When you make the following app and find out your exact latitude and longitude, you can check if you were right.

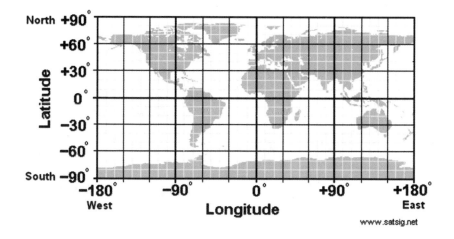

www.satsig.net

Lost & Found app

PURPOSE OF THIS APP
This app lets you find out exactly where you are (latitude, longitude, and address) with the click of a button.

APP RATING

 3

ASSETS YOU'LL NEED
Map image.

Lost & Found			
Screen1 properties	**AlignHorizontal**: Center **AlignVertical**: Center **ScreenOrientation**: Portrait **Scrollable**: Yes (selected) **Title**: Lost & Found **BackgroundColor**: Orange		
Components	**What do I rename it?**	**What does it do?**	**What properties do I set?**
Vertical- Arrangement	Vertical- Arrangement1	Allows you to position the image and labels down the page	
Button	Locationbutton	When clicked, the current location is recalled	**FontSize**: 20 **Text**: "Click twice to find out where you are"
Image	MapImage	Displays a map image	**Picture**: foldedmap.png
6 Labels	Addresslabel Addressdatalabel Latitudelabel Latitudedatalabel Longitudelabel Longitudedatalabel	Displays **Text** Displays the address Displays **Text** Displays the latitude Displays **Text** Displays the Longitude	**Text**: "Address" **Text**: "Address will appear here" **Text**: "Latitude" **Text**: "Latitude will appear here" **Text**: "Longitude" **Text**: "Longitude will appear here"
LocationSensor Palette group: Sensors	Locationsensor1	Identifies the current location of the phone	

Media files

1 file downloaded from our website:
   Mapimage.png

If you get the design of the screen right, the Components panel should look like this.

As you aren't storing any data, making any lists, or doing too much, this whole clever little app can be achieved in one event handler. The following single step shows how you get the button's **Click** event handler and call the readings from the location sensor that tell you the address, latitude, and longitude of your location. Job done!

1. Get the `Locationbutton.Click` block.

2. Set the three location labels to the `LocationSensor1.CurrentAddress`, `Latitude`, and `Longitude`, respectively.

This app displays the latitude and longitude using GPS and then finds the street address by connecting to Google Maps online. So, you'll need an internet connection in order to see the address; the latitude and longitude will display even without an internet connection. You need a Wi-Fi or phone internet connection for any location-aware app that uses the current address or links out to Google Maps (like the next two apps).

That's it for this app. GPS apps don't work on the emulator, but you can use it to check how the layout looks; then link the app to your phone and try it.

Learning Point: GPS settings

You need a clear view of the sky to get a reading from the GPS satellites. But if you're indoors and don't have a view of the sky, you can still get a good reading through your Wi-Fi or mobile phone network. Have GPS enabled on your phone, select Use Wireless Networks, and then select from your phone's choices.

Remember that when you started this app, we suggested that you use the grid to estimate your latitude and longitude and then check it with Lost & Found? Were you right? We were close!

Taking it further

Apps can be presents! Why not make the Lost & Found app for someone you know with a photo of them as the image instead of the map?

Homing Pigeon app

PURPOSE OF THIS APP
This app lets you find out exactly where you are (address, latitude and longitude address). Then if you're on a school trip, for example, you can record this meeting point location, go off exploring, and with the press of another button be directed back to a meeting point.

APP RATING

3

ASSETS YOU'LL NEED
Homingpigeonimage.png, foldedmap.png.

This app has quite a few components, but it's worth the effort. We've included a screen shot of the Components Palette that you can use as a great checklist to make sure that once you've put in all the hard work, you get paid back with an app that does something pretty clever!

As we said earlier, GPS apps don't work on the emulator; but while you're designing Homing Pigeon, you can have the emulator open to check that the layout looks right.

Homing Pigeon			
Screen1 properties	**AlignHorizontal**: Center **BackgroundColor**: Cyan **Icon**: Homingpigeonimage.png **Scrollable**: Yes (selected) **Title**: Homing Pigeon		
Components	**What do I rename it?**	**What does it do?**	**What properties do I set?**
Horizontal-Arrangement	Horizontal-Arrangement1	Arranges images	**Width**: Fill Parent
Image	PigeonImage	Shows an image of a pigeon	**Width**: 200 **Height**: 200 **Picture**: Homingpigeon-image.png
Image	MapImage	Shows an image of a map	**Width**: 120 **Height**: 200 **Picture**: Foldedmap.png
Label	CurrentLocation-Label	Displays the section title	**Font**: Bold **FontSize**: 20 **TextAlignment**: Center **Text**: "Current Location" **Width**: Fill Parent **Height**: Fill Parent
Table-Arrangement	TableArrangement1	Arranges the current location results	**Columns**: 4 **Rows**: 2 **Width**: Fill Parent
6 **Label**s	CurrentAddressTitle CurrentGPSLabel CurrentLatLabel CurrentLongLabel CurrentAddressLabel CurrentCommaLabel	Displays **Text** Displays **Text** Displays the latitude Displays the longitude Displays the address Displays **Text**	**Text**: "Address" **Text**: "GPS" **Text**: "0" **Text**: "0" **Text**: "Unknown" **Text**: "," **TextColor**: Blue (for all labels)
Button	RememberCurrent-LocationButton	When clicked, the current location is saved into TinyDB and becomes the remembered location	**FontSize**: 14 **Shape**: Rounded **Text**: "Remember my current location" **TextAlignment**: Center **Width**: Fill Parent **Height**: Fill Parent

Components	What do I rename it?	What does it do?	What properties do I set?
Label	Remlocationlabel	Displays the section title	**FontSize**: 20 **Text**: "Remembered Location" **TextAlignment**: Center **Width**: Fill Parent **Height**: Fill Parent
Table-Arrangement	TableArrangement2	Arranges the remembered location results	**Columns**: 4 **Rows**: 2 **Width**: Fill Parent
6 Labels	RemAddressTitle RemGPSLabel RemLatLabel RemLongLabel RemAddressLabel RemCommaLabel	Displays **Text** Displays **Text** Displays the latitude Displays the longitude Displays the address Displays **Text**	**Text**: "Address" **Text**: "GPS" **Text**: "0" **Text**: "0" **Text**: "Unknown" **Text**: "," **TextColor**: Blue (for all labels)
Button	GetDirectionsButton	Opens Google Maps, and finds a route from the new current location to the remembered location	**FontSize**: 20 **Shape**: Rounded **Text**: "Get directions" **TextAlignment**: Center **Width**: Fill Parent **Height**: Fill Parent
LocationSensor Palette group: Sensors	LocationSensor1		
TinyDB	TinyDB1		
ActivityStarter Palette group: Connectivity	ActivityStarter1		**Action**: **android.intent.action** **.VIEW** **ActivityClass**: **com.google.android** **.maps.MapsActivity** **ActivityPackage**: **com.google.android** **.apps.maps** This section is case sensitive, so be precise!

Media files

2 files downloaded from our website:
Foldedmap.png
Homingpigeonimage.png

ActivityStarter

In chapter 12, we looked at the **ActivityStarter** component in detail. But we thought it might be useful to zero in on its properties in this app to make sure you get it just right. When you drag the **ActivityStarter** component onto the screen, you have to make sure you copy the **Action**, **ActivityClass**, and **ActivityPackage** exactly as shown here, including lowercase and uppercase:

```
Action: android.intent.action.VIEW
ActivityClass: com.google.android.maps.MapsActivity
ActivityPackage: com.google.android.apps.maps
```

Layout of the screen

TableArrangement1 and **TableArrangement2** are laid out as follows:

CurrentAddressTitle	CurrentAddresslabel	(Leave empty)	(Leave empty)
CurrentGPSLabel	CurrentLatLabel	CurrentCommaLabel	CurrentLongLabel

Due to the use of table arrangements, the design of this app is a bit fiddly. This diagram, used with the screen grabs at right of the Components Palette and the app, should help you understand how everything lines up.

Coding the blocks

To code the Homing Pigeon app, you'll be dealing with five different blocks and event handlers. First, drag out the **LocationSensor1.LocationChanged** event handler, which takes data from the Android location sensor and displays it in the labels you've set up. Next you code the **RememberCurrentLocationButton.Click** event handler, which saves the data from the current location into the TinyDB database in your phone (we talked about TinyDB in chapter 11). Then code the

`GetDirectionsButton.Click` event handler to take the data from the remembered location and the new current location and search Google Maps for a route back to the Homing Pigeon meeting point. As with many apps, you need to set a starting point, or baseline, when the app is first opened; and in this case, you need to put in a **Screen1.Initialize** block that checks to see if there is a remembered address before the user attempts to find their way back to the Homing Pigeon point.

1. Recording the starting location

Using the **LocationSensor** block, you populate the current address, latitude, and longitude labels with data. This means as soon as the app opens, without the user even needing to click a button, the sensor realizes that the user is in a new place and puts that information in **CurrentAddressLabel** and the other labels.

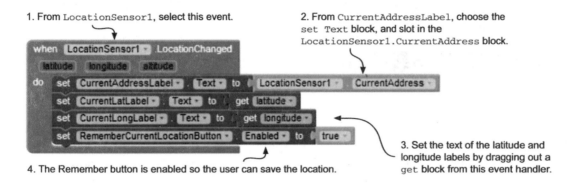

1. From LocationSensor1, select this event.

2. From CurrentAddressLabel, choose the set Text block, and slot in the LocationSensor1.CurrentAddress block.

3. Set the text of the latitude and longitude labels by dragging out a get block from this event handler.

4. The Remember button is enabled so the user can save the location.

2. The Remember Current Location button

In this step, you use the event handler **RememberCurrentLocationButton.Click** that means something will happen when the user clicks the button. You'll set the remembered address, latitude, and longitude label text to the current address details. This means you're setting the location to get back to: your meeting point.

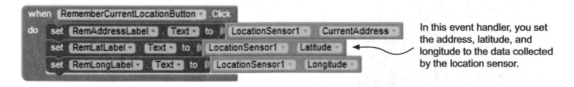

In this event handler, you set the address, latitude, and longitude to the data collected by the location sensor.

3. Saving the location to Tiny DB, and activating the directions button

Next you want to save the location into Tiny DB. We looked at this in detail in chapter 11, and you know Tiny DB enables the user to save data to the mobile device for future use. In this case, the user is taking the current location information, displaying it as the remembered location, and saving it to Tiny DB so that once the user changes location, they can find their way back to their first destination.

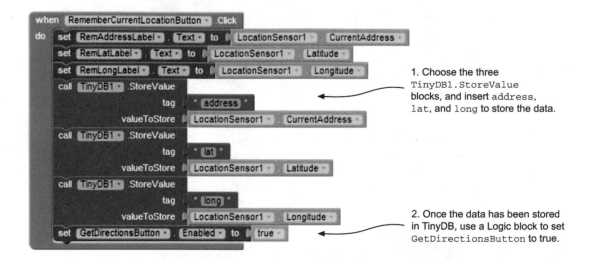

1. Choose the three TinyDB1.StoreValue blocks, and insert address, lat, and long to store the data.

2. Once the data has been stored in TinyDB, use a Logic block to set GetDirectionsButton to true.

4. The Get Directions button

In order to get directions to the remembered location, you need to use an activity starter. As you know from the Book Finder app in chapter 10, the **ActivityStarter** component launches other apps. In this case, you're creating blocks that put together a search that launches Google Maps using the two locations: current and remembered.

1. From within My Blocks, choose the ActivityStarter1.DataUri block, and insert a make block from Built-in > Text.

2. Make the complete text string by carefully copying the text and inserting the blocks as shown.

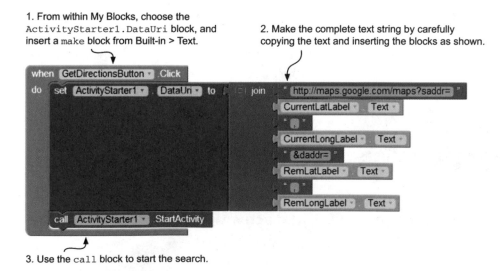

3. Use the call block to start the search.

For simplicity, imagine that the current location has latitude 0 and longitude 1 and the remembered location has latitude 2 and longitude 3. The whole URL would be

```
http://maps.google.com/maps?saddr=0,1&daddr=2,3
```

Aren't **make** Text blocks brilliant? You can mix text with data and search for anything!

5. Creating the tempaddress variable

You've already done some work with variables earlier in the book. But to remind you, some-times you need to create a variable that hasn't already been created by a component. In this case, you need to create a variable called **tempaddress**. When the user opens the app, this variable's purpose is to test whether a location is already saved as the remembered loca-tion. It'll become clearer in a minute.

1. Choose a `define variable` **block, and type** `tempaddress` **over the word** *variable*.

2. Insert a Text block from the Built-in blocks.

initialize global **tempaddress** to `" text "`

6. Initializing the app

For some apps, this one included, you need to do some checks as the screen opens. In this case, you need to put some blocks together to check whether the user has already saved a location in TinyDB. Then, if they have saved a location, you want to populate the remem-bered location table with the address, latitude, and longitude.

1. Because you've set a variable called `tempaddress`, **a** `global` **block is available in Variables.**

2. Call the `TinyDB1.GetValue` **block, and slot in a Text block, typing in** `address`.

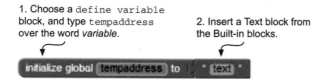

when **Screen1** .Initialize
do   set **global tempaddress** to   call **TinyDB1** .GetValue
                                                    tag `" address "`
                                         valueIfTagNotThere `" ■ "`

7. The if block

To complete the `Screen1.Initialize` block, you insert an **if** statement. The **if** state-ment checks whether there is an address in TinyDB. There will of course be an address in TinyDB only if the user previously saved their current location. The next step the user will probably want to take is to find their way back to this remembered location, so the **Screen1.Initialize** block ends by enabling the **GetDirections** button.

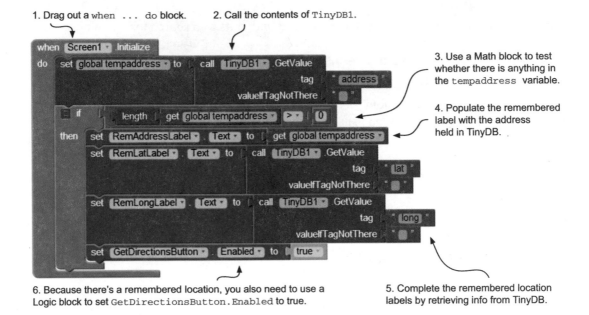

1. Drag out a when ... do block.   2. Call the contents of TinyDB1.

3. Use a Math block to test whether there is anything in the tempaddress variable.

4. Populate the remembered label with the address held in TinyDB.

6. Because there's a remembered location, you also need to use a Logic block to set GetDirectionsButton.Enabled to true.

5. Complete the remembered location labels by retrieving info from TinyDB.

Taking it further

1 You could extend Homing Pigeon by letting users add locations to a list so they can choose which location to return to, rather than having just one.

2 Improve the interface of Homing Pigeon by generating better buttons. Use a site like Button Maker (www.grsites.com/generate/group/2000/).

What did you learn?

In this chapter, you learned about the following:

- How phones know where they are
- What latitude and longitude are
- How to use the location sensor
- How to access Google Maps in an app using the activity starter

Test your knowledge

1   Why are **make** Text blocks so useful?
2   Where is the 0,0 location?
3   What is the imaginary line around the center of the globe called?
4   How many GPS satellites are there?
5   Who used the GPS system first?
6   How do you check if there is anything in a variable when you initialize an app?

Taking it further

Try creating a different sort of QR treasure hunt that enables the user to use the location sensor.

CHAPTER 14

From idea to app

Now that you have the skills and knowledge of an App Inventor, we'll look at how you can turn your ideas into fully working apps. This is a process, and the finished app may be different from what you first imagined—and that's OK! Almost all the apps in this book started out as slightly different ideas on paper: as we worked them through, we changed the way they looked or functioned. Sometimes App Inventor worked in a way we hadn't thought of and had us really scratching our heads. On the flip side, we also often discovered a great smartphone feature that we went on to add to an app.

So far, you've built apps that are fairly simple—this was so you could learn a couple of features or concepts at a time and concentrate on those. If you've tackled some of the "Try It Out" challenges at the end of each chapter, you probably feel that making apps on your own is very different from following instructions in a book. You'll notice that as your apps get bigger, they quickly become more complicated—as this graph shows.

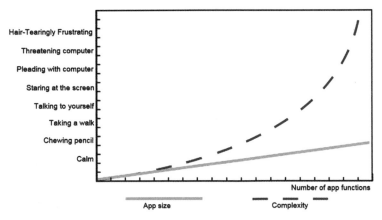

General problem-solving strategies (useful for app inventing)

The difference between following instructions and creating something yourself is a little like the difference between a baby being fed by its parents and learning to feed itself. This increasing complexity can result in things getting messy very quickly! But messy is good—it means you're learning; the trick is to keep things manageable (like the top baby) and not get frustrated if something goes wrong early on (like the baby with a spoon on its head).

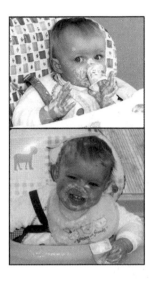

So how do you keep problems manageable and monitor your progress? We've put together some general strategies for any problem-solving activity—including app building. Which one you choose depends on what you're working on and how you work as an individual. For that reason, you'll find them scattered throughout this chapter—see how many you can spot:

- *Decompose*—Break hard problems into smaller chunks. Are those chunks still too hard? Then break those down, too. Keep going until you've solved it! This strategy is also called *divide and conquer*. You'll see *decomposition* a lot in this chapter.
- *Get out your pencil*—Some programmers find it helpful to write out steps in plain language. Others draw a flowchart of part of the app to check that it makes sense.
- *Prototype*—Start small with some of the basic functions of the app, get them to work, and then add extra bits afterward.
- *Recycle*—Chances are, someone has already written an app that's a little like yours—or at least has solved some of your problems. There are heaps of helpful people out there making videos and writing tutorials about what they've done. Use their stuff, give them credit, and return the favor when you've solved a problem or written an app.
- *Comment your programs*—Use comments on blocks to make it clear how they're meant to work.
- *Involve the users*—Find people who might use your app and get them involved early on, so you don't waste time designing a lovely app that is never used.
- *Test*—One of the great features of App Inventor is that unlike with other programming languages, you can live-test your app as you build it. You can try different approaches and also attempt to "break" an app: for example, by putting text in a text box when the app expects a number.
- *Talk about it*—Work with a partner, and be sure you can explain to each other how you think the program should work.

These strategies can be combined. You might do them several times, adding detail as you solve problems. For example, you might make a rough prototype of how an app works, then talk about it with a friend, and finally refine it into a more detailed prototype.

In this chapter we'll show you how to build two complex apps, using some of these strategies to help keep you on track. For the Alarm Clock app, we'll share with you how we went about things, what the problems were, and how we solved them (or not!). We'll give you the full app component table at the end of the Alarm Clock section—but don't rush straight there; see if you can solve the problems we came across. The important thing we hope you learn is that making the apps wasn't easy, but we got there using some of the strategies we listed and a little patience.

In the second half of the chapter, you'll develop a full game with levels. But first comes a revamp of your smartphone's basic alarm clock.

Zombie Alarm! app

Smartphone alarm clocks can be boring. That's a shame, because here's a device that can play any sound and display any picture or animation. We figured it was time for a fun alarm clock aimed at kids that would get them up in the morning. The basic idea was to have a clock displayed onscreen and a way for the user to enter an alarm time. When that time was reached, an animation would activate with sound—and that would repeat until the user switched off the alarm. Now what we needed was some inspiration. Time for …

User involvement

End users often have brilliant ideas, and if you're designing an app for someone else, you need to ask them what they want. The following template can help you interview your users or focus your thoughts on what potential end users might want. For an alarm clock aimed at an age group of 7–12, we came up with the following questions and answers:

Name of app idea	
Fun Alarm Clock	
Section 1: Introduction	
What is the problem or opportunity that the app will solve?	The user wants a fun alarm clock designed just for them, to help them wake up in time for school.
Are there any similar apps?	Shrek Alarm

Section 2: Users	
What age group is the app aimed at?	7–12
What other types of interests do the users have?	Computer games, theme parks, Minecraft, music, TV, comic books
What other apps do the users like?	Temple Run, Flappy Bird

Section 3: What does the app do?	
If you had to describe the app in the time it takes an elevator to go up five floors, what would that description be?	The alarm is a fun way to wake up. Instead of just an audible alarm going off, the alarm has an animation. The idea is that the user enjoys the graphic so much that they wake up fully in time to see the end animation.
What are the inputs?	Boxes to set the alarm time Check box to set the alarm on or off
What are the outputs?	The current time Animation and sound effects

Section 4: Design	
Are there any specific images or icons that need to be used in the app?	Original artwork would be good, with the color scheme and fonts matching the animation in style.
What does the app need to do?	1 Display the current time. 2 Record the alarm time. 3 Enable the user to activate and deactivate the alarm. 4 At the alarm time, trigger the current-time alarm. 5 The alarm trigger causes the animation to start and sound effects to be played. 6 The alarm repeats until the user deactivates it.

Now that the basic idea was in place, we needed some inspiration for what the central animation should be. We doodled a bit and chewed our pencils. One idea we liked was a flower clock with animated petals that dropped off—but it didn't feel like something that would appeal to kids or get them out of bed. Inspiration came when we combined the idea of things falling off with a hand-drawn cartoon that Carl's son left on his computer desk. And so the idea of a zombie alarm clock was born (eek!). When the alarm was activated, the zombie's body parts would start falling off, and some suitable squelchy noises and moans of "Brainzzz!" would hopefully be enough to wake the dead (or at least 7–12-year-old kids).

Decomposing: get out your pencil

To get the zombie to decompose, you first need to decompose the problems that this app idea gives you. So before hitting App Inventor, it's time to take out those pencils and make a list of the problems and questions you can see. Here are some that we saw:

1 How to update an onscreen clock.
2 How to trigger an alarm at the time the user selected.
3 How to get the zombie image into the computer.
4 How to make parts fall off the zombie.
5 What happens to the zombie parts that fall off?
6 Once the zombie has fallen completely apart, how do you start again?
7 How to warn the user if they quit the alarm app.
8 When the user switches off the alarm, how do you reset everything back to the beginning?

That list was just for starters, and it's looking complicated already, but at least you have some specific things to solve. By working out what the problems are, you can focus on solving them bit by bit, and you can decide what to spend your time tackling first.

TIP
Making lists isn't just useful for coding; you can use it to solve any problem. This was brilliantly illustrated by the genius Albert Einstein: when asked by a journalist what he would do if he had only 60 minutes to save the planet, he responded, "I would spend 55 minutes defining the problem and then 5 minutes solving it!"

You can group related problems together: for instance, you have timer problems (1 and 2), then graphics and animation problems (3, 4, 5, 6, and 7). Let's tackle these problems one at a time by prototyping and testing each part.

Solving the timer problems

In this section we'll decompose and tackle the timer problems.

PROBLEM 1: HOW TO UPDATE AN ONSCREEN CLOCK

This is easy to solve because you can recycle some code from chapter 7, where you figured out how to display the system time whenever the user clicked a button. Now, rather than updating the clock on a button click, you can use a timer to update the clock. We prototyped this by starting a new app with a **Label** called **TimeLabel** in a **Horizontal-Arrangement** and a **Clock** called **TimeNowClock**. Next we copied the code from chapter 7 into the **TimeNowClock.Timer** event, like so:

Every 200 ms, update `TimeLabel` to display the current system time, formatted in hours, minutes, and seconds.

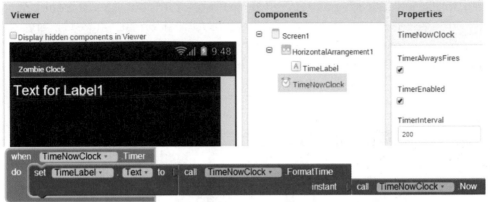

Why 200 milliseconds (ms) for the timer interval? Well, this came from a bit of trial and error: firing it more slowly meant that every now and then, the **TimeLabel** display would skip a second onscreen. That's probably because when a clock timer event fires, it needs to complete all its blocks before the timer restarts—so if you set the timer to update once a second, and updating the label takes 50 ms, the timer only restarts after 1,050 ms. Eventually, all those extra 50 ms add up, and the seconds skip a beat. Choosing a faster trigger of 200 ms means you'll definitely finish updating the screen and restarting the clock before the next system time second ticks by.

Learning Point: Timer wait time

You can test our theory about timers waiting for blocks to fire by putting a big counting loop that updates a label inside a fast-firing timer trigger, as shown here.

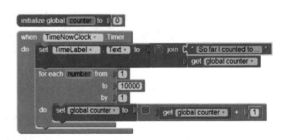

No matter how fast you set the **TimeNowClock** timer interval, you'll find that the message you see onscreen updates slowly—the speed is limited by how fast your phone can count to 10,000.

If you run the code so far, you'll see that the screen displays the time; but if you look carefully, there's something odd. Can you spot it?

The system time in the top-right corner of the screen reads 22:01, but the reported time in the app is 10:01:09 PM. At first this looked like a problem—the user needs to know that if they set the alarm time to 07:30, they will be woken up in the morning; and we wondered whether such an alarm would also be triggered at 19:30. As it turns out, it's just a quirk of App Inventor—the **FormatTime** block always defaults to AM/PM format, whereas everything else in App Inventor uses 24-hour format. We tested this by swapping the **FormatTime** block in our code to blocks of code that output the hours, minutes, and seconds separately, like so:

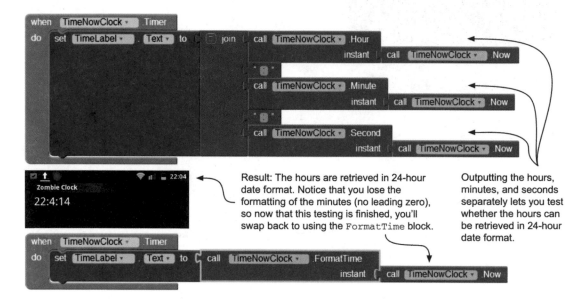

Result: The hours are retrieved in 24-hour date format. Notice that you lose the formatting of the minutes (no leading zero), so now that this testing is finished, you'll swap back to using the FormatTime block.

Outputting the hours, minutes, and seconds separately lets you test whether the hours can be retrieved in 24-hour date format.

PROBLEM 2: HOW TO TRIGGER AN ALARM AT THE TIME THE USER SELECTED

Next we added some additional objects to our horizontal arrangement so the user has two text boxes in which to set their alarm time's hours and minutes. We also added a check box so the user can control when the alarm is active.

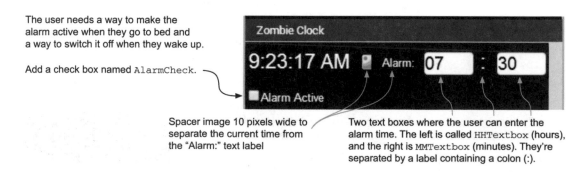

The user needs a way to make the alarm active when they go to bed and a way to switch it off when they wake up.

Add a check box named AlarmCheck.

Spacer image 10 pixels wide to separate the current time from the "Alarm:" text label

Two text boxes where the user can enter the alarm time. The left is called HHTextbox (hours), and the right is MMTextbox (minutes). They're separated by a label containing a colon (:).

We selected the **NumbersOnly** property of the text boxes to stop the user from typing letters by mistake.

Time to prototype some blocks to make the alarm go off. You won't worry about the zombie animation yet—first let's get the phone to make a noise. Add a sound object called **Alarm-Sound**, and choose a sound file source (such as the "baaa" sound from chapter 2). This is temporary; later you'll replace it with zombie sounds.

Now you have a couple of questions to answer. Before you read the answers, think the questions through, get out your pencil and/or talk to someone else about them, and see if you can work out some solutions:

1 What conditions need to be true to play the sound?

2 What event checks to see whether the alarm sound should be played?

For question 1, three conditions all have to be true before the alarm sounds:

- The **AlarmCheck** check box needs to be selected. If the user didn't select it at bedtime, they don't want to be woken up.
- The system time's hours needs to equal the value entered in **HHTextbox**.
- The system time's minutes needs to equal the value entered in **MMTextbox**.

For question 2, the trigger event to check whether the alarm should be played has to be a timer. Think about it: the user isn't going to be interacting with the phone (for example, pushing a button) while they're asleep, so the only option is a regular timed event. You can add a new **Clock** called **AlarmCheckClock** to do this. How often should it check whether the alarm time is reached (the timer **interval** property)? It needs to be less than a minute; otherwise you might miss the alarm time. We opted for once a second (1,000 ms) so the alarm will trigger almost as soon as the alarm time is reached. Here's everything put together:

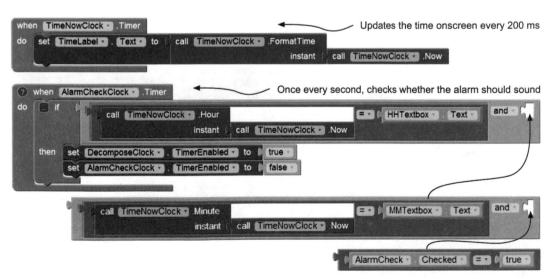

There are three test conditions for the `if` block, and we had to split them up here to fit them on the book page. The arrows show how you fit them together to make an awfully long set of blocks! Hopefully in a future update App Inventor will let you add **and** statements below each other so it's easier to view this kind of thing. We also added comments to the code so that we didn't get confused about what the two timers are doing.

Time to test: run the app, enter the current time in the hour and minute text boxes, and click the check box. What happens? You should hear your sound play—and it will repeat until the current time changes to one minute after the alarm time. This is *almost* what you want; but if the user doesn't wake up in the first minute, you want the alarm to keep sounding forever (or at least until they turn it off). To solve this problem, you can recycle an idea from the Splat the Rat app—remember how you have one timer that shows the rat and another that hides the rat? You can use that idea of one timer handing off to another in a sort of relay here. Try working this out with pencil and paper now.

Here's the way we thought it could work:

1 Every second, check to see whether the alarm should fire (we've already worked this out).

2 If all the conditions for starting the alarm are met, stop the **AlarmCheckClock** timer and start a new timer (you'll call this **DecomposeClock** because later you'll use it to make the zombie fall apart).

3 Every time **DecomposeClock** fires, it will do the following:

   a Play the alarm sound.

   b Check to see if the **AlarmCheck** check box has been switched off. If so, **DecomposeClock** switches off and the **AlarmCheckClock** timer switches on.

To try this, add a new clock to your app. Call it **DecomposeClock**, and set its **TimerInterval** property to 3,000 ms and its **Enabled** property to False. Here are the steps we've worked out, turned into blocks:

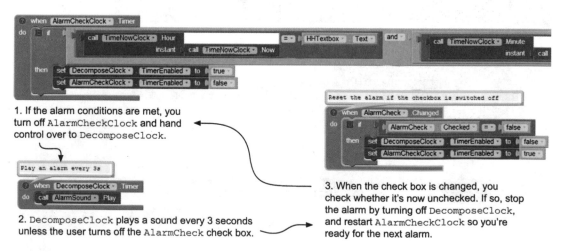

1. If the alarm conditions are met, you turn off AlarmCheckClock and hand control over to DecomposeClock.

2. DecomposeClock plays a sound every 3 seconds unless the user turns off the AlarmCheck check box.

3. When the check box is changed, you check whether it's now unchecked. If so, stop the alarm by turning off DecomposeClock, and restart AlarmCheckClock so you're ready for the next alarm.

Re-test the app, and you'll find that the alarm goes off as it did before—but now it continues to sound every 3 seconds until the user switches it off.

Solving the graphics and animation problems

That's solved all the timer-related problems (fingers crossed). Let's move on to the graphics and animation problems.

PROBLEM 3: HOW TO GET THE ZOMBIE IMAGE INTO THE COMPUTER

One idea was to simply scan or photograph the zombie image and turn it into a sprite. Can you see any problems with that? You want pieces to drop off the zombie, and to do that you need to turn it into a jigsaw puzzle of separate sprites.

There are a couple of ways you can do this. One option is to scan the image and then cut out pieces using a graphics editor like Paint. That gives you something like the image on the left, where we've used the freeform selection tool in Microsoft Paint to roughly chop up the image. It's quick to do, but any areas you chop out end up leaving a hole in the original image. We also felt it would be good to color the image, and that wasn't easy on a scanned graphic.

We found that a better option was to use the scanned image, but we redrew over it using a vector drawing program (we used Serif DrawPlus, but there are lots of alternatives). You can see how it worked on the right.

Using a vector drawing package means it's easy to resize the image so it fits the phone's screen. You can use the built-in fill effects to color the image; and because the parts are traced separately, when an eye or nose falls off, you won't see a gaping hole. We used the drawing package to draw a mud bank for the zombie to stand on—this also provided an easy (and slightly sneaky) way to solve problem 5.

In the end, we split the zombie into 12 different parts plus the mud bank. You can download them as separate images from the website.

Now you need to put the zombie back together again in the app. This is exactly like putting a jigsaw puzzle together, and frankly it's a little tedious—but trust us, it'll all be worthwhile when you wake up to a moaning zombie. First you need to create 13 sprites on a canvas and then upload the 12 zombie parts and the mud bank as their image properties. Then you need to get all 13 sprites in just the right place onscreen—it's handy to use a phone for live testing here, because it's annoying to have the app look great on your PC only to find out it looks terrible on your phone. Our top tip when you're doing this is that any sprite you move will come to the foreground—so you need to work from the back to the front (do the head first, then the hair, eye, and nose). If you don't do this, you'll end up with an even weirder-looking zombie—for example, with a nose that is behind its face.

Once the zombie was back together in the app and standing on the mud bank, we set the background color of the canvas to dark grey to add a suitably gloomy atmosphere. You could try adding a spooky background image to the canvas—say, a scary castle, a swamp, or (worst of all) a shopping mall. Here you can see how we re-composed the jigsaw zombie:

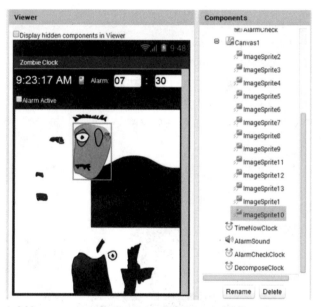

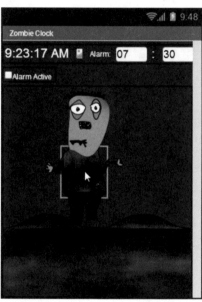

1. Add a `Canvas`, and set `Height` and `Width` to Fill Parent.

2. Create 13 sprites. Set the `Image` property of sprites 1–12 to images Zombie1.png through Zombie12.png.

3. Set sprite 13's `Image` property to mud.png.

4. Put the zombie back together by dragging the pieces in the Designer window, just like completing a jigsaw.

Tip: If a sprite is tricky to get into place manually, change its `X` and `Y` properties.

PROBLEM 4: HOW TO MAKE PARTS FALL OFF THE ZOMBIE
The situation so far is that you have an alarm that plays a sound and a zombie made of 12 parts. You need to link them so the alarm plays zombie-type sounds and triggers an animation of each part of the zombie dropping off in turn.

Setting up the zombie sounds is pretty easy. We used a microphone and some sound-editing software (Audacity) to make a suitable squelchy sound that plays whenever a body part drops off and a spooky "brainzz" sound that plays when the zombie has completely fallen apart. You can download the files from the website. Change your **AlarmSound Source** property to the squelch.mp3 file, and add a new sound object called **Brainzz** and set its source to the Brainzz.mp3 file.

To animate all the body parts, you'll set their **Heading** property to 290 (drifting toward bottom right of the canvas) and their **Speed** property to 6 to start them moving. You need an efficient solution here because coding separate blocks for all 12 body parts is a big task—and what if you wanted a more complex image, maybe one with 50 parts? In the Hungry Spider app, you saw how lots of fly sprites can be efficiently animated using a *list* of sprite objects; and you can recycle that idea here, too. Here are the steps behind the blocks:

1 Set up a list called **ZombieParts** that contains all the zombie part sprites.

2 Set up a variable called **Counter** with a value of 0.

3 When **DecomposeClock** fires, do the following:

  a Add 1 to **Counter**.

  b If **Counter** is less than 13, there are still parts to animate. So:

    ○ Play the alarm sound (you'll play a "squelch" sound).

    ○ Animate the sprite in the **ZombieParts** list that's at **Counter**'s index position, by setting its **Speed** to 6 and **Heading** to 290.

  c Else (if **Counter** is 13 or more, meaning all the parts have dropped off):

    ○ Play a new sound called **Brainzz**.

    ○ Reset all the sprites to their start positions so the zombie is whole again, ready to repeat the decomposition.

    ○ Reset the **Counter** variable to 0.

Step 1 sets up the **ZombieParts** list. You'll create a new variable **ZombieParts** as an empty list; then, at screen-initialize time, you'll add all 12 zombie **ImageSprite**s to the list. We've shown you the first and last image sprites here—in between, you need to add **ImageSprite**s 2–11.

Steps 2 and 3 deal with what happens when the **DecomposeClock** timer fires every 3 seconds. Just like in Hungry Spider, you're going to use Any Component blocks to set properties of all the zombie image sprites. The difference is that in Hungry Spider, you used a **for each** loop to start all the flies moving at once, whereas in this case you want to animate a new zombie part every time **DecomposeClock** fires. That's why you're using the global variable **Counter** that keeps track of which part has just been animated —between the times when **DecomposeClock** fires. Here are the blocks:

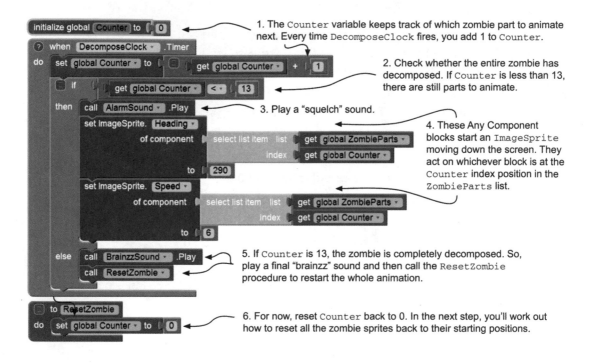

1. The Counter variable keeps track of which zombie part to animate next. Every time DecomposeClock fires, you add 1 to Counter.

2. Check whether the entire zombie has decomposed. If Counter is less than 13, there are still parts to animate.

3. Play a "squelch" sound.

4. These Any Component blocks start an ImageSprite moving down the screen. They act on whichever block is at the Counter index position in the ZombieParts list.

5. If Counter is 13, the zombie is completely decomposed. So, play a final "brainzz" sound and then call the ResetZombie procedure to restart the whole animation.

6. For now, reset Counter back to 0. In the next step, you'll work out how to reset all the zombie sprites back to their starting positions.

NOTE

You could have set the **Heading** property of all the sprites in the Designer window, but why do something 12 times when you can have the blocks do it for you?

Why did you set up a separate **ResetZombie** procedure? Couldn't you reset the **Counter** to 0 right after playing the **Brainzz** sound? You do this because you don't only reset the zombie when it's fully decomposed—you also want to reset it when the user turns off the alarm, so that you have a fully formed zombie ready to go again the next time the alarm triggers.

By making a **ResetZombie** procedure, you can call it from the previous blocks *and* from the **AlarmCheck.Changed** event, too. That means you save yourself some time. Let's make that addition now before we forget.

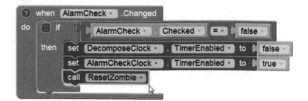

If you try the app now, you'll see that it's almost complete. When the alarm time is reached, the zombie falls apart with squelchy sounds and calls for "Brainzz!" But all its body parts just sit at the bottom of the screen and don't re-form into a whole zombie. The first problem is easy to solve, but the second is pretty hard!

PROBLEM 5: WHAT HAPPENS TO THE ZOMBIE PARTS THAT FALL OFF?

One of the reasons we put a thick mud bank at the bottom of the screen is so you don't have to worry about programming blocks to hide the 12 zombie parts as they reach the bottom of the screen. Instead you can just let them drop *behind* the mud bank. You know that image sprites have **x** and **y** properties for their position. They also have a **z** property that controls how the sprites are layered. The higher the **z** number, the closer the sprite is to the front of the screen. So if you set the **z** property of the mud bank to 2, it will be in front of all the other sprites (which have a **z** value of 1).

Setting the mud-bank image sprite's z property to 2 makes it appear in front of the other image sprites.

Test the app now, and the zombie should slide out of view—if he's still peeking from behind, make the mud bank a little larger.

PROBLEM 6: ONCE THE ZOMBIE HAS FALLEN COMPLETELY APART, HOW DO YOU START AGAIN?

How would you tackle this problem? You need all the zombie parts to go back to the positions they started in. Think about how you might do that before reading further …

… Nope, too soon—think a little more, please. ☺ Did you think about x and y positions?

One solution that is fairly easy from a programming point of view is to write down the x and y positions of all the sprites from the Designer screen. Then you could store them in two lists—say, **ZombieX** and **ZombieY**. A **for each** loop could then be added to the **ResetZombie** procedure that would set the x and y positions of each image sprite. That's a good solution, but it could be improved. Here are the problems with it:

1 Writing down x and y coordinates of 12 image sprites is tedious—and the app *already knows* all the x and y image sprite coordinates when it starts.

2 What if you move the zombie around in the Designer window? You have to remember to change the x and y positions in the list blocks, too.

There's a clever solution to these problems: use blocks to record all the x and y positions directly when the screen initializes. Then, later on, you can use a **for each** block, just as you originally worked out. Here we've added the blocks that record all the image sprite positions during the **Screen1.Initialize** event:

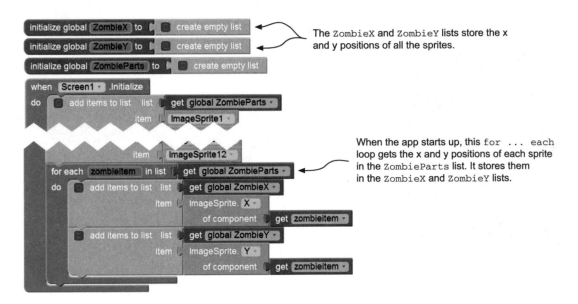

The ZombieX and ZombieY lists store the x and y positions of all the sprites.

When the app starts up, this for ... each loop gets the x and y positions of each sprite in the ZombieParts list. It stores them in the ZombieX and ZombieY lists.

Don't forget that the two blocks that have an **of component** socket are special Any Component blocks—that's why you can reuse them for all the image sprites.

The last big piece of the jigsaw puzzle is to reset the zombie. The next set of blocks shows how to cycle through the 12 image sprites, setting their speed back to 0 and their x/y coordinates back to the values you collected. This took a few attempts to get right, because at first we tried the same sort of "for each in list" loop that you can see in the previous example. We hadn't thought about the fact that to reset the sprites, we needed to access three lists at the same time: **ZombieParts** (the list of sprites) as well as **ZombieX** and **ZombieY**.

That meant we needed a common index number to access the same position in all three lists. The solution was a regular **for each** loop with a range from 1 to 12; we could then use the loop's counter (which we renamed **zombiepart**) as an index to access all three lists. Now that we've figured that out, you can recycle that idea whenever you need to work with several lists at once. Here are the blocks:

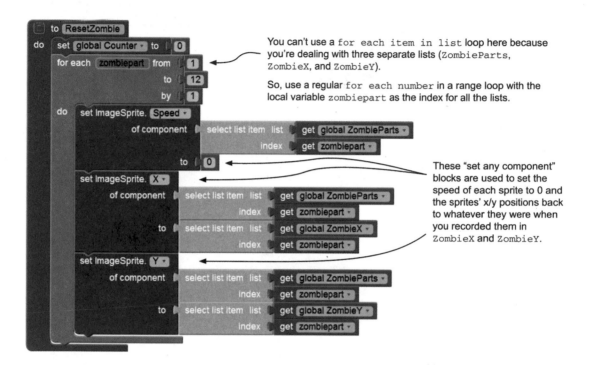

You can't use a for each item in list loop here because you're dealing with three separate lists (ZombieParts, ZombieX, and ZombieY).

So, use a regular for each number in a range loop with the local variable zombiepart as the index for all the lists.

These "set any component" blocks are used to set the speed of each sprite to 0 and the sprites' x/y positions back to whatever they were when you recorded them in ZombieX and ZombieY.

If you run the app, it works, but there is one final twist (literally)—all the zombie parts are rotated when they're put back together! This is because we forgot to change the **Rotate** property of the image sprites to be false (unselected). You could add blocks in the screen's **Initialize** event to fix this, but it's just as quick to simply unselect the **Rotates** box for each sprite in the Designer window. It took us literally less than 30 seconds—ready, steady, go!

PROBLEM 7: HOW TO WARN THE USER IF THEY QUIT THE ALARM APP

To solve this problem, we recycled code from another App Inventor website. Pura Vida Apps by Taifun had a solution we could use: we just added a `Notifier` object (`Notifier1`) and then copied the blocks from http://mng.bz/KHno.

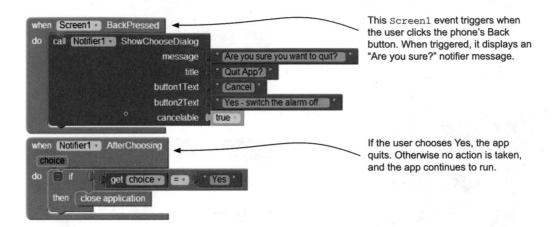

This `Screen1` event triggers when the user clicks the phone's Back button. When triggered, it displays an "Are you sure?" notifier message.

If the user chooses Yes, the app quits. Otherwise no action is taken, and the app continues to run.

OK, on to our final problem …

PROBLEM 8: WHEN THE USER SWITCHES OFF THE ALARM, HOW DO YOU RESET EVERYTHING BACK TO THE BEGINNING?

… which turns out not to be a problem at all—or rather, we'd already solved it. That's because we made a general `ResetZombie` procedure, and we'd already added a call to it from the `AlarmCheck.Changed` event. So whenever the user unchecks the check box, the zombie automatically resets. That's the power of reusable procedures.

The next section gives you the full specification of what the program does and the objects and properties we invented.

NOTE

App Inventor can't wake up your phone's screen or stop your screen from sleeping. But even when the screen sleeps, you'll still hear the alarm sounds. You could cancel the screen timeout manually in your phone settings, but make sure your phone is fully charged—or, even better, plugged in to a power source.

We hope you enjoy Zombie Alarm! as much as we do—we particularly like when his eyeball drops out. Now use your imagination to come up with your own animated alarm clock.

Zombie Alarm!
app: full specification

PURPOSE OF THIS APP

Almost everything can be enhanced by the inclusion of a zombie—
and this alarm clock is no exception. The app displays the current
time. The user enters their alarm time and selects a check box to set
the alarm, and at the appropriate time, bits start dropping off the
zombie with a squelchy alarm sound (and the occasional "Brainzz").
When all 12 parts of the zombie have fallen in the mud, he is resur-
rected. This loop continues until the user wakes up and unchecks the
Alarm Active check box.

APP RATING

5

ASSETS YOU'LL NEED

12 zombie parts (kindly drawn by Carl's son, Daniel); "brainzz" and "squelch" sounds.

Zombie Alarm!			
Screen1 properties	`ScreenOrientation`: Portrait `Title`: Zombie Alarm! `BackgroundColor`: Dark Grey `Icon`: zombie.png (downloaded from our website)		
Components	**What do I rename it?**	**What does it do?**	**What properties do I set?**
`Horizontal-Arrangement`	`HorzArr1`	Contains the current time, alarm labels, and two text boxes	Default settings (no changes needed)
`Label`	`TimeLabel`	Shows the time	**Text**: Default **FontSize**: 24 **TextColor**: White
`Label`	`AlarmLabel`	Displays "Alarm"	**Text**: "Alarm:" **FontSize**: 14 **TextColor**: White
`Label`	`ColonLabel`	Puts a colon (:) between the hours and minutes	**Text**: ":" **FontSize**: 24 **TextColor**: White

Components	What do I rename it?	What does it do?	What properties do I set?
Image	Image1	Spacer between **TimeLabel** and **AlarmLabel**	**Width**: 10 pixels
2 **TextBox**es	HHTextBox MMTextBox	User inputs hours (HH) and minutes (MM) of the alarm time	**FontSize**: 20 **NumbersOnly**: Yes (selected) **Hint**: **HHTextBox**: "HH" **MMTextBox**: "MM" **Width**: 50 pixels
CheckBox	AlarmCheck	Activates/Deactivates the alarm	**Checked**: No **FontSize**: 14 **Text**: "Alarm Active" **TextColor**: White
Canvas	Canvas1	Displays the zombie animation	**BackgroundColor**: Dark Grey **Height**: Fill Parent **Width**: Fill Parent
12 **ImageSprites**	ImageSprite1– ImageSprite12	Display the zombie body parts	**Speed**: 0 **Rotates**: No (unselected) **Picture**: The matching zombie image. For ImageSprite1, it's Zombie1.png; and so on.
Clock Palette group: User Interface	TimeNowClock	Displays the current time	**TimerAlwaysFires**: Yes (selected) **TimerEnabled**: Yes (selected) **TimerInterval**: 200
Clock Palette group: User Interface	AlarmCheckClock	Checks whether the current time equals the set alarm time	**TimerAlwaysFires**: Yes (selected) **TimerEnabled**: Yes (selected) **TimerInterval**: 1000
Clock Palette group: User Interface	DecomposeClock	Causes a part of the zombie to fall off at regular intervals	**TimerAlwaysFires**: Yes (selected) **TimerEnabled** = No (unselected) **TimerInterval**: 3000
Sound	AlarmSound	Plays a sound whenever a zombie part falls off	**Source**: Squelch.mp3
Sound	BrainzzSound	Says "Brainzzz!" once the zombie has completely decomposed	**Source**: Brainzz.mp3
Notifier	Notifier1	Checks whether the user wants to quit the app	Default

Media files

12 image files downloaded from our website: Zombie1.png–Zombie12.png
   Squelch.mp3
   Brainzz.mp3

Taking it further

Give the user a choice of wake-up sound effects for the Zombie Alarm! app.

Designing a complete game

In the final app of the book, we decided to get really ambitious and create a multilevel game that uses both the phone's orientation sensors and the touch screen. At some point, we used all our problem-solving strategies to deal with this app's complexity (decomposing problems, getting out a pencil, prototyping, recycling, commenting our programs, involving users, and testing).

The final game took about a week to make from scratch, but prior to that we had a bunch of ideas and prototypes.

Here's Paula's early prototype of the game that inspired the final app. The idea is to tilt the phone so the ball rolls between the blocks until it reaches the bottom of the screen. At the same time, the blocks can be moved around by dragging them with your finger.

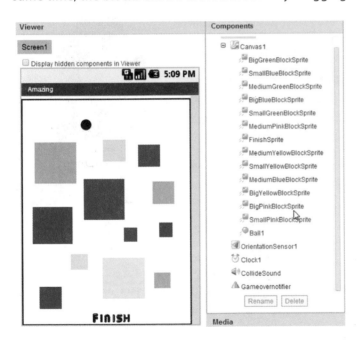

From start to finish, we made lots of small prototypes of the way the app looked and the way it played. Here are some of the problems we encountered along the way:

1 What should the rules of the game be?

2 How can we get the user interested in winning, so they want to keep playing?

3 How will one level be different than another?

4 How can we write code blocks that make it easy to add levels without programming lots of extra code?

Learning Point: Prototyping

The first computer mouse was designed using a roll-on deodorant tube and a butter dish. It didn't work with a computer, of course, but the prototype helped people understand the idea and think about how a computer mouse might work.

In app development, you might prototype a user interface to see how an app would look, without worrying about the blocks. You could also prototype some of the blocks to see how the app would work, without worrying about the interface. App prototypes are just early versions of part of the app to help programmers and users find and solve problems.

Developing the characters and rules

The prototype was great to demonstrate that our idea worked, but it looks like a basic puzzle game—the user had no emotional investment in getting the ball through the maze, other than a sense of accomplishment. If you think of games that people enjoy, there are usually characters that they identify with. Nintendo is particularly good at this: many players feel a connection with Mario, Luigi, or Princess Peach. Inspiration for our main character came from a coffee mug.

A penguin sliding about on ice made sense in the context of the game—the motion is similar to a ball rolling around a maze. We would start the penguin at the top of the screen, and it would have to slide around obstacles to reach an exit point at the bottom of the screen. We named our penguin Gentoo, after a species of Antarctic penguins, and she's female (because there are so many male game characters).

This was a good start, but Mario faces Bowser, Pac-Man is hunted by ghosts, and those Angry Birds are angry at the pesky pigs—what we needed was a villain. Our idea was to make a Yeti that had the power to turn Gentoo into a block of ice, sending her back to the beginning. The rules of the game developed from these ideas, and here's what we ended up with:

- Gentoo must travel along an icy path from top left on the screen to bottom left. She starts with five lives.
- If Gentoo falls into the sea, she loses a life and starts back at the beginning of the current level.

- A Yeti moves randomly along the path. If it touches Gentoo, she freezes, loses a life, and returns to the beginning.
- Gentoo has a stock of five snowballs that she can fire at the Yeti. A snowball hit freezes the Yeti for 5 seconds. During this time, Gentoo can touch the Yeti without freezing.
- A fish appears and disappears at random intervals. If Gentoo eats the fish, she gains a life.
- Gentoo scores 10 points for hitting the Yeti with a snowball, 50 points for completing a level, and 500 points for completing all the levels.
- If Gentoo completes all the levels, the game cycles back to the first level and resets the number of snowballs to five.

Now we needed some graphics. The character graphics were developed by starting with some public domain vector images and making some changes—for instance, the Yeti was a smooth blob, so we made him spiky (a bit like a snowflake).

We also made stop-frame animations in which we changed the images a little at a time to generate a series of images that could be uploaded to App Inventor. (You already know from the Creepy Spider app how to turn these images into animated sprites.) Once we had an animation for Gentoo and Yeti walking around, we created animations for Gentoo splashing in the sea and being frozen. Finally we created a fish image, a goal post, and a snowball splat to a single Yeti image for when Gentoo freezes him with a snowball (we only needed one image because the Yeti isn't animated when he is splatted). We used Serif DrawPlus to do this—but there's lots of other software you could use. Here are some examples of the graphics we created:

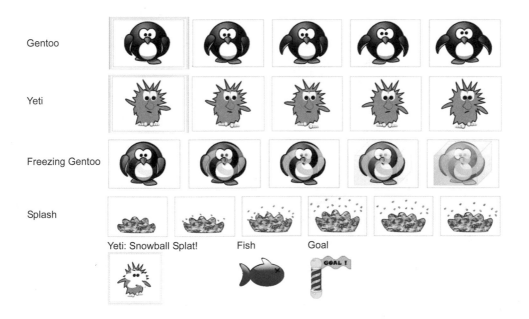

TIP

Have you noticed that Gentoo and the Yeti face forward rather than left or right? That helps you because, as you saw in the Hungry Spider app, if you want sprites that can face left and right, you have to produce two sets of images and write blocks of code that can switch between them depending on which direction the sprite is travelling. Having the characters face the player means you cut down on a lot of coding! If you're familiar with MIT's Scratch programming interface (http://scratch.mit.edu/), you know there are sprite controls to do this hard work automatically—hopefully we'll see something similar in App Inventor very soon.

Designing the levels

What could you change about each level to make it more challenging? You have lots of choices here: make the Yeti faster, add more Yetis, add ice that is more slippery, reduce the number of times the fish appears, and so on. We settled on a simple example to start with, which changes the following items with each new level:

- The path that Gentoo travels gets narrower and more complicated.
- The Yeti's speed increases.
- The Yeti's starting point changes.
- The fish appears in a different place on each level.

Once we had the level changes working, we could try out additional ideas to make each level harder.

Changing Gentoo's path on each level is the hardest to achieve. In the prototype at the beginning of this section, all the wall blocks were separate sprites. That means for every new level, we would need to set the x and y positions of all the wall sprites; and that's not really a pathway, it's just a collection of blocks. For a complicated path with joined-up walls, we might have 20 or more sprites to set for each level—and that's a lot of coding even if you use lists of x and y positions. Fortunately, we had a cunning solution. App Inventor lets you test the background color of any x, y point on the canvas using a method called `Canvas.GetBackgroundColor`. So if Gentoo starts on a white, icy path, you can use a timer to keep checking whether a point under her feet is still white. If it isn't, you can assume that she has fallen into the water. This approach has a massive advantage: you can *draw* each level in your favorite drawing package and upload it as a canvas background in App Inventor. As long as the path is white, the game will work—no complicated x, y coordinates and collision detection needed. See? We told you it was cunning. You can use exactly the same trick to keep the Yeti from falling off the path. Here are the three increasingly difficult levels we drew.

We had the rules and graphics; now it was time to make the app.

A-Mazeing Penguin app

PURPOSE OF THIS APP
Help Gentoo escape the Yeti by tilting your phone to move her along the icy path from the top of the screen to the goal at the bottom. Sneak past the Yeti by touching the screen to throw a snowball. Eat blue fish to gain extra lives.

APP RATING

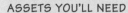

5

ASSETS YOU'LL NEED
3 level images, 9 penguin images (animation), 7 freezing penguin images (animation), 15 splash images (animation), 6 Yeti images (animation), 1 splatted Yeti image, 1 fish image, 1 goal image, and 8 sound effects—phew!

A-Mazeing Penguin	
Screen1 properties	`ScreenOrientation`: Portrait `AlignHorizontal`: Center `Scrollable`: No (unselected) `Title`: A-Mazeing Penguin `BackgroundColor`: Black `Icon`: penguin1.gif (downloaded from our website)

Components	What do I rename it?	What does it do?	What properties do I set?
`Horizontal-` `Arrangement`	`HorzArr1`	Contains the player information text (see the next eight labels)	Default settings (no changes needed)

8 **Label**s	`LevelLabel`
	`LevelNumLabel`
	`LivesLabel`
	`LivesNumLabel`
	`SnwblLabel`
	`SnwblNumLabel`
	`ScoreLabel`
	`ScoreNumLabel`
		Display the four pieces of player information	**FontBold**: Yes (selected)
			Fontsize: 9
			TextColor: White
			
			Text:
			LevelLabel: "Level:"
			LevelNumLabel: "0"
			LivesLabel: "Lives:"
			LivesNumLabel: "5"
			SnwblLabel: "Snowballs:"
			SnwblNumLabel: "5"
			ScoreLabel: "Score:"
			ScoreNumLabel: "0"

`Canvas`	`Canvas1`	Displays the game area	**BackgroundColor**: None **BackgroundImage**: icemaze1.png **Height**: Fill Parent **Width**: Automatic

4 **ImageSprite**s	`PenguinSprite`
	`GoalSprite`
	`YetiSprite`
	`FishSprite`
		Display the game elements	**Rotates**: No (unselected)
			Picture: See the Media Files list
			PenguinSprite: **X**: 6, **Y**: 3
			GoalSprite: **X**: 10, **Y**: 326

`Ball` Palette group: Drawing and Animation	`SnowBall`	Can be launched at the Yeti	**PaintColor**: Light Gray **Radius**: 8 **Speed**: 15 **Visible**: No (unselected)
`Orientation-` `Sensor`	`Orientation-` `Sensor1`	Detects how the phone is tilted. Gentoo will always head toward the ground. Bigger tilt = faster movement.	**Enabled**: Yes (selected)

Components	What do I rename it?	What does it do?	What properties do I set?

6 **Clock**s
Palette group: User Interface
	`Anim_PenguinClock`
	`Anim_SplashClock`
	`Anim_YetiClock`
	`Anim_FreezeClock`
		Control game animations. **`Anim_PenguinClock`** and **`Anim_YetiClock`** also check whether Gentoo and the Yeti have reached the edge of the icy path.	**`Anim_PenguinClock`** and **`Anim_YetiClock`**:
			`TimerEnabled`: True (selected)
			`TimerInterval`: 100
			
			`Anim_SplashClock`:
			`TimerEnabled`: False (unselected)
			`TimerInterval`: 10
			
			`Anim_FreezeClock`:
			`TimerEnabled`: False (unselected)
			`TimerInterval`: 300

	`FishClock`	Makes the fish appear at random intervals	**`TimerEnabled`**: True (selected) **`TimerInterval`**: 6000
	`SplatClock`	Times how long the Yeti is splatted and frozen	**`TimerEnabled`**: False (unselected) **`TimerInterval`**: 6000
`Notifier`	`Notifier1`	Used for all game notifications: Level Complete, All Levels Complete, and Game Over	No changes needed
9 **Sound**s	See Media Files	Used for game sound effects	See Media Files

Media files

Canvas level backgrounds: Upload images icemaze0.png–icemaze2.png.

Static (not animated) sprites:
Set the **Picture** property of **FishSprite** and **GoalSprite** to fish.png and goal.png, respectively. Upload the file yetisplat.gif—this is the image you'll show when the Yeti is hit with a snowball.

Animated sprites:
Gentoo: Upload the image files penguin1.gif–penguin9.gif. Set the **Picture** property of **PenguinSprite** to penguin1.gif.
Yeti: Upload the image files yeti1.gif–yeti6.gif. Set the **Picture** property of **YetiSprite** to yeti1.gif.
Freezing Gentoo: Upload images icepenguin1.gif–icepenguin7.gif.
Splashing Gentoo: Upload images splash1.gif–splash15.gif.

Sounds: Create these **Sound** objects, and set their **Source** property as follows:
SplashSound: splash.mp3
FreezeSound: freeze.mp3
VictorySound: victor.mp3
SplatSound: splat.mp3
GameOverSound: gameover.mp3
OneUpSound: oneup.mp3
YetiSound: yeti.mp3
LevelSound: LevelUp.mp3
WhooshSound: whoosh.mp3

1. Setting up the screen

The screen setup is straightforward, but there are a lot of media files to import. Take your time doing this; wait for each one to upload fully before moving on to the next one.

Here's the layout:

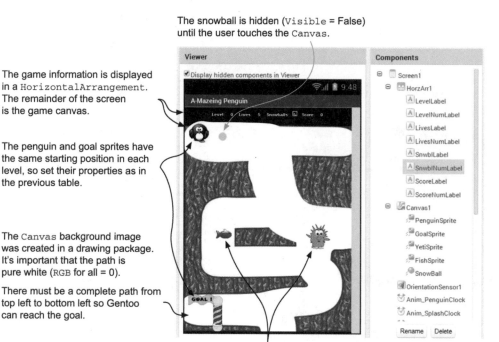

The snowball is hidden (Visible = False) until the user touches the Canvas.

The game information is displayed in a HorizontalArrangement. The remainder of the screen is the game canvas.

The penguin and goal sprites have the same starting position in each level, so set their properties as in the previous table.

The Canvas background image was created in a drawing package. It's important that the path is pure white (RGB for all = 0).

There must be a complete path from top left to bottom left so Gentoo can reach the goal.

The fish and yeti sprite start positions are set by the app blocks at the beginning of each level.

2. Coding the blocks: setting up the variables

You'll have a lot to keep track of in this game. Make a quick list now of the variables you think you'll need. Following you'll find our final list. We have three sorts of variables: those that keep track of gameplay information like the score, those that set the speed of sprites, and those that control the animation of sprites. The variable **penguinspeed** isn't changed anywhere in the program, but it's a useful variable when you want to test what speed works best on your phone. You could also use it to change the difficulty of each level: for example, you could create a red fish that makes Gentoo move at half speed for 30 seconds.

Here are the variables used throughout the app:

These four variables keep track of game-play information for the number of lives remaining, current score, snowballs remaining, and current level number.

There are four animations in the game. These counters keep track of which image should be shown each time a corresponding clock fires.

This variable stores the total number of levels in the game. Levels start at 0, so a value of 2 means there are three levels: 0, 1, and 2.

3. Updating the game information

There will be lots of times in the game when you want to update the information at the top of the screen. For example, when a snowball is fired, you'll reduce the number of snowballs by one; or you'll indicate when the player loses or gains a life. It makes a lot of sense to write a general procedure to do this that you can call on all these occasions—you'll call it **UpdateInfo**, and it will set each of the text labels to the value of the matching variable, like so:

```
to UpdateInfo
do  set LevelNumLabel . Text to   get global currentlevel
    set LivesNumLabel . Text to   get global lives
    set SnwblNumLabel . Text to   get global snowballs
    set ScoreNumLabel . Text to   get global score
```

4. Animating and moving the penguin

Most of the code here, you've seen before. You can recycle much of it from previous apps in the book.

Animating the penguin works exactly as in Hungry Spider. Each time the timer fires, you add 1 to a picture counter variable. If you've reached the last of the nine images, you reset

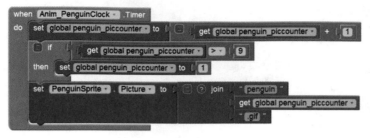

the counter to 1. Then you set
PenguinSprite's **Picture**
property to a filename made
of the word *penguin* + the
current counter + *.gif*. So if the
counter is 5, **PenguinSprite**
.Picture="penguin5.gif".

If you run the app, you should see a flapping Gentoo. Now you need to make her move
around by responding to the orientation sensor. This is the same thing you did in Hungry
Spider—but here, each time Gentoo moves, you also need to check that she is still on the
white ice path. To do this, you'll test the color of the canvas between her feet every time the
orientation sensor changes. The color white has a value of -1 in App Inventor; so if during
any of your tests the color doesn't equal -1, you'll play a "splash" animation (because the
path is surrounded by the sea), reduce Gentoo's lives by one, and send her back to the
beginning of that level.

Step 1 is to figure out how to check the color of the canvas between Gentoo's feet. You can
use a canvas block called **GetBackgroundPixelColor**, which has sockets for an x and a y
coordinate. If you feed in Gentoo's x and y positions, that'll tell you the color at the top left
of the sprite. Here's how to modify **PenguinSprite.X** and **Y** and feed them into
Canvas1.GetBackgroundPixelColor:

3. Add half of PenguinSprite's Width property to get the x coordinate.

2. PenguinSprite's X
and Y properties give
you the sprite's top-left
coordinates.

4. Add all of PenguinSprite's Height property
to get the y coordinate (because y increases as
you go down the screen).

1. You want to check whether the background color of the canvas is white at this point.

5. Turn this calculation into a code block.

Now you can make a decision based on whether the result of this block is -1 (white) and combine this with the Hungry Spider blocks that used the orientation sensor to move the character around.

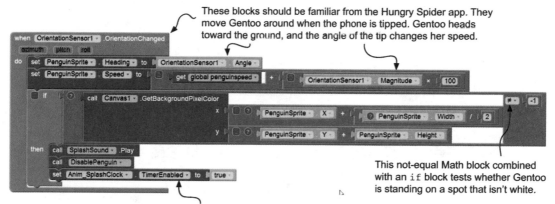

These blocks should be familiar from the Hungry Spider app. They move Gentoo around when the phone is tipped. Gentoo heads toward the ground, and the angle of the tip changes her speed.

This not-equal Math block combined with an `if` block tests whether Gentoo is standing on a spot that isn't white.

If Gentoo isn't standing on a white pixel, do the following:
1. Play a "splash" sound.
2. Stop Gentoo from moving and interacting with other sprites.
3. Enable `Anim_SplashClock` to play a "splash" animation.

5. Making a splash

At the moment, you haven't defined the procedure **DisablePenguin** that you see in the previous blocks, and **Anim_SplashClock** currently does nothing. To stop Gentoo in her tracks, you need to do four things:

1. Disable the orientation sensor. This stops the **OrientationSensor.Changed** event from triggering, which would start Gentoo moving again.
2. Disable **Anim_PenguinClock** to turn off Gentoo's walking animation.
3. Set **PenguinSprite.Speed** to 0.
4. Disable **PenguinSprite**, in case the Yeti collides with Gentoo.

If you put all this in a procedure then you can also call the same procedure when Gentoo is frozen by the Yeti. The blocks are shown at right.

You now have a penguin that stops moving and interacting whenever it steps on a non-white pixel. Next you need to play a "splash" animation, but unlike your other animations, you only want it to play once—one big splash. To do this, you can adapt the Gentoo animation blocks you've already made, but insert a decision that asks whether you've reached the last frame of the animation. When you do reach the last frame, you'll stop the splash animation, deduct a life, and decide whether it's Game Over or whether the player has lives left to play. You'll see a new procedure in the following blocks: **LoseALife**. Create the procedure now (we'll tell you what to add in a moment). Here are the blocks:

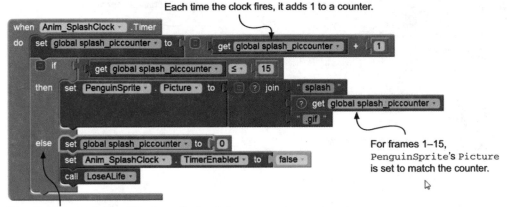

Each time the clock fires, it adds 1 to a counter.

For frames 1–15, PenguinSprite's Picture is set to match the counter.

When the last splash picture has been displayed, the program does the following:

1. Resets the counter to 0
2. Stops Anim_SplashClock from firing
3. Calls the LoseALife procedure

6. How to lose a life

You've played the "splash" sound and animation. Now you need to deduct a life from the **lives** variable. You'll also reset the number of snowballs to five, because if the player runs out of snowballs and the Yeti is close by, the player should only die once and then have a fighting chance to win the level. It's also important at this point to update the information bar at the top of the screen by calling **UpdateInfo**.

Now you have to make a decision:

1 If the player has zero lives remaining, it's Game Over. You'll need to pause the game and give them a chance to play again. You can do this using a notifier. You'll then need to reset all the variables back to the beginning.

2 If the player has lives remaining, you'll reset Gentoo—we call this *respawning*. To respawn, you need to reverse the changes you made when Gentoo first made a splash. Here's the **Respawn** procedure that does the reset.

Here's the **LoseALife** procedure that carries out the steps we described and calls the **Respawn** procedure if the player has lives remaining:

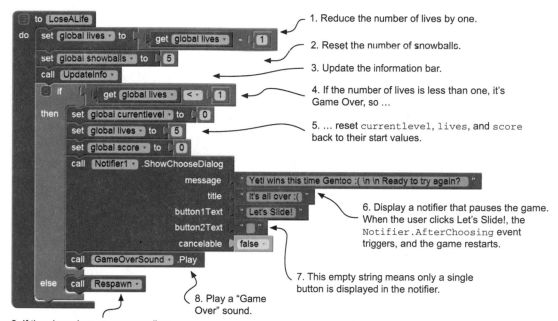

1. Reduce the number of lives by one.

2. Reset the number of snowballs.

3. Update the information bar.

4. If the number of lives is less than one, it's Game Over, so ...

5. ... reset `currentlevel`, `lives`, and `score` back to their start values.

6. Display a notifier that pauses the game. When the user clicks Let's Slide!, the `Notifier.AfterChoosing` event triggers, and the game restarts.

7. This empty string means only a single button is displayed in the notifier.

8. Play a "Game Over" sound.

9. If the player has one or more lives remaining, call a `Respawn` procedure to reset Gentoo to the beginning of the level.

At the moment, the game won't restart after Gentoo has lost all her lives, because you haven't yet programmed the **Notifier1.AfterChoosing** event. You'll do this in section 10, which looks at how you start a new level or restart the game.

7. A fishy interlude

After all that complexity, let's take a more manageable bite out of the game and do something easy—you want to make the (life-giving) blue fish appear at random intervals. It isn't animated and doesn't move around, so you just need to set **FishSprite**'s **Visible** property to true or false at random intervals. To do this, you have **FishClock** fire every 6 seconds. When it fires, you'll pick a number between 1 and 10. If it's 6, you'll show the fish. That means at any moment, there is a 1 in 10 chance that the fish will be onscreen. Here are the blocks.

At the moment, Gentoo doesn't interact with the fish, but you'll deal with this shortly in a single procedure that handles what happens if Gentoo collides with the fish, the Yeti, or the goal. Before that, let's …

8. Get that Yeti moving

The Yeti's movement recycles lots of the penguin code. The only difference with the Yeti is that he doesn't respond to the phone's movement—he just wanders around randomly, bumping off the sides of the ice path. For that reason, you can do the Yeti's animation and movement blocks all together in one event, which is triggered when `Anim_YetiClock` fires. The Yeti's initial position and speed are set later in the program, but for testing purposes make sure he's on the white path in the Designer window and set his `Speed` property to 3.

If you run the app now, you'll see the Yeti glide across the screen—you need to keep him on the path, though. To do this, you'll detect the color of the canvas at a spot between his feet. Sound familiar? It's exactly what you did with Gentoo. If the spot isn't white, you'll change his direction to keep him on the path.

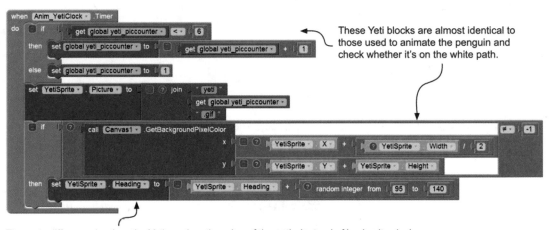

These Yeti blocks are almost identical to those used to animate the penguin and check whether it's on the white path.

The main difference is when the Yeti reaches the edge of the path. Instead of having it splash in the sea, you change its direction (heading) by adding to its current heading a random value between 95 and 140 degrees. This makes it turn around and continue on the path.

So far so good—the Yeti should now roam around randomly like, well, like we imagine a Yeti should do. Sometimes we did find that our Yeti got stuck in a corner; that was because he was still on the path but couldn't go any further because he reached the screen edge. You can solve that by recycling the code from the flies in Hungry Spider so the Yeti bounces off screen edges.

9. When penguins collide ...

Most of your gameplay elements are now onscreen and moving around, but they aren't interacting with each other. Gentoo can touch the Yeti, the fish, and the goal—but nothing happens. It's time to write blocks that detect a penguin collision. There are three possibilities to think through:

- *Gentoo collides with the Yeti.* Oh no! If this happens, you'll do exactly the same process as when Gentoo falls in the water—the only difference is that this time, you'll play a "freeze" animation and sound rather than a "splash" animation and sound.
- *Gentoo collides with the fish.* Yum yum! If this happens, you'll make the fish disappear, add 1 to the number of lives, play a "one-up" sound, and update the information bar.
- *Gentoo collides with the goal.* Hooray! Gentoo has completed the level. You'll need to load the next maze.

Because only one of these three things can take place at a time, you can use an **if** ... **then** ... **else** ... **if** decision block. This works just like an **if** ... **then** ... **else** block, but each time a condition is false, you ask a different **if** question, like so:

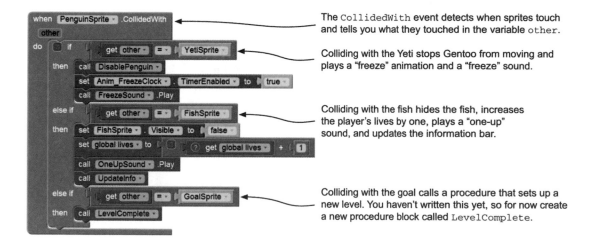

The CollidedWith event detects when sprites touch and tells you what they touched in the variable other.

Colliding with the Yeti stops Gentoo from moving and plays a "freeze" animation and a "freeze" sound.

Colliding with the fish hides the fish, increases the player's lives by one, plays a "one-up" sound, and updates the information bar.

Colliding with the goal calls a procedure that sets up a new level. You haven't written this yet, so for now create a new procedure block called LevelComplete.

For now, you'll leave part of **PenguinSprite.CollidedWith** as calling an empty procedure (define a new procedure called **LevelComplete**, but don't add any blocks yet). The reason is that if you finish your last gameplay elements—**Anim_FreezeClock** and throwing a snowball—you'll have a working game for level 1. It's then much easier to add the final code that creates as many levels as you can draw.

Here's the **Anim_FreezeClock.Timer** code that activates when Gentoo and the Yeti collide as you've just seen. Can you spot the difference between this and **Anim_SplashClock**?

They're virtually identical—this is recycling in action. The only changes are that there are seven frames of animation and the image files all start with the word *icepenguin*.

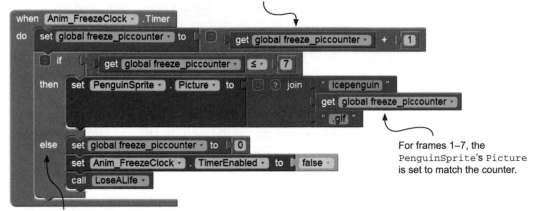

Each time the clock fires, it adds 1 to a counter.

For frames 1–7, the `PenguinSprite`'s `Picture` is set to match the counter.

When the last icepenguin picture has been displayed, the program does the following:

1. Resets the counter to 0
2. Stops `Anim_SplashClock` from firing
3. Calls the `LoseALife` procedure

10. The snowballs strike back!

At the moment, Gentoo is helpless—she has to run around avoiding the Yeti. Let's give her some ammunition to splat him with, in the form of five fat snowballs. The idea is that the player touches the screen (`Canvas1.Touched` event), and a snowball is launched toward the point they touched (hopefully the Yeti).

Before you can let Gentoo fire a snowball, three conditions must be met:

- Gentoo must have some snowballs left to fire.
- There must not be a snowball already in flight—these aren't rapid-fire snowballs.
- **PenguinSprite** must be "active"—you can't fire snowballs when you're frozen or underwater!

As long as these three conditions are all true, you'll move the snowball to Gentoo's current position, make it visible, and set its heading toward the point the user touched. The snowball already has speed (you set that in properties), so it fires immediately. Here's the code to throw the snowball, update the number of snowballs remaining, and play a "whoosh" sound:

These are the three conditions that must be met before a snowball can be fired. Plug them into the three and sockets of the if statement below.

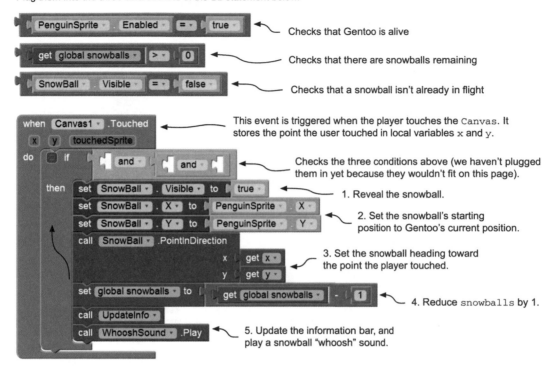

PenguinSprite . Enabled = true ← Checks that Gentoo is alive

get global snowballs > 0 ← Checks that there are snowballs remaining

SnowBall . Visible = false ← Checks that a snowball isn't already in flight

when Canvas1 .Touched ← This event is triggered when the player touches the Canvas. It stores the point the user touched in local variables x and y.

x y touchedSprite

do if and and ← Checks the three conditions above (we haven't plugged them in yet because they wouldn't fit on this page).

then set SnowBall . Visible to true ← 1. Reveal the snowball.

set SnowBall . X to PenguinSprite X ← 2. Set the snowball's starting position to Gentoo's current position.

set SnowBall . Y to PenguinSprite Y

call SnowBall .PointInDirection

x get x ← 3. Set the snowball heading toward the point the player touched.

y get y

set global snowballs to get global snowballs - 1 ← 4. Reduce snowballs by 1.

call UpdateInfo

call WhooshSound .Play ← 5. Update the information bar, and play a snowball "whoosh" sound.

Once the snowball is in flight, there are two possibilities:

- The snowball misses the Yeti and reaches the edge of the screen. You can detect that as an event and make the snowball invisible. Here are the blocks:

when SnowBall .EdgeReached

edge

do set SnowBall . Visible to false

- The snowball collides with the Yeti (which you can detect with a **SnowBall.Collided-With** event). When this is triggered, you'll hide the snowball and switch off the Yeti animation, replacing it with a single image of a Yeti with snow on his face. The Yeti will be disabled so Gentoo can touch him without being frozen. You'll also update the player's score and then set a timer to wait 6 seconds before you let the Yeti be enabled and start moving again.

Disabling the Yeti is exactly the same as disabling Gentoo when she's frozen (more recycling). The only difference is that you don't want to disable the phone's orientation sensor—the player can still move Gentoo. Here's the new procedure:

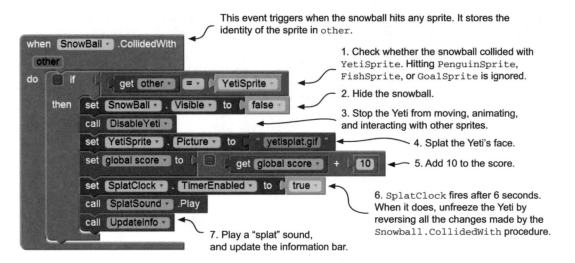

You'll call **DisableYeti** whenever a snowball collides with **YetiSprite**, along with the other changes we just discussed. Here are the blocks:

This event triggers when the snowball hits any sprite. It stores the identity of the sprite in other.

1. Check whether the snowball collided with YetiSprite. Hitting PenguinSprite, FishSprite, or GoalSprite is ignored.

2. Hide the snowball.

3. Stop the Yeti from moving, animating, and interacting with other sprites.

4. Splat the Yeti's face.

5. Add 10 to the score.

6. SplatClock fires after 6 seconds. When it does, unfreeze the Yeti by reversing all the changes made by the Snowball.CollidedWith procedure.

7. Play a "splat" sound, and update the information bar.

The final part of the snowball section is to have the Yeti unfreeze. To do this, you'll play **YetiSound** so the player knows the Yeti is unfreezing, and set his animation back to the beginning frame. Then you just need to reverse the **DisableYeti** blocks and turn off **SplatClock** (until the next time the Yeti gets a snowball in the nose).

That's it—you should have a fully functioning level 1. Try it out!

11. Level up!

Earlier you created a procedure called **LevelComplete** that is called when Gentoo reaches **GoalSprite**. At the moment, **LevelComplete** is empty. This procedure needs to do the following:

1 Stop Gentoo and the Yeti from moving.
2 Decide whether the player has reached the end of a level or the end of the game. If the player has levels left to play, then **currentlevel** will be less than **num_of_levels**.
   a If there are levels left to play, you'll increase **currentlevel** by 1 and increase the score by 50.
   b If all levels are complete, you'll set **currentlevel** back to 0, increase the score by 500, and give Gentoo 5 new snowballs.
3 In both the level-complete and game-complete cases, you'll also show a notifier congratulating the player.

Here are the blocks:

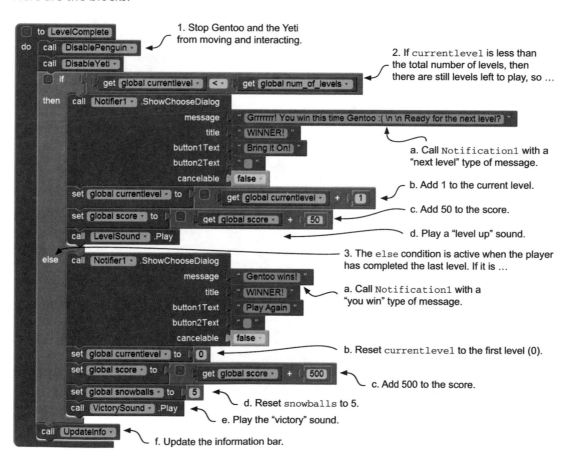

Notice that you show a notification, play some sounds, and change some variables, but at this stage a new level hasn't been loaded. It's time to …

12. Load a new level

The final part of this gigantic jigsaw puzzle of blocks is to figure out how to start a new level. There are three situations when you need to load a new level:

1 When the app first starts (**Screen1.Initialize** event)
2 When Gentoo reaches **GoalSprite**
3 When it's Game Over for the player (to restart at level 0)

For situation 1, you can use the **Screen1.Initialize** event to trigger a procedure that updates the level. Let's call the procedure **StartLevel**—create it now as an empty procedure.

For situations 2 and 3 (reaching the goal or Game Over), you'll call a notifier to pause the game and tell the player what happened. If you look back at the **LoseALife** and **LevelComplete** procedures, you'll see that you already have the notifier set up. You can use the notifier **After-Choosing** event to trigger a procedure that updates the level as shown at right.

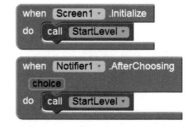

So what does **StartLevel** do? The previous "Designing Levels" section in this chapter said that each new level should change the canvas background to be a narrower and more complicated path. Also changing in each level are the Yeti's speed and the starting coordinates (x, y) of the fish and the Yeti.

Save your levels with the same name structure as the animated sprites: *icemaze* + a level number + *.png*. So if you set the current level to 2 and set **canvas1 .back-groundimage** to *ice-maze* + **currentlevel** = *.png*, level 2 will be loaded.

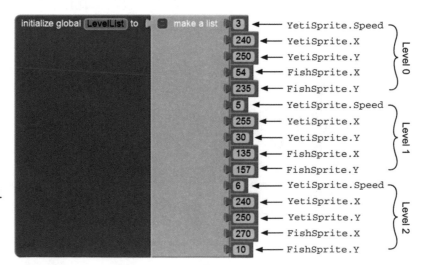

The other items (Yeti speed, Yeti x, Yeti y, fish x, and fish y) can all be stored in lists. In fact, they can all be stored in one giant list, as long as you keep the order of these items the same for each level. You'll call this **LevelList**. The beauty of this system is that if you want to create 15 levels, you just add the Yeti and fish variables to the bottom of the list for each level and upload the relevant ice maze background images numbered from 1–15.

There are five variables for each level. So if you know your current level number and the order of the variables, you can find any variable in the list using these steps:

1 Multiply **currentlevel** by 5 (because there are 5 variables).
2 Add a position number to find a variable, as follows: **YetiSpriteSpeed** = +1, **YetiSpriteX** = +2, **YetiSpriteY** = +3, **FishSpriteX** = +4, **FishSpriteY** = +5.

Sound complicated? Try it out. Let's say you're on level 2, and you want to know what **YetiSprite.Speed** should be set to. Multiply **currentlevel** (2) by 5: 2 x 5 = 10. Now add 1 because you want to find out the **YetiSpriteSpeed**: 10 + 1 = 11. Look at the list. What is in the 11th position? It's 6—so you set **YetiSprite**'s **speed** to 6.

You can use this idea to read and use all these variables at the start of each level. In addition, at the start of a level, you'll need to respawn Gentoo, enable the Yeti, and update the information bar. Here are the blocks:

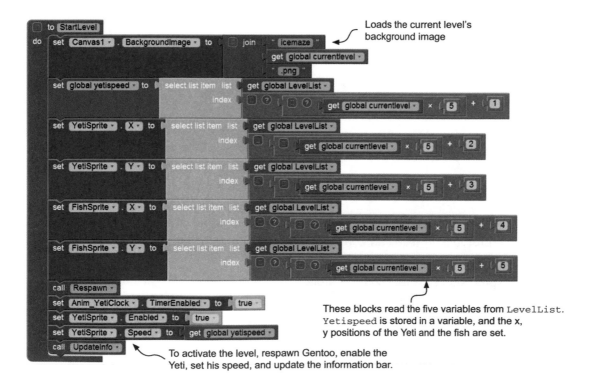

Loads the current level's background image

These blocks read the five variables from LevelList. Yetispeed is stored in a variable, and the x, y positions of the Yeti and the fish are set.

To activate the level, respawn Gentoo, enable the Yeti, set his speed, and update the information bar.

And that is the final block of the game! It's a lot of work, but we think the result is worth it. Although there are only three levels right now, adding more is easy. The game has a couple of small glitches: the sound effects can take a moment to load, meaning you sometimes get a warning message when the app starts; sometimes the snowball disappears in flight; and occasionally the Yeti gets stuck. But those are tiny problems that can be ironed out with a little time and testing. If you find the game too hard, you can change Gentoo's and the Yeti's **speed** variables.

We hope you think the game is fun to play and that the apps in this chapter inspire you to experiment and invent your own complete apps and games. When you do, let us know on the Manning Hello App Inventor! forum (www.manning.com/beer/Author Online)—we'd love to see them.

Taking it further

1   Stop the A-Mazeing Penguin app from being cancelled by a Back key click, just like you did in Zombie Alarm!.

2   Draw another three levels and add them to the app.

3   Add a timer so the player has to get to the goal before time runs out.

4   Make up your own additional A-Mazeing Penguin rules and add them to the blocks. For example, players must eat a fish before they can exit a level.

5   Add a high score to A-Mazeing Penguin, and give the player a chance to tweet or text their score.

What did you learn?

In this chapter, you learned about the following:

- Techniques to help you build complex apps: decomposing problems, getting out your pencil, prototyping, recycling, commenting your programs, involving users, and testing
- How to test and debug blocks
- Using procedures to make code reusable
- How to prepare your own graphics and animations for use in apps
- How to store the positions of sprites in a list and then restore the sprites back to their start positions

- How to stop an app from quitting just because the Back button is clicked
- How to develop game rules and turn them into blocks of code

Test your knowledge

1 How does user involvement help you make better apps?

2 How might these people use decomposition in their jobs?

   a Chef

   b Architect

   c Lawyer

   d Scientist

3 How do procedures help app designers?

CHAPTER 15

Publishing and beyond

In this chapter, we'll set you off on the road to publishing your finished apps. If you're ever flagging in your quest for early fame and fortune in the app world, we've drafted some support in the form of quotes and profiles of some teen and preteen programmers and app developers. Then, to wrap up, we'll talk about the future of App Inventor and consider whether there are other app-development tools out there for you.

Publishing apps

OK, so you've made an app that is going to sweep the nation, or perhaps you just think it's pretty good and would be fun to share. As an expert app inventor, you already know that you can email the .apk file to your friends or share the file on your website, via Twitter, or on your Facebook account. But what if you want to take things further and share your inspiration with the world? You can upload your app to the Google Play Store for a one-time cost of $25.00.

If you're serious about uploading your app to the Google Play Store, you must access Google's own resources via the Web to ensure that your understanding of the process is as up to date as possible. Many developers use app-publishing experts to help them publish to the Web in the most effective way, because there are so many potential complications and opportunities (like creating screenshots in the requested formats and writing a good description of the app). We'll provide a starting point to help you understand the steps in the process. But first let's see what some inspiring teens and preteens have been up to.

Young app developers

Many young app developers and programmers have been making an impres-
sion in the world of computer science
and beyond. We've included profiles of
five of them here, although there are
many more to choose from.

Thomas Suarez: believes in sharing knowledge with others[1]

In 2011, a 12-year-old American named Thomas Suarez
spoke about his passion for technology and apps in front of
a very appreciate audience during a TED talk. TED talks are
conferences during which speakers from a multitude of different backgrounds talk about "ideas worth spreading."
Thomas talked about two iPhone apps he had developed
and posted to the app store. He believes in the power of
sharing knowledge and how kids can help teachers in this
area. During his TED talk, Thomas said, "These days students

usually know a little bit more than teachers with the technology so … sorry … so this is a
resource [for] teachers. Educators should recognize this resource and make good use of it."

Nick D'Aloisio: app development millionaire[2]

English born Nick D'Aloisio was just 17 when he sold his
app to Yahoo! for an unconfirmed sum of $30 million. In an
interview with news agency Reuters, D'Aloisio encouraged
other entrepreneurs, saying, "If you have a good idea, or
you think there's a gap in the market, just go out and
launch it because there are investors across the world right
now looking for companies to invest in."

---

[1]   Photo by MakerBot Industries: http://mng.bz/oO7Y. Thomas's TED talk: http://mng.bz/YQzp.
[2]   Photo by Puramyun31: http://mng.bz/cNqV.

His app idea was inspired when, while studying for history exams, he found it very time consuming to trawl through lots of web pages looking for information. His iPhone app called Summly (originally called Trimit) automatically reduces the content of web pages to 400 words to be read on a mobile device.

With technical know-how and incredible persistence, he attracted investors who helped further develop his app and also helped him become a very rich young man and Yahoo!'s youngest employee—all while still in school and planning to go to college.

Jordan Casey: My Little World

At the age of 12, Irish boy Jordan Casey had published four games to the Google Play Store. Since then he has written more apps, including some using iOS. He explained that his app My Little World took eight months to program. He advises young developers that they should "Never give up" when trying to get their apps published.

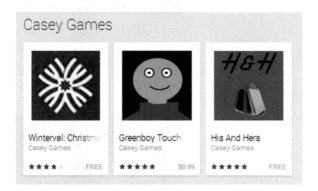

Charley Hutchinson: "Why don't I make my own app?"

At the age of 11, Charley Hutchinson of Mississippi wrote an iPhone app to keep track of the Flickr photos posted by his friends. In 2012, he was interviewed on CNN and talked about the race to get the app published to the App Store before his 12th birthday. He had published an app called Doodles to the Google Play Store the year before. Asked how he decided to make an app for the iPhone, he said, "I've always been really interested in computers.

Then my parents had an iPhone, and I really loved playing with apps on there, so I decided, why don't I make my own app?" Charlie continued, "If there's so many already on the store, surely I can make one myself."

Where are the girls?[3]

If you're a girl reading this book, don't be down-hearted that we didn't immediately find any semi-famous young girl app developers in the media. If you look at the App Inventor website's news page (http://mng.bz/J1Yw) or search the Web for the words "girls in computing," you'll find that lots of people are desperate to get girls involved in computing. Research shows that although fewer girls than boys choose to study computing, when they do, they achieve just as well or better than boys. In fact, the world's first computer programmer was female. Ada Lovelace lived in the mid-19th century and wrote "Notes" that are understood to have included the first algorithm that was intended to be processed by Charles Babbage's early mechanical general-purpose computer, the Analytical Engine.

Given Ada Lovelace (first program), Grace Hopper (first compiler), and Adele Goldberg (first object-oriented language), why would anyone think women aren't in computing?

Amy Mather is an accomplished and passionate young programmer. We first met Amy in 2012 when she came to a school event and wowed our teacher trainees with her computer science knowledge. She first learned HTML and then joined other organizations in the UK that engage young computer scientists. She has had some great mentors but is mostly self-taught, using a free resource called Codecademy (www.codecademy.com) to teach herself Python programming. When talking at an event for enthusiasts of the Raspberry Pi computer (known as a Raspberry Jam), she explained what first caused her to get interested in programming: "It's all very well to use iPads and

---

[3] Ada Lovelace photo by Duncan Hull: http://mng.bz/5PsP.

stuff. But I thought, how could I get it to do what I want it to do?" If you want to see Amy demonstrating how she developed a pretty complicated Python program, which links to some LED lights to represent a concept called Conway's Game of Life, watch this video: http://mng.bz/txd5.[4]

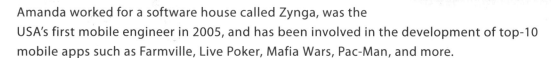

A career in app development?

Where could a career in app development take you? Let's take, for example, Amanda Wixted.

Amanda worked for a software house called Zynga, was the USA's first mobile engineer in 2005, and has been involved in the development of top-10 mobile apps such as Farmville, Live Poker, Mafia Wars, Pac-Man, and more.

Amanda left Zynga and in 2012 created her own company called Meteor Grove Software where she continues to successfully develop apps for customers in Brooklyn, New York. Interestingly, she says that when she was in college, she "randomly took a class in computer science and decided to change (my) major from dance to computer science."[5]

Steps in the publishing process

Google provides very detailed guidance about preparing your app for release that you can find at http://mng.bz/dGU4. This diagram gives you some idea of the different steps involved in the process. If you're a teen reading this book, run things by an adult, particularly because there is a cost involved!

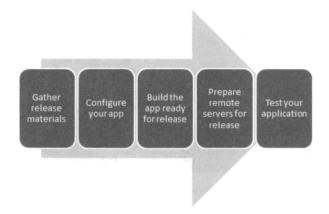

---

[4]   Photo by Alan O'Donohoe.

[5]   See http://amanda.wixted.usesthis.com/.

As you'll notice, there are terms in these steps that we haven't talked about, so we'll go over them a little here. You may have to learn more about them directly from the Google site if you want to do more, but this will get you started.

Step 1: gather materials for release

This first step includes a few tasks to get materials including cryptographic keys (explained in a moment), license agreements, and graphics ready for release.

CRYPTOGRAPHIC KEYS

Sounds exciting, like perhaps it has to do with an Egyptian tomb, but in this context a *cryptographic key* means a unique code that links to your app and your app only. App Inventor sorts this out for you when the .apk file is being written. But it's sensible to make a backup of your keystore as part of the process of backing up your app.

When you're in the My Projects page, select the app you intend to publish, and select More Options/Download Keystore. Export the keystore to a computer, rather than relying solely on MIT's cloud servers … just in case. If your keystore gets lost, it can't be re-created, even if you've re-created the source code of the app when upgrading the app on the Google Play Store. The keystore needs to be the original one; otherwise you'll have to completely republish, which means existing users won't get the upgrade. Experienced programmers save the keystore several times. Possibilities are on a USB stick, on cloud storage, and via email to yourself or trusty people like parents or caregivers.

APPLICATION ICON

In the Designer with the **Screen1** component selected in the Properties panel, choose Icon and select a suitable image to be your application icon.

EULA

A EULA is an end user license agreement that lets users know what they're agreeing to in downloading your app. It also protects your property. You've most likely agreed to hundreds of them yourself by clicking through and "accepting" at the end of the text. If you want to see what a commercial EULA looks like, search for "end user license agreement" and the name of an app. One very typical item to include is that your users can't copy or resell your app, which seems fair enough!

MISCELLANEOUS MATERIALS

These include promotional materials such as images or video of your app in action plus some promotional text selling your app to the public. Google has some strict guidelines about the quality of images and type of promotional material required. You're required to provide a minimum of two screenshots as follows:

- JPEG or 24-bit PNG (no alpha)
- Minimum dimension of 320 px

- Maximum dimension of 380 px
- Maximum dimension can't be twice as long as the minimum

To maximize the usage of your app, it does make sense to provide screen shots for other devices such as 7-inch and 10-inch tablets. Google permits you to upload up to eight screenshots. In addition, there is more guidance about designing for tablets. Read up on this to maximize the likelihood that your app is successful.

VERSION CODE AND VERSION NAME
Every app you publish must have a **VersionCode** and a **VersionName**. You can set these in the Designer in the Properties panel for the **Screen1** component. The **VersionCode** is an integer (whole number) that, although invisible to users, can be used by other apps to check whether your app has been upgraded. Now you know how your phone tracks upgrades automatically!

The **VersionCode** always starts at 1 and increases by 1 each time a small or large upgrade is made. The **VersionName** is a string (number, symbols, or text) that also changes inline with upgrades. It's common for the first **VersionName** to be a decimal number 1.0: when a small upgrade is made, it changes to 1.1; and when a large upgrade is made, it changes to 2.0. It's essential that your users be able to track what version of your app they have installed and to be able to automatically access upgrades.

SAVING THE .APK FILE
From the design screen of the app that you want to publish, choose Download to This Computer. The .apk file will be saved to your Downloads folder.

Step 2: configuring your application for release

At the very minimum, ensure that there are no bug warnings in your blocks, and remove any deactivated blocks. When you're in the home screen of your app in App Inventor, select Debugging and select Clear to remove any messages or developer messages.

Step 3: building your application for release

Good news: App Inventor does this bit for you. In the home screen of your app, select Build/ App (Save .apk to My Computer) and download the file to your computer. App Inventor automatically compiles the .apk file for you and saves it into your Downloads folder.

Step 4: preparing external servers and resources

If your application relies on another server, ensure that the server is secure and suitable for production use. If you're intending to bill from your app, this is of course essential. The type of mistake that could be made here is a developer leaving the app pointing to a test server rather than the live server that will be used for a content feed or billing.

Any apps containing TinyWebDB are dependent on external servers maintained by MIT. In chapter 12, you developed the Dream Sharer app, which allows the user to share the contents of their dreams with their friends via the web using the `TinyWebDB` component. But the default server accessed by TinyWebDB is a test service that isn't suitable for apps that will be published, because the contents will be eventually overwritten. So if you produce a published app that will use TinyWebDB, you can create a customized TinyWebDB service. Follow the instructions at this link: http://mng.bz/Oq12.

Step 5: testing your application for release

Google Play Store requests that you have tested your app on at least one handset-sized device and one tablet-sized device. But if you have friends with Android devices, why not try it on a few different-sized screens to see how it looks and works? The types of things you could consider are the fit of the screen, changes in orientation, and different settings such as languages available for the app. In addition, if your app is dependent on other external resources such as SMS or Bluetooth, what happens when these aren't available?

The future of App Inventor

In August 2011, Google handed over control and development of App Inventor to MIT (Massachusetts Institute of Technology). Since then, interest in and use of App Inventor has taken off across the world. In 2013, there was a big upgrade of App Inventor, which is also known currently as App Inventor 2. If you see any mention of App Inventor Classic, this was the first version of App Inventor, which has now been replaced. The current App Inventor team is very interested in making App Inventor a fantastic resource for the world of computer science education, engaging young people in developing their own apps.

Other platforms

If you really want to get into programming, it's a good idea to be part of a programming community. Have you tried Scratch programming yet? Scratch is similar to App Inventor in that it involves slotting together blocks to create programs for laptops/desktops. It's a free download available at http://scratch.mit.edu/. What is particularly great about Scratch is that its attitude is concerned with sharing and remixing each other's work. You're encouraged to upload your projects and download the source code of other programmers' projects and adapt it with your ideas. There are also plenty of tutorials, education resources, and forums available on the site to keep you busy and happy.

Or you can try Codecademy, which is another free resource. The young programmer Amy Mather (mentioned earlier) used Codecademy to teach herself Python. Once you've created an account and signed in, it keeps track of your progress and encourages you as you learn to code in Python, HTML, and JavaScript. The website address is www.codecademy.com/.

If you want to expand your app inventing experience, take a look at other platforms that are available. If you want to progress down the Apple route and develop apps that can be used on iPhones or iPads, you'll need to purchase the iOS developer program (http://mng.bz/K1an). There are plenty of support materials to help you learn the skills necessary to become an Apple developer at http://mng.bz/T7nQ, although these materials are targeted more at experienced developers rather than beginners.

If the up-front cost of the iOS developer's kit puts you off and you're looking for something free, a program called Lua is available at www.lua.org/download.html. We have seen this taught in a school. Again, the resources aren't set up with younger developers in mind, but it's worth the persistence to spread your wings a bit. Lua is a powerful, fast, lightweight, embeddable (can be used inside other applications) scripting language. It's powerful enough to be used in applications that you may have heard of, like Photoshop and Lightroom, and it's been used in some complex and successful games such as World of Warcraft and apps like Angry Birds. The website Lua for Kids (http://luaforkids.com/) contains a couple of tutorials to get you started. One of the special things about Lua is that you get to choose which platform you write your app for. So, you can produce apps for Android or Apple.

Another option is TouchDevelop (www.touchdevelop.com/), which is also free and enables users to develop apps on iPad, iPhone, Android, PC, Mac, and Windows Phones. A colleague of ours has used the interactive tutorials with high school students, who produced their first app within one hour.

Staying with App Inventor for the time being?

If you've created all the apps in this book but want to develop further, you can backtrack through the book and do the Try It Out challenges. These are extensions of the original tutorials that expect you to really think about what components and blocks will be needed to adapt the apps. For example, in chapter 6, we suggest that you create a slot-machine game using three lists of fruit. Award points and play a sound when three matching fruits are selected—then take it further by adding delays and animation sprites. Give it a go!

What about trying some advanced features?

In the pages of this book, we have used 38 of the 46 (counting LEGO Mindstorms as one!) components. But there are a few left that you could have fun investigating for yourself:

- **Slider** *(Palette group: User Interface)*—The only component from the User Interface group that we haven't used in a tutorial is **Slider**. A slider is a progress bar that adds a draggable thumb. You can touch the thumb and drag left or right to set the slider thumb position. You can use a slider to change other component properties such as font size or radius of a ball.

  > APP IDEA   Produce a drawing app in which the user uses sliders to tailor their own screen.

- **Camcorder** *(Palette group: Media)*—This component allows you to open the device's camcorder record and save a video file.

  > APP IDEA   Combining this functionality with TinyDB, set up a video diary app to record a holiday diary.

- **VideoPlayer** *(Palette group: Media)*—As long as the video is under 1 MB and in WMV, 3GP, or MPEG-4 format the **VideoPlayer** component appears as a rectangle on the device screen; when tapped, it displays video controls.

  > APP IDEA   Perhaps adapt the Inspiration Scrapbook app from chapter 11 and include a video of your hero rather than just text to speech, or build a Snapchat.

- **SoundRecorder** *(Palette group: Media)*—Just like it sounds! This component allows you to record audio.

  > APP IDEA   "Good ideas get lost, just like good pens." Why not create an ideas app and, when you get an idea, record it? It'll be fun to listen to later.

- **NearField** *(Palette group: Sensors)*—This component allows you to use near-field technology to read and write text to another device in the immediate vicinity (only a few inches away).

  > APP IDEA   Create an app that enables you to share contact details immediately, without using SMS texts.

- **PhoneCall** *(Palette group: Social)*—Often used with a list picker, this component allows you to make phone calls.

  > APP IDEA   Create an app that picks from your social phone list and automatically calls friends on their birthdays.

- **FusionTablesControl** *(Palette group: Storage)*—This non-visible component communicates with Google Fusion Tables. Google Fusion Tables let you query, store, share, and visualize data tables. This component lets you query, create, and modify these tables.

> **APP IDEA**   Create an app that looks at the weather in all your favorite holiday destinations.

- **BluetoothClient** *and* **BluetoothServer** *(Palette group: Connectivity)*—Both components enable you to connect to other devices wirelessly.

> **APP IDEA**   Create an app that enables you to share contact details immediately, without using SMS texts.

- *LEGO Mindstorms*—This group of components lets you control LEGO Mindstorms robots using Bluetooth technology.

There is a forum for this book on the publisher website (www.manning.com/beer > Author Online). If you have some success with these other components, why not share what you think about them? Also consider posting some tutorials yourself to the App Inventor 2 website.

Final words

At the beginning of the book, we shared with you this quote:

> *Any sufficiently advanced technology is indistinguishable from magic.*
>
> —Arthur C. Clarke's Third Law of Prediction[6]

We hope you've found some magic in the creation of your own apps. From the simple Getting to Know Ewe starter app in chapter 2 to the more complicated A-Mazeing Penguin app in chapter 14, we hope you've learned plenty about what you can do with App Inventor. You'll find that once you've followed the tutorials and learned the basics, you can see what is possible and become more creative and adventurous in your programming ideas. Keep experimenting, coding with your friends, and enjoying what App Inventor has to offer.

---

[6]   In the essay "Hazards of Prophecy: The Failure of Imagination," in *Profiles of the Future* (Gollancz, 1962).

Index

MORE TITLES FROM MANNING

Hello World! Second Edition
Computer Programming for Kids
and Other Beginners

by Warren Sande and Carter Sande

ISBN: 9781617290923
464 pages
$39.99
December 2013

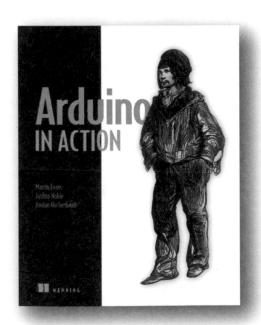

Arduino in Action
by Martin Evans, Joshua Noble,
  and Jordan Hochenbaum

ISBN: 9781617290244
368 pages
$39.99
May 2013

For ordering information go to www.manning.com